PARA SERVIRLE

Spanish Conversation and Grammar for Beginners

Max Novitz

Former Chairman, Department of Foreign Languages
Cody High School, Detroit, Michigan

Former Instructor in Spanish
Wayne State University, Detroit, Michigan

Dedicated to serving
AMSCO
our nation's youth

When ordering this book, please specify:
either **R 243 W** *or*
PARA SERVIRLE / WORKBOOK

AMSCO SCHOOL PUBLICATIONS, INC.
315 Hudson Street / New York, N.Y. 10013

FRONT COVER: Mexican students entertaining themselves in Chapultepec Park, Mexico City

PHOTO CREDIT: Beryl Goldberg

ISBN 0-87720-523-X

Printed in the United States of America

Preface

PARA SERVIRLE is a workbook in Spanish for beginners. It is designed for two purposes: to make students converse in Spanish and to provide instruction in Spanish grammar. Conversation is taught in the most direct way by using pairs of simple questions and answers in repetitive patterns that can be learned with a minimum of effort.

Each unit of conversation is introduced by a Topic Question—a question in Spanish derived from the interests and everyday experiences of boys and girls in high school—followed by a set of related *preguntas y respuestas,* which are to be memorized and used in the classroom as grist for conversation. These sets of questions and answers are supplemented by short *Lecturas* dealing with related themes, and by mastery exercises in *Conversación* to be performed in class without the help of books or notes. Included among the *Lecturas* are brief glimpses of some aspects of Hispanic culture.

There are 47 Topic Questions in all, distributed among 72 lessons. The lessons are arranged in a cumulative sequence from the easiest to the most difficult.

Repetition being the soul of learning, most of the Spanish expressions and conversational patterns introduced in PARA SERVIRLE are used over and over again in different contexts throughout the book.

PARA SERVIRLE contains a wide variety of exercises, including a number of games and crossword puzzles to entertain as well as instruct.

The units on Spanish grammar include the grammar topics that are taught in most first-year courses.

It is recommended that teachers begin every class hour with a review of the *preguntas y respuestas* that were learned in the previous class session. Students should try to master all 47 Topic Questions and their answers. Those who achieve even this minimal objective will have gained considerable facility in speaking Spanish.

—MAX NOVITZ

Table of Contents

Introduction: Some Useful Expressions

To the student: It takes time and effort to learn a foreign language. You can learn it more quickly if you speak it at every opportunity, using as many expressions as you can. It is also more fun that way. Spanish is the native language of 20 million Americans, so you may often get the chance to greet a neighbor with a few words of Spanish. Do not be shy; even a single word of greeting can make a friend. And if you have no one else to practice your Spanish on, your classmates are always available. (You need not be shy with *them*!) You do not have to be told that Spanish, like every language, is meant to be *spoken*.

Let us begin by learning a few basic expressions that are used every day in the Spanish-speaking world. You may already know most of them. Learn to pronounce them correctly by imitating your teacher.

A. *Greetings and Good-byes*

***¡Hola!**	Hello! Hi!
Buenos días.	Good morning.
Buenas tardes.	Good afternoon.
Buenas noches.	Good evening.
***¿Qué tal?**	How goes it? How are things?
Bien, gracias.	Fine, thanks.
Así así.	So-so.
¿Y usted?	And you?
No muy bien.	Not very well.
Lo siento.	I'm sorry.
Adiós.	Good-bye.
Hasta luego.	See you later.
Hasta la vista.	I'll be seeing you.
Hasta mañana.	Until tomorrow.

B. *Other Useful Expressions*

Por favor.	Please.
Muchas gracias.	Thanks very much.
De nada.	You're welcome.
¡Salud!	(1) Bless you! *Gesundheit!* (Said when someone sneezes.) (2) To your health! (Said in giving a toast.)

Para servirle is the title of this book. Its literal meaning is "to serve you," that is, *I am at your service*. The expression is often used in Spanish-speaking countries as a polite reply to *Gracias*.

---

*Questions in Spanish begin with an upside-down question mark (¿). Exclamations begin with an upside-down exclamation point (¡). These are placed at the beginning of the question or exclamation. For that reason, they sometimes occur in the middle of a sentence: "Buenos días, Juan, ¿qué tal?"

C. *Titles of Address*

señor	Mr.
señorita	Miss
señora	Mrs.
señores	gentlemen
los señores Smith	Mr. and Mrs. Smith

These titles may be abbreviated:

Sr.	Mr.
Srta.	Miss
Sra.	Mrs.

Exercise

Learn all the Spanish expressions listed in this introduction. Can you translate these sentences into Spanish without looking at the lists? Write each translation on the blank line.

1. Good morning, Miss García. Buenos días, senorita Garcia.
2. I'll be seeing you. Hasta la vista.
3. Thanks very much. Muchas gracias.
4. I'm sorry. Lo siento.
5. How are things? ______
6. Fine, thanks. ______
7. So-so. ______
8. Not very well. ______
9. Good afternoon. ______
10. Mr. and Mrs. Mendoza ______
11. Good evening, gentlemen. ______
12. You're welcome. ______
13. To your health! ______
14. Hello! ______
15. See you later. ______

Lesson 1

llamarse, *to be named*

TOPIC QUESTION 1

¿Cómo se llama usted? What is your name?

The lessons in this book will show you how to ask questions about everyday activities. The first question you will learn deals with names. Practice saying the following six questions easily without reference to notes. Correct pronunciation and accent are important, so imitate your teacher as well as you can.

Each question is followed by an answer. Write the rest of the answer on the blank line.

A. 1. **¿Cómo se llama usted?**
What is your name?
Yo me llamo ____
My name is . . .

2. **¿Cómo se llama su padre?**
What is your father's name?
Mi padre se llama____
My father's name is . . .

3. **¿Cómo se llama su madre?**
What is your mother's name?
Mi madre se llama ____
My mother's name is . . .

4. **¿Cómo se llaman sus hermanos?**
What are the names of your brothers and sisters?
Mis hermanos se llaman____
My brothers' and sisters' names are . . .

5. **¿Cómo se llama su amigo favorito?**
What is the name of your favorite (male) friend?
Mi amigo favorito se llama ____
My favorite (male) friend's name is . . .

¿Cómo se llama su amiga favorita?
What is the name of your favorite (female) friend?
Mi amiga favorita se llama ____
My favorite (female) friend's name is . . .

RELAYED ANSWER

6. **¿Cómo se llama él?** — **Él se llama** ________________________________
What is his name? — His name is . . .
¿Cómo se llama ella? — **Ella se llama** ________________________________
What is her name? — Her name is . . .

To obtain a relayed answer, ask a classmate for the name of someone in your class. Your classmate will turn to the person whose name you want to know, and will ask: "¿Cómo se llama usted?" When the question is answered, your classmate will relay the answer to *you*: "Él/Ella se llama . . ."

B. Read these sentences aloud. Learn to pronounce them correctly and easily:

Yo me llamo Ricardo González, para servirle.*
My name is Richard González, at your service.

Mi padre se llama Tomás.
My father's name is Thomas.

Mi madre se llama Margarita.
My mother's name is Margaret.

Mis hermanos se llaman Pepe, María y Lucía.
The names of my brother and sisters are Joey, Mary and Lucy.

Mi amigo favorito se llama Miguel.
My favorite friend's name is Michael.

Mi amiga favorita se llama Anita.
My favorite friend's name is Annie.

Mi madre se llama Margarita.

C. Using the sentences above as models, write a paragraph in which you tell the names of some important people in your life. The following comments may help you in writing your paragraph:

1. In the phrase **Yo me llamo** ("I call myself"), the word **yo** ("I") may be omitted.
2. **Hermanas** means *sisters* but **hermanos** may mean either *brothers* or any combination of brothers and sisters. Similarly, in **mis amigos se llaman . . .** ("my friends' names are . . ."), **amigos** may mean only male friends or any mixed group of male and female friends.

Write your paragraph on the lines below. Then read it aloud for practice, and be ready to repeat it orally in class without looking at your paper.

____

____

____

____

____

*When you tell someone your name for the first time, it is considered polite to add "para servirle."

Lesson 2

llamarse, *to be named (continued)*

A. *Lectura* (Reading)

Me llamo José. Mi padre se llama Juan. Mi madre se llama María. Mis hermanos se llaman Pablo y Margarita. Mi amigo favorito se llama Tomás. Mi amiga favorita se llama Josefina.

Vocabulario

el muchacho, the boy
la muchacha, the girl
mi, **mis** } my
su, **sus** } his, her, your, their

Preguntas (Questions). For each answer, write a complete Spanish sentence.

Me llamo José.

1. ¿Cómo se llama el muchacho?

----

2. ¿Cómo se llama su padre?

----

3. ¿Cómo se llama su madre?

----

4. ¿Cómo se llaman sus hermanos?

----

5. ¿Cómo se llama su hermano?

----

6. ¿Cómo se llama su hermana?

----

7. ¿Cómo se llama su amigo favorito?

----

8. ¿Cómo se llama su amiga favorita?

B. *Traduzca usted al español* (Translate into Spanish):

1. My father's name is José.

----

2. What is your mother's name?

----

3. The name of my favorite friend is María.

---

4. What is the name of your favorite (male) friend?

---

5. What is your father's name?

---

6. My mother's name is Anita.

---

7. What are the names of your brother and sister?

---

8. The names of my brother and sister are Bob and Mary.

---

9. My sister's name is Inés.

---

10. My brother's name is Bob.

C. *Preguntas y respuestas* (Questions and answers)

Read these questions and answers aloud as correctly and easily as you can:

1. ¿Cómo se llama usted?
Yo me llamo Ricardo González.

2. ¿Cómo se llama su padre?
Mi padre se llama Tomás.

3. ¿Cómo se llama su madre?
Mi madre se llama Margarita.

4. ¿Cómo se llaman sus hermanos?
Mis hermanos se llaman Pepe, María y Lucía.

5. ¿Cómo se llama su amigo favorito?
Mi amigo favorito se llama Miguel.

6. ¿Cómo se llama él?
Él se llama José.

¿Cómo se llama ella?
Ella se llama María.

Mi padre se llama Tomás.

D. *Preguntas personales* (Personal questions)

These questions are addressed to *you*. Answer them in complete Spanish sentences:

1. ¿Cómo se llama Ud.? (*Ud.* is the abbreviation for *usted*.)

----

2. ¿Cómo se llama su madre?

----

3. ¿Cómo se llama su padre?

----

4. ¿Cómo se llaman sus hermanos?

----

5. ¿Cómo se llama su amigo favorito?

----

6. ¿Cómo se llama su amiga favorita?

E. *Conversación*. Ask a student in your class each of the six questions following Topic Question 1 on page 3, starting with *¿Cómo se llama Ud.?*

Lesson 3

SPANISH NAMES

In the Spanish-speaking world, everybody uses two surnames (family names). The first surname is that of the father and the second is the maiden name of the mother. In the name *María Mendoza Gutiérrez,* Mendoza is the name of María's father and Gutiérrez is the maiden name of María's mother. María would be addressed as *señorita Mendoza,* for short.

Let us suppose that María marries Antonio García y Rodríguez; she would then become *María Mendoza de García*. The *de* means *of,* thus showing to whom María "belongs." She would be addressed as *señora García,* for short.

Listed below are some of the more popular Spanish surnames that you may encounter in your travels. Practice pronouncing them aloud. You will be seeing and hearing them a great deal.

los apellidos españoles **(Spanish surnames)**

Alarcón
Ávila
Calderón
Cárdenas
Castillo
Cervantes
Cisneros
Cruz
Chapa
Fernández
García
Gómez
Guevara
Gutiérrez
Guzmán
Herrero
Ibáñez
Jiménez
López
Marín
Martínez
Medina
Mendoza
Navarro
Pérez
Quintero
Ramírez
Reyes
Rivas
Rodríguez
Salinas
Sánchez
Torre
Treviño
Valdés
Vargas
Vázquez
Villalobos
Villareal

nombres de pila **(first names)**

MUCHACHAS (girls)

Adela
Alicia
Amada
Ana
Anita
Antonia
Bárbara
Beatriz
Berta
Blanca
Carlota
Carolina
Catalina
Cecilia
Clara
Concha
Constanza
Cristina
Chavela
Dorotea
Elena
Elisa
Emilia
Enriqueta
Esperanza
Ester
Eva
Felipa
Florencia
Francisca
Gertrudis
Gracia
Inés
Isabel
Josefina
Juana
Julia
Leonor
Lucía
Luisa
Manuela
Margarita
Mariana
Marianela
Paula
Paulina
Pilar
Raquel
Rebeca
Rosa
Rosalía
Sara
Sofía
Susana
Teresa
Virginia

MUCHACHOS **(boys)**

Abrahán	Edmundo	Heriberto	Miguel
Alberto	Eduardo	Jaime	Nicolás
Alejandro	Emilio	Jerónimo	Pablo
Alfredo	Enrique	Joaquín	Patricio
Alonso	Ernesto	Jorge	Pedro
Andrés	Esteban	José	Ramón
Antonio	Eugenio	Juan	Raúl
Arturo	Federico	León	Renaldo
Benjamín	Felipe	Leonardo	Ricardo
Bernardo	Fernando	Lorenzo	Roberto
Carlos	Francisco	Luis	Rogerio
Cristóbal	Gregorio	Manuel	Teodoro
Diego	Gualterio	Marcos	Timoteo
Dionisio	Guillermo	Martín	Tomás
Domingo	Haroldo	Mateo	Vicente

A. Create your own "cast of characters" by combining names chosen from the list of *apellidos* and *nombres de pila* on pages 8 and 9. Write the full Spanish names of five boys in column *A* and five girls in column *B*. Then imagine that each boy marries the girl whose name appears opposite his in column *B*. In column *C*, write the girl's full name as a married woman.

	A	*B*	*C*
EXAMPLE:	*Andrés Marín Rivas*	*Ana Cisneros Cruz*	*Ana Cisneros de Marín*
1.	____________________	____________________	____________________
2.	____________________	____________________	____________________
3.	____________________	____________________	____________________
4.	____________________	____________________	____________________
5.	____________________	____________________	____________________

B. In exercise A, above, you wrote the names of five married couples: the husband's name in column *A*, the wife's name in column *C*. Now choose a *nombre de pila* for their first child, and write his or her name in full. (Remember that a child has two *apellidos*: his father's name followed by the name of his mother's father.)

For example, the first child of Andrés Marín Rivas and Ana Cisneros de Marín is a girl, Berta. Her full name is . . .

Berta Marín Cisneros
____

1. ____

2. ____

3. ____

4. ____

5. ____

Lesson 4

estar, *to be*

TOPIC QUESTION 2A

¿Cómo está Ud.?
How are you?

present tense of ***estar***	
yo **estoy**	I am
Ud. **está**	you are
él **está**	he is
ella **está**	she is
ellos **están**	they are

A. *Preguntas y respuestas*

Practice reading aloud the following questions and answers:

1. ¿Cómo está Ud.?
Yo estoy bien, gracias. ¿Y Ud.?

2. ¿Cómo está él?
Él está bien.

3. ¿Cómo está ella?
Ella no está bien.

4. ¿Cómo están ellos?
Ellos están así así.

Vocabulario

bien, well, fine
así así, so-so
ellos, they
gracias, thank you
sí, yes
Diego, James

Learn to ask and answer these questions easily, without looking at the page.

Here are some more questions to learn. Write the missing parts of the answers:

5. ¿Cómo está Ud.?
Yo --

6. ¿Cómo está su padre?
Mi padre --

7. ¿Cómo está su madre?
Mi madre --

8. ¿Cómo están sus hermanos?
Mis hermanos ______________________________

9. ¿Cómo está su amigo favorito?
Mi amigo favorito ______________________________

10. ¿Cómo está su amiga favorita?
Ella ______________________________

Ask a classmate these questions about a girl and a boy in your class:

RELAYED ANSWER

11. ¿Cómo está ella? ______________________________

12. ¿Cómo está él? ______________________________

TOPIC QUESTION 2B

¿Está Ud. bien de salud?
Are you in good health?

B. Learn these questions too:

1. ¿Está Ud. bien de salud?
Sí, yo estoy ______________________________

2. ¿Está su padre bien de salud?
Sí, mi padre ______________________________

3. ¿Está su madre bien de salud?
Sí, mi madre ______________________________

4. ¿Están sus hermanos bien de salud?
Sí, mis hermanos ______________________________

5. ¿Está su amigo favorito bien de salud?
No, mi amigo favorito no ______________________________

6. ¿Está su amiga favorita bien de salud?
Sí, ella ______________________________

Ask a classmate these questions about a boy and a girl in your class:

RELAYED ANSWER

7. ¿Está él bien de salud? ______________________________

8. ¿Está ella bien de salud? ______________________________

C. *Lectura*

Mi hermana no está bien.

Me llamo Diego. Yo estoy bien. Mi padre está bien. Mi madre está así así. Mi hermano está bien. Mi hermana no está bien. Mi amigo favorito está así así. Mis amigos Alberto y Martín están muy bien.

Preguntas

1. ¿Cómo se llama el muchacho? ____________________
2. ¿Cómo está Diego? ____________________
3. ¿Cómo está su padre? ____________________
4. ¿Cómo está su madre? ____________________
5. ¿Cómo está su hermano? ____________________
6. ¿Cómo está su hermana? ____________________
7. ¿Cómo está su amigo favorito? ____________________
8. ¿Cómo están Alberto y Martín? ____________________

D. *Preguntas personales*

Mi amigo Alberto está bien de salud.

1. ¿Cómo está Ud.?

   ____

2. ¿Cómo está su padre?

   ____

3. ¿Cómo está su madre?

   ____

4. ¿Cómo están sus hermanos?

   ____

5. ¿Cómo está su amigo favorito?*

   ____

E. *Traduzca Ud. al español:*

1. I'm fine, thank you. ____________________
2. How are you? ____________________
3. He's not well. ____________________
4. How is she? ____________________
5. She is so-so. ____________________

---

*If your favorite friend is a *girl,* use the feminine form in your answer: ''Mi amig**a** favorit**a** está . . .''

6. How is your brother? ______________________________
7. He isn't well. ______________________________
8. How is your sister? ______________________________
9. My father is in good health. ______________________________
10. My brothers are in good health. ______________________________
11. Are you in good health? ______________________________
12. How are they? ______________________________

F. *Conversación*

Ask a student in your class the questions listed under Topic Questions 2A and 2B.

Lesson 5

tener, *to have*

TOPIC QUESTION 3

¿Tiene Ud. un coche? Do you have a car?

present tense of ***tener***	
yo **tengo**	I have
Ud. **tiene**	you have
él **tiene**	he has
ella **tiene**	she has
ellos **tienen**	they have

A. *Preguntas y respuestas*

Practice reading aloud the following questions and answers:

1. ¿Tiene Ud. un coche?
Sí, yo tengo un coche.
No, yo no tengo coche.*

2. ¿Tiene él un coche?
Sí, él tiene un coche.
No, él no tiene coche.

3. ¿Tiene ella un coche?
Sí, ella tiene un coche.
No, ella no tiene coche.

4. ¿Tienen ellos un coche?
Sí, ellos tienen un coche.
No, ellos no tienen coche.

Vocabulario

coche, car
también, also
es, is, it is
usado, used
¿Qué marca es? What make is it?

Mi hermana tiene un coche usado.

*When **tener** is used negatively, it is not followed by the indefinite article (**un** or **una**): "yo **no** tengo coche," I don't have *a* car.

Learn to ask and answer these questions easily, without looking at the page.

For questions 5 to 10, write the missing parts of the answers:

5. ¿Tiene Ud. un coche?

No, yo no ______________________________

6. ¿Tiene su padre un coche?

Sí, mi padre ______________________________

7. ¿Tiene su madre un coche?

Sí, mi madre ______________________________

8. ¿Tienen sus hermanos un coche?

No, mis hermanos no ______________________________

9. ¿Tiene su amigo favorito un coche?

No, mi amigo favorito ______________________________

10. ¿Tiene su amiga favorita un coche?

Sí, ______________________________

Ask a classmate these questions about a girl and a boy in your class. (Write the girl's name in #11, the boy's name in #12.)

	RELAYED ANSWER
11. ¿Tiene ______________ un coche?	______________________________
12. ¿Tiene ______________ un coche?	______________________________

B. *Lectura*

Yo me llamo Enrique.
Yo no tengo coche.

Mi padre tiene un coche.
Es un Chevrolet.

Mi madre tiene un coche también.
Es un Ford.

Mi hermana Margarita tiene un coche usado.
Es un Pinto.

Mis hermanos se llaman Roberto y Tomás.
Ellos no tienen coche.

Mi amigo favorito se llama Alberto.
Alberto tiene un coche.
Es un Mercedes.

*Preguntas**

1. ¿Tiene Enrique un coche?

----

2. ¿Tiene su padre un coche? ¿Qué marca es?

----

3. ¿Tiene su madre un coche? ¿Qué marca es?

----

4. ¿Tienen Roberto y Tomás un coche?

----

5. ¿Cómo se llama la hermana de Enrique?

----

6. ¿Tiene Margarita un coche? ¿Qué marca es?

----

7. ¿Tiene Alberto un coche?

C. *Preguntas personales*

1. ¿Tiene Ud. un coche? --

2. ¿Tiene su padre un coche? ------------------------------------

3. ¿Tiene su madre un coche? ------------------------------------

4. ¿Tienen sus hermanos un coche? --------------------------------

5. ¿Tiene su amigo favorito un coche? ----------------------------

D. *Tema* (Composition)

Write a composition entitled *¿Tiene Ud. un coche?* Start with *Yo me llamo . . . Yo tengo un coche. Es un. . . .* Then give the same kind of information about the following people, in the order given:

mi padre
mi madre
mis hermanos
mi amigo favorito (*or* amiga favorita)

----

*Throughout this book, always answer a **pregunta** with a *complete Spanish sentence*.

E. *Traduzca Ud. al español:*

1. My mother doesn't have a car. ______________________

2. My brother has a car. ______________________

3. Does your sister have a car?______________________

4. Your sister has a used car. ______________________

5. I don't have a car.______________________

6. Does your friend have a car? ______________________

7. He doesn't have a car. ______________________

8. Does she have a car? ______________________

9. Yes; it's a Cadillac. ______________________

10. My brothers and sisters have a car. ______________________

11. What make is it? ______________________

F. *Conversación.* You and your classmates take turns asking one another questions 5 to 10 on page 15. Students should reply in Spanish without looking at the page.

Lesson 6

manejar, *to drive*

TOPIC QUESTION 4

¿Maneja Ud.? Do you drive?

present tense of ***manejar***	
yo **manejo**	I drive
Ud. **maneja**	you drive
él **maneja**	he drives
ella **maneja**	she drives
ellos* **manejan**	they drive
ellas* **manejan**	they drive

A. *Preguntas y respuestas*

Practice reading aloud the following questions and answers:

1. ¿Maneja Ud.?
Sí, yo manejo.
No, yo no manejo.

2. ¿Maneja él?
Sí, él maneja.
No, él no maneja.

3. ¿Maneja ella?
Sí, ella maneja.
No, ella no maneja.

4. ¿Manejan ellos?
Sí, ellos manejan.
No, ellos no manejan.

Vocabulario
bastante, quite
esposo, husband
hija, daughter
hijo, son
nuevo, new
viejo, old
porque, because

Mi hermano tiene un coche nuevo.

---

*__Ellos__ refers to males *or* to a mixed group of males and females. **Ellas** refers only to females.

Learn to ask and answer these questions easily, without looking at the page.

For questions 5 to 12, write the missing parts of the answers:

5. ¿Maneja Ud.?
No, yo no ____________________________

6. ¿Maneja su padre?
Sí, mi padre __________________________

7. ¿Maneja su madre?
Sí, ella __________________________

8. ¿Manejan sus hermanos?
No, mis hermanos ________________________________

9. ¿Maneja su amiga favorita?
Sí, mi amiga favorita __________________________

10. ¿Maneja su amigo favorito?
No, él ________________________________

11. ¿Maneja María?
No, ____________________________________

12. ¿Maneja Alberto?
Sí, ____________________________________

B. *Lectura*

Yo me llamo Margarita.
Yo no manejo.

Mi padre maneja.
Él no maneja bien.

Mi madre maneja.
Ella maneja bien.

Mi amiga favorita, Rosita, maneja.
Ella no maneja muy bien.

Mi padre no maneja bien.

Preguntas

1. ¿Cómo se llama la muchacha? ____

2. ¿Maneja Margarita? ____

3. ¿Maneja su padre? ____

4. ¿Maneja él bien? ____

5. ¿Maneja su madre? ____

6. ¿Maneja ella bien? ____

7. ¿Cómo se llama su amiga favorita? ______________________________

8. ¿Maneja bien Rosita? ______________________________

C. *Preguntas personales*

1. ¿Maneja Ud.? ______________________________

2. ¿Maneja su padre? ______________________________

3. ¿Maneja su madre? ______________________________

4. ¿Manejan sus hermanos? ______________________________

5. ¿Maneja su amigo favorito? ______________________________

D. *Tema*

Write a composition entitled *¿Maneja Ud.?* Start with *Yo me llamo. . . . Yo manejo un coche. Es un. . . . Yo manejo bien.* Then give the same kind of information about the "cast of characters" in exercise D on page 16. After you have written the *tema,* prepare to give it orally.

____

____

____

____

____

E. Here is a *tema* written by a teacher. Read it carefully; then make up five questions in Spanish about what you have read. Example: *¿Maneja bien Carol Smith?* Write your questions on the lines below; then read them aloud to a classmate, who will answer them in Spanish.

¿Maneja Ud.?

Me llamo Carol Smith. Yo manejo. Manejo bastante bien.

Mi esposo se llama Robert. Él maneja. No maneja bien.

Yo tengo una hija. Se llama Sue. Ella maneja. Maneja bien.

Yo tengo dos hijos. Un hijo se llama Joe. Él maneja. Maneja así así. El otro hijo se llama Curly. Curly no maneja.

Curly no maneja.

1. ____

2. ____

3. ____

4. ____

5. ____

F. *Traduzca Ud. al español:*

1. Do you drive? ____
2. She doesn't drive. ____
3. He drives. ____
4. I don't drive. ____
5. Does your mother drive? ____
6. Do your brothers and sisters drive? ____
7. You don't drive. ____
8. They drive. ____
9. Do they drive? ____
10. No, they don't drive. ____

G. Complete the sentences:

1. "¿Cómo ________________ usted?" "Yo ________________ muy bien, gracias."

2. "¿Cómo ________________ sus hermanas?"
   "Ellas ________________ Anita y Juana."

3. Mi padre no tiene un* coche nuevo; él tiene un coche ________________.
   Yo no ________________ coche porque yo no ______________________________.

4. "¿Manejan Rosita, Clara y Alberto?"
   "Sí, ________________ manejan muy bien."
   (they)

5. Yo me llamo José Martínez Guzmán. La señora ________________ es mi madre.

La columna personal de Anita Gómez (1)

(Anita Gómez's Personal Column)

Anita Gómez.

Anita Gómez writes a column for the newspaper *El Diario* in Mexico City. If you have any problem concerning your family or affairs of the heart, be sure to write to her. Letters to Anita Gómez must be written in Spanish and include a self-addressed return envelope. Postage to Mexico costs the same as within the United States.

Read Juan Enfermo's letter below. Also read the candid advice offered by Anita Gómez in her reply.

---

*The indefinite article is used if the object of **no tener** is modified by an adjective: "Yo no tengo coche" *but* "Yo no tengo **un** coche **nuevo**."

el 2 de febrero

Querida Anita Gómez:

Mi padre no está bien. Mi madre no está bien. Mis hermanos no están bien. Mi amigo favorito no está bien. Mi burro no está bien.

¿Qué debemos hacer?

Juan Enfermo

el 10 de febrero

Querido Juan Enfermo:

¡Ustedes deben ir a un médico, claro!

Anita Gómez

P.D. Yo no estoy bien tampoco.

Vocabulario

querido, **querida** dear
burro, donkey
debemos, we ought
hacer, to do
¿Qué debemos hacer? What should we do?
enfermo, **enferma** sick
deben, you (*pl.*) ought
ir, to go
médico, doctor
¡claro! of course!
P.D. (posdata), P.S.
tampoco, either
por eso, for that reason, therefore
dice que, says that

H. Complete the sentences:

1. Juan no está bien. Por eso él se llama Juan ____________________.
2. "¿Están enfermos sus hermanos?" "Sí, ellos no ________________ bien."
3. Su madre también está ________________. Ella no ________________ bien.
4. ¿Qué debe hacer Juan? Anita Gómez dice que Juan debe ______________________ ______________.
5. ¿Cómo está Anita Gómez? Ella dice que ____________________________________.

Lesson 7

licencia para manejar, *driver's license*

A. *Lectura*

Yo me llamo Lupe. Yo no manejo y no tengo licencia para manejar.

Mi padre maneja. Él tiene una licencia para manejar.

Mi madre maneja. Ella no tiene licencia para manejar. No tiene licencia para manejar porque no maneja bien.

Mi hermano Guillermo maneja y tiene una licencia para manejar.

Mis hermanos Margarita y Tomás no tienen licencia para manejar.

Mi amigo favorito, Pepe, tiene una licencia para manejar. Él no maneja mucho porque no tiene coche.

Vocabulario

Lupe (short for **Guadalupe**), girl's name
Pepe (nickname for **José**), Joey
Guillermo, William
la madre de Lupe, Lupe's mother

Mi madre maneja. No tiene licencia para manejar.

Preguntas

1. ¿Cómo se llama la muchacha?

____

2. ¿Maneja Lupe?

____

3. ¿Tiene el padre de Lupe una licencia para manejar?

____

4. ¿Por qué no tiene licencia para manejar la madre de Lupe?

____

5. ¿Maneja Guillermo?

____

6. ¿Cómo se llama el amigo favorito de Lupe?

____

7. ¿Por qué no maneja mucho Pepe?

____

B. *Traduzca Ud. al español:*

1. Do you have a driver's license?

---

2. They don't have a driver's license.

---

3. I don't have a driver's license.

---

4. Lupe's mother doesn't drive.

---

5. Does your mother have a driver's license?

Review Exercises

(Lessons 1–7)

Preguntas y respuestas

C. Here are some answers. What are the questions?

EXAMPLE: Ella se llama María. *¿Cómo se llama su amiga favorita?*

1. No, yo no tengo coche.

---

2. No, mi hermana no maneja.

---

3. No, él está bien de salud.

---

4. Sí, mi padre tiene un coche.

---

5. Ellos se llaman José y Marta.

---

6. Sí, Juan y Jorge manejan bien.

---

7. Yo me llamo José García, para servirle.

---

8. María está bien.

Verb Review

D. Write the form of the verb that goes with the indicated subject:

	tener	*estar*	*llamarse*
1. Ud.	________________	________________	________________
2. yo	________________	________________	________________
3. ellas	________________	________________	________________
4. él	________________	________________	________________

Ricardo no maneja bien.

Lesson 8

quiere decir, *it means;* **se dice,** *one says*

TOPIC QUESTION 5	**TOPIC QUESTION 6**
¿Qué quiere decir . . . ? What does . . . mean?	**¿Cómo se dice . . . ?** How does one say . . . ? How do you say . . . ?

A. *Preguntas y respuestas*

Practice reading aloud the following questions and answers:

(1) **1.** ¿Qué quiere decir *padre?*
Padre quiere decir *father.*

2. ¿Qué quiere decir *madre?*
Madre quiere decir *mother.*

3. ¿Qué quiere decir *amigo?*
Amigo quiere decir *friend.*

4. ¿Qué quiere decir *hermano?*
Hermano quiere decir *brother.*

5. ¿Qué quiere decir *tener?*
Tener quiere decir *to have.*

6. ¿Qué quiere decir *manejar?*
Manejar quiere decir *to drive.*

(2) **1.** ¿Cómo se dice *friend?*
Se dice *amigo.*

2. ¿Cómo se dice *to drive?*
Se dice *manejar.*

3. ¿Cómo se dice *father?*
Se dice *padre.*

4. ¿Cómo se dice *mother?*
Se dice *madre.*

5. ¿Cómo se dice *sister?*
Se dice *hermana.*

6. ¿Cómo se dice *I have?*
Se dice *yo tengo.*

B. Make up six questions in Spanish: three that ask what something means, and three that ask "how does one say . . . ?" Write your questions and their answers in the blanks below:

	QUESTIONS	ANSWERS
1.	________________________________	________________________________
2.	________________________________	________________________________
3.	________________________________	________________________________
4.	________________________________	________________________________
5.	________________________________	________________________________
6.	________________________________	________________________________

C. *Traduzca Ud. al español:*

1. What does "casa" mean? "Casa" means "house."

----

2. How do you say "Good morning"? You say "Buenos días."

----

3. What does "no tengo dinero" mean? It means "I don't have any money."

COGNATES (1)

Americans may find Spanish easier to learn than other languages because many Spanish words look like English words and have similar meanings. Such resemblances are due to a common origin. About half of the English vocabulary comes from Latin. Since Spanish was originally a form of Latin, it is not surprising that Spanish and English have many words in common.

If an English word is similar to a Spanish word in form and meaning, the two words are called *cognates*. For example, *remedio* is a cognate of "remedy" (and vice versa). About 65% of the Spanish words that you will learn have English cognates.

Not all cognates have the same meaning; for instance, a *lectura* is not a lecture but something that is read.

COGNATE TYPE 1: Spanish nouns that end in **-dad** or **-tad** have English cognates ending in *-ty*.

Here are some examples:

la* **sociedad,** society
la **prosperidad,** prosperity
la **majestad,** majesty
la **oportunidad,** opportunity
la **ciudad,** city
la **trinidad,** trinity
la **nacionalidad,** nationality

How do you think the following words are written in Spanish? Can you write them correctly without consulting a dictionary?

D. 1. formality ______________________
2. unity ______________________
3. curiosity ______________________
4. liberty ______________________
5. personality ______________________
6. capacity ______________________

*The definite article (*the* in English) has different forms in Spanish; for example, "**el** padre," "**la** madre." **El** is used before a masculine noun, **la** before a feminine noun. (All Spanish nouns are either masculine or feminine—even nouns that refer to *things* rather than persons.) Nouns that end in **-dad** or **-tad** are feminine. (See Lesson 30.)

Lesson 9

nosotros / nosotras } *we;* ustedes, *you (pl.)*

The Spanish word for *we* ends in **-os** when referring to males or to a mixed group of males and females; it ends in **-as** when referring only to females. For example, María would refer to herself and her girl friends as "nosotr**as**."

The word **nosotros** does not have to be expressed:

nosotros tenemos or simply **tenemos** } = we have

Usted, *you,* becomes **ustedes** when speaking to more than one person. The abbreviation for **ustedes** is **Uds.** If a question is directed to **ustedes,** you must answer with the **nosotros** form of the verb.

nosotros forms:
nos llamamos, our names are **estamos,** we are **tenemos,** we have **manejamos,** we drive
The **ustedes** form is the same as that for **ellos:** **Uds.** / ellos / ellas } **están, tienen, manejan**

A. *Preguntas y respuestas*

Practice reading aloud the following questions and answers:

1. ¿Cómo se llama Ud.?
Yo me llamo Enrique, para servirle.

2. ¿Cómo se llaman Uds.?
Nosotros nos llamamos María y José.

3. ¿Cómo está Ud.?
Yo estoy bien.

4. ¿Cómo están Uds.?
Nosotros estamos bien.

5. ¿Tiene Ud. un coche?
No, yo no tengo coche.

6. ¿Tienen Uds. un coche?
No, nosotros no tenemos coche.

7. ¿Maneja Ud.?
No, yo no manejo.

8. ¿Manejan Uds.?
No, nosotros no manejamos.

B. Write the proper form of the verb:

llamarse

1. yo ____________________
2. Ud. ____________________
3. él ____________________
4. nosotros ____________________
5. Uds. ____________________
6. ellas ____________________

estar

7. yo ____________________
8. Ud. ____________________
9. ella ____________________
10. nosotras ____________________
11. Uds. ____________________
12. ellos ____________________

tener

13. yo ____________________
14. Ud. ____________________
15. él ____________________
16. nosotros ____________________
17. Uds. ____________________
18. ellas ____________________

manejar

19. yo ____________________
20. Ud. ____________________
21. ella ____________________
22. nosotras ____________________
23. Uds. ____________________
24. ellos ____________________

C. *Traduzca Ud. al español:*

1. My name is Tomás. ____________________
2. What is your name? *(Ud.)* ____________________
3. What are your names? *(Uds.)* ____________________
4. Their name is González. ____________________
5. Our names are Pepe and Lupe. ____________________
6. How are you? *(Uds.)* ____________________
7. We are fine. ____________________
8. They aren't well. ____________________
9. You have a car. *(Ud.)* ____________________
10. Do you have a car? *(Uds.)* ____________________

Vocabulary Review

D. Write these expressions in Spanish:

1. Mr. ____________________
2. Mrs. ____________________
3. Miss ____________________
4. Good morning. ____________________
5. Good afternoon. ____________________
6. Good evening. ____________________
7. Hi! ____________________
8. How goes it? ____________________
9. So-so. ____________________
10. Thank you. ____________________

11. Very well. ______________________
12. Good-bye. ______________________
13. I'll be seeing you. ________________
14. You're welcome. _______________
15. Bless you! ______________________
16. to be named ___________________
17. at your service _________________
18. your __________________________
19. father _________________________
20. mother ________________________
21. brother ________________________
22. sister _________________________
23. friend _________________________
24. her ___________________________
25. his ___________________________
26. to be _________________________
27. he ____________________________
28. she ___________________________
29. they __________________________
30. you (singular) _________________
31. you (plural) ___________________
32. Thomas ________________________
33. I _____________________________
34. to have _______________________
35. car ___________________________
36. it is __________________________
37. to drive _______________________
38. driver's license ________________
39. What does . . . mean? ___________
40. How do you say . . . ? _________

La columna personal de Anita Gómez (2)

el 12 de mayo

Querida Anita Gómez:

Yo no manejo. Mi padre no maneja. Mi madre no maneja. Mis hermanos no manejan. Mi amigo favorito no maneja. Nosotros tenemos cinco coches.
¿Qué debemos hacer?

Juan No Maneja

el 20 de mayo

Querido Juan No Maneja:

Uds. deben emplear a cinco chóferes.

Anita Gómez

P.D. ¿Por qué no aprenden Uds. a manejar?

Vocabulario

cinco, five
emplear, to hire, employ
chóferes, chauffeurs, drivers
aprender, to learn

E. Complete the sentences:

1. Juan se llama ''Juan No Maneja'' porque ______________________________
2. Juan, su familia y su amigo tienen ______________________________
3. Anita Gómez dice que ellos deben aprender ______________________________

Frases revueltas (Scrambled sentences)

F. Unscramble the following sentences:

1. ? Ud. llama ¿ cómo se

____

2. y llaman hermanos mis se Jorge Ricardo .

____

3. favorito se amigo Juan llama mi .

____

4. ? muchacho cómo el está ¿

____

5. Catalina usado coche hermana un mi tiene .

____

6. coche ? él ¿ un tiene

____

7. tienen sí coche ellos un .

____

8. marca ? es qué ¿

____

9. maneja no bien él .

____

10. ? padre maneja su ¿

____

11. tengo no yo para manejar licencia .

____

12. maneja tiene porque mucho coche no no Pepe .

____

13. mucho ¿ por maneja qué ? Pepe, no

----

14. decir "tener" *have to* quiere .

----

15. *friend* ? se dice ¿ cómo

----

16. quiere "madre" *mother* decir .

----

17. tenemos nosotros no coche .

----

18. servirle yo llamo Timoteo me para .

----

19. Miguel nosotros y Anita nos llamamos .

----

20. están ¿ cómo ? Uds.

Lesson 10

proverbios y refranes, *proverbs and sayings*

The Spanish language has a rich store of proverbs and sayings. Here are some of the more popular sayings along with their English equivalents. Practice reading these proverbs aloud until you can pronounce them accurately and easily. Then try to learn a few of them by heart.

1. **En boca cerrada no entran moscas.**
("Into a closed mouth flies do not enter.")
Don't put your foot in your mouth.
(It's safer to keep your mouth shut.)

Dime con quien andas y te diré quién eres.

2. **Dime con quien andas y te diré quien eres.**
("Tell me with whom you go and I will tell you who you are.")
Birds of a feather flock together.

3. **Más vale pájaro en mano que cien volando.**
("A bird in the hand is worth more than a hundred flying.")
A bird in the hand is worth two in the bush.

4. **Perro que ladra no muerde.**
A barking dog doesn't bite.

5. **A caballo regalado no le mires el diente.**
("Don't look at the tooth of a gift horse.")
Don't look a gift horse in the mouth.

Más vale tarde que nunca.

6. **Más vale tarde que nunca.**
Better late than never.

7. **Antes que te cases, mira lo que haces.**
("Before you marry, watch what you're doing.")
Marry in haste, repent at leisure.

8. **Del dicho al hecho hay gran trecho.**
("From the said to the done there is a great distance.")
It's easier said than done.

9. **Todo lo que brilla no es de oro.**
All that glitters is not gold.

10. **Cortesía de boca mucho vale y poco cuesta.**
(''Courtesy of the mouth is worth much and costs little.'')
It pays to be polite.

11. **Ver es creer.**
Seeing is believing.

12. **Hay que llamar al pan pan y al vino vino.**
(''One must call bread bread and wine wine.'')
Let's call a spade a spade.

13. **Salud, pesetas y amor.** (a toast)
Here's to health, money and love.

14. **A buena hambre no hay pan duro.**
(''When one is really hungry, there's no such thing as hard bread.'')
Beggars can't be choosers.

15. **Querer es poder.**
(''To want is to be able.'')
Where there's a will, there's a way.

Exercise

Write a Spanish proverb that would be suitable for each situation:

1. Juan is tardy when he arrives in class. He tells the teacher, ''I'm sorry I'm late.'' She answers:
'' -- ''

2. ''Thanks for the watch, it's a nice present,'' says María. ''But I really wanted a bicycle.'' Her friend answers:
'' -- ''

3. Alberto wants to refuse the third prize in a TV game show in order to take a chance on winning the first prize. But his friend advises:
'' -- ''

4. Anita says: ''I can easily earn an *A* in Spanish; I just don't feel like studying.'' Pepe replies, ''It's easy to *say* you can, but you know the old proverb:
-- ''

5. "This umbrella broke the first time I opened it. I'm going to return it to the store and demand my money back!"

"All right, but don't sound so angry. As they say in Spanish,

--."

6. "That's a pretty ring you have," says Susana to Lupita, "but you know the old saying:

--."

"You mean it's not a real diamond?" asks Lupita.

7. Señora Mendoza tells her son: "I'd have a better opinion of your friend Raúl if he didn't always hang around with *that* crowd. You know the saying:

--."

8. Tomás says: "I'd love to visit Spain, but it's hopeless; where would I get the money for the trip?" His friend Ramón replies: "If you want to, you'll find a way. As the Spanish say:

--."

9. Pepe tells Ramón about the wonderful girl he met last night: "She is my dream girl and I am planning to propose to her tonight." Ramón warns:

" --."

10. "What does he do for a living?"

"He's a specialist in mortuary science."

"You mean he's an *undertaker*. Why don't you say so? After all,

--."

Lesson 11

los números cero a diez, *numbers zero to ten*

TOPIC QUESTION 7A

¿Cuántos son _____ y _____?
How much is ___ plus ___?

TOPIC QUESTION 7B

¿Cuántos son _____ menos _____?
How much is ___ minus ___?

A. Learn the Spanish words for 0–10:

0 **cero**	6 **seis**
1 **uno**	7 **siete**
2 **dos**	8 **ocho**
3 **tres**	9 **nueve**
4 **cuatro**	10 **diez**
5 **cinco**	

B. *Un poco de aritmética* (A little arithmetic)

1. ¿Cuántos son 5 y 3? — How much is 5 and 3? / How much is 5 + 3?

5 y 3 son 8. — 5 and 3 is (equals) 8. / 5 + 3 = 8.

2. ¿Cuántos son 5 menos 3? — How much is 5 − 3?

5 menos 3 son dos. — 5 − 3 = 2.

C. *Lea Ud.* (Read):

1. Uno y uno son dos.
2. Dos y tres son cinco.
3. Cuatro y dos son seis.
4. Siete menos cinco son dos.
5. Diez menos tres son siete.
6. Cinco y cinco son diez.

Vocabulario

número, number
cuente Ud., count
desde . . . hasta, from . . . to
en inglés, in English
en español, in Spanish

D. *Preguntas*

1. ¿Qué quiere decir *nueve* en inglés?
   En inglés *nueve* quiere decir ____.
2. ¿Qué quiere decir *seis* en inglés?

   ____

3. ¿Cómo se dice *five* en español?

---

4. ¿Cómo se dice *eight* en español?

---

5. ¿Cuántos son tres y seis?

---

6. ¿Cuántos son ocho menos cinco?

---

7. ¿Cuántos son diez menos uno?

---

8. ¿Cuántos son cinco menos cinco?

Cuente Ud. . . .

9. Cuente Ud. desde uno hasta cinco.

---

10. Cuente Ud. desde cuatro hasta nueve.

E. *Traduzca Ud. al español:*

1. Four and six is ten.

---

2. Six minus four equals two.

---

3. Count from three to eight.

---

4. Count from two to six.

---

5. How do you say *nine* in Spanish?

---

6. What does *cinco* mean?

---

7. Five and two is seven.

---

8. Ten minus seven is three.

---

9. How much is four and five?

____

10. How much is ten minus two?

____

F. Write three addition problems in blanks 1 to 3 and three subtraction problems in blanks 4 to 6. (Make up your *own* problems; be original.) Write all numbers as Spanish words. Then read each problem aloud to a classmate, who will answer them in Spanish.

1. ______________________________
2. ______________________________
3. ______________________________
4. ______________________________
5. ______________________________
6. ______________________________

G. Make up three commands in the form *Cuente Ud. desde* _____ *hasta* _____.

1. ______________________________
2. ______________________________
3. ______________________________

COGNATES (2)

COGNATE TYPE 2: Spanish words ending in **-ción** have English cognates ending in *-tion*.

Spanish nouns ending in **-ción** are feminine. Here are some examples:

la **transportación,** transportation
la **civilización,** civilization
la **organización,** organization
la **comunicación,** communication
la **meditación,** meditation

H. Write these words in Spanish:

1. conservation ______________
2. condition ______________
3. imitation ______________
4. nation ______________
5. section ______________
6. information ______________
7. separation ______________

Lesson 12

ir, *to go*

TOPIC QUESTION 8

¿Va Ud. mucho al cine? Do you go to the movies much?

present tense of *ir*			
yo **voy**	I go	nosotros **vamos**	we go
Ud. **va**	you go	Uds. **van**	you go
él **va**	he goes	ellos } **van**	they go
ella **va**	she goes	ellas } **van**	they go

A. *Preguntas y respuestas*

Practice reading aloud the following questions and answers:

1. ¿Va Ud. mucho al cine?
Sí, yo voy mucho al cine.
No, yo no voy mucho al cine.

2. ¿Van Uds. mucho al cine?
Sí, nosotros vamos mucho al cine.
No, nosotros no vamos mucho al cine.

3. ¿Va él mucho al cine?
Sí, él va mucho al cine.
No, él no va mucho al cine.

4. ¿Va ella mucho al cine?
Sí, ella va mucho al cine.
No, ella no va mucho al cine.

5. ¿Van ellos mucho al cine?
Sí, ellos van mucho al cine.
No, ellos no van mucho al cine.

Vocabulario

Mateo, Matthew
escuela superior, high school
(escuela) primaria, elementary school
universidad, college, university
padres, parents
las afueras, the outskirts, suburbs
la ciudad de México, Mexico City
La Ciudad Universitaria, University City

Learn to ask and answer these questions without looking at the page.

For questions 6 to 12, write the missing parts of the answers:

6. ¿Va Ud. mucho al cine?
No, yo no ____

7. ¿Van Uds. mucho al cine?
Sí, nosotros ____

8. ¿Va su padre mucho al cine?

No, mi padre no ______________________________________

9. ¿Va su madre mucho al cine?

No, mi madre ______________________________________

10. ¿Van mucho al cine sus hermanos?

Sí, mis hermanos ______________________________________

11. ¿Va mucho al cine su amigo favorito (amiga favorita)?

Sí, mi amigo(-a) favorito(-a) ______________________________________

12. ¿Va ella mucho al cine?

No, ella ______________________________________

B. *Lectura*

Yo me llamo Mateo. Yo tengo dos hermanos y una hermana.

Mi hermana Carlota y yo vamos a la escuela superior.

Mi hermano Ramón va a la primaria y mi hermano Eugenio va a la universidad.

La universidad se llama la Universidad Nacional de México. Se llama también la Ciudad Universitaria. Está en las afueras de la ciudad de México.*

Mis padres no van a la escuela.

Ramón va a la primaria.

Preguntas

1. ¿Cuántas hermanas tiene Mateo?

____

2. ¿Va Eugenio a la escuela superior?

____

3. ¿Quién (*Who*) va a la primaria?

____

C. *Traduzca Ud. al español:*

1. I go to school.

____

2. Does your father go to the movies much?

____

*Actually, "la ciudad de México" is an expression rarely heard *inside* Mexico, where people call the city simply *México*. (It is also called *México, D. F.* See Lesson 46.)

3. Mary and Louis don't go to high school.

____

4. Do your brothers and sisters go to elementary school?

____

5. The National University is on the outskirts of Mexico City.

____

6. We go to school.

____

7. You *(Ud.)* go to high school.

____

8. You *(Uds.)* go to University City.

____

9. Do you *(Ud.)* go to school?

____

10. Does your favorite friend go to college?

____

D. *Diálogo*. In the following dialogue, play the role of María. Write her responses in the blanks.

JUAN: ¿Van usted y su hermano a la escuela superior?

MARÍA: ____

JUAN: Yo voy a la escuela superior también. Mi hermana Rosita va a una universidad en México.*

MARÍA: ____

JUAN: Se llama la Universidad Nacional. ¿Qué quiere decir en inglés?

MARÍA: ____

JUAN: ¿Va usted al cine hoy?

MARÍA: ____

JUAN: ¿Con quién va usted?

MARÍA: ____

---

*As María, try to respond to this comment in a way that leads to Juan's *next* remark: "It's called the National University." Juan has no reason to say this unless María has asked him about the name of Rosita's university.

When you fill the blanks in the *Diálogo* exercises, check your work to make sure that each response makes sense in two "directions": as a reply to what the other person has just said and also as a possible reason for what the other person *is going to say next*.

La columna personal de Anita Gómez (3)

el 3 de marzo

Querida Anita Gómez:

Yo no tengo dinero. Yo no tengo coche. Yo no tengo novia.

¿Qué debo yo hacer?

Pobre Pepe

Vocabulario

novia, sweetheart, girlfriend, fiancée
pobre, poor
trabajar, to work

el 14 de marzo

Querido Pobre Pepe:

¡Ud. debe trabajar!

Anita Gómez

E. Complete the sentences:

1. Pepe no tiene coche porque ______________________________________.

2. Pepe no tiene ____________________ tampoco.

3. Anita Gómez dice que Pepe ______________________________________.

Lesson 13

THE POSSESSIVE ADJECTIVE su (sus)

A. Learn all the possible meanings of **su (sus):** { *your*, *his*, *her*, *its*, *their* }

Vocabulario

libro, book
página, page

The *intended* meaning can be determined only from what is said earlier in the conversation. Read the following sentences. Can you tell the meaning of **su** or **sus** in each case?

meaning of su (sus)

1. Roberto tiene un coche. Su amigo Martín tiene un coche también. _______________
2. Roberto, ¿cómo están sus padres? _______________
3. Yo no uso mi libro porque sus páginas están rotas *(torn)*. _______________
4. María tiene cinco pesos. Sus amigas Inés y Margarita tienen diez pesos. _______________
5. El padre de María y Antonio tiene un coche nuevo. María y Antonio van al cine en su coche porque ellos no tienen coche. _______________
6. María y Antonio tienen un coche nuevo. Ellos van al cine en su coche. _______________

B. **Su** becomes **sus** before a noun in the plural: *their friend* = **su amigo;** *their friends* = **sus amigos.**

Change the phrase from the singular to the plural or vice versa:

1. su libro ____________________________________
2. sus hermanas ____________________________________
3. su burro ____________________________________
4. sus amigos favoritos ____________________________________
5. su madre ____________________________________

C. *Traduzca Ud. al español:*

1. I have your book. ____________________________________
2. He doesn't have your books. ____________________________________
3. He drives his car. ____________________________________
4. His sisters go to school. ____________________________________
5. Her father drives. ____________________________________
6. Her parents drive. ____________________________________
7. Their father is not well. ____________________________________
8. Their sisters have a car. ____________________________________

D. Complete these sentences with the names of your friends and their parents. (Use first names only.) Start #1 with the name of a boyfriend, #2 with the name of a girlfriend.

Read the sentences aloud for practice, and be ready to repeat them orally in class without looking at your paper.

1. __________________ es mi amigo.
Su padre se llama __________________.
Sus padres se llaman __________________ y __________________.

2. __________________ es mi amiga.
Su padre se llama __________________.
Sus padres se llaman __________________ y __________________.

3. __________________ y __________________ son hermanos.
Su padre se llama __________________.
Sus padres se llaman __________________ y __________________.

E. Since **su (sus)** has several meanings, the intended meaning can be made clear by replacing **su (sus)** with a more specific expression:

your his her their	book = **su** libro *or*	**el libro de Ud.** **el libro de Uds.**	your book
		el libro de él,	his book
		el libro de ella,	her book
		el libro de ellos **el libro de ellas**	their book

your his her their	books = **sus** libros *or*	**los libros de Ud.** **los libros de Uds.**	your books
		los libros de él,	his books
		los libros de ella,	her books
		los libros de ellos **los libros de ellas**	their books

For example, in the sentence ''Raúl y sus padres van en su coche,'' it may not be clear in whose car they are going: Raúl's? His parents'? To avoid confusion, one can say instead:

Raúl y sus padres van en el coche de él (in *his* car).

or

Raúl y sus padres van en el coche de ellos (in *their* car).

—depending on which meaning of **su** is the one intended.

Replace *su (sus)* with a more specific expression.

EXAMPLE: (*su* = her) su libro *el libro de ella*

1. (*su* = their) su coche ________________________

2. (*su* = his) su madre ________________________

3. (*sus* = your, *pl.*) sus amigos ________________________

4. (*sus* = her) sus hermanos ________________________

5. (*su* = its, *f.*) su precio *(price)* ________________________

Lesson 14

los días de la semana, *the days of the week*

Vocabulario

ayer, yesterday
hoy, today
mañana, tomorrow
fue, was
el **día,** day
la **semana,** week
¿Qué día? What (Which) day?
lunes, Monday
martes, Tuesday
miércoles, Wednesday
jueves, Thursday
viernes, Friday
sábado, Saturday
domingo, Sunday
si, if

TOPIC QUESTION 9A — **¿Qué día es hoy?** What day is today?

TOPIC QUESTION 9B — **¿Qué día es mañana?** What day is tomorrow?

TOPIC QUESTION 9C — **¿Qué día fue ayer?** What day was yesterday?

A. *Lectura*

Los días de la semana son: lunes, martes, miércoles, jueves, viernes, sábado y domingo.

Hoy es martes. Mañana es miércoles. Ayer fue lunes.

Yo me llamo Juan. Yo voy a la escuela los* lunes, los martes, los miércoles, los jueves y los viernes.

Yo no voy a la escuela los sábados y los domingos.

Preguntas

1. ¿Cómo se llama el muchacho?

____

2. ¿Va Juan a la escuela los martes?

____

3. ¿Va a la escuela los domingos?

____

4. Si mañana es miércoles, ¿qué día es hoy?

____

*__Los__ is the plural form of **el.** Both forms, of course, mean *the*. To express *on* with a day of the week, the definite article must be used: **el** martes, on Tuesday; **los** martes, on Tuesdays.

5. Si ayer fue lunes, ¿qué día es mañana?

____

6. Si hoy es martes, ¿qué día fue ayer?

____

B. *Preguntas personales*

1. ¿Va Ud. a la escuela los jueves?

____

2. ¿Van Uds. a la escuela los sábados?

____

3. ¿Cómo se dice *Wednesday* en español?

____

4. ¿Qué quiere decir *viernes* en inglés?

____

5. Hoy es martes. ¿Qué día es mañana?

____

6. Ayer fue domingo. ¿Qué día es hoy?

____

7. Mañana es viernes. ¿Qué día es hoy?

C. *Traduzca Ud. al español:*

1. What day is today?

____

2. Today is Tuesday.

____

3. Do you *(Ud.)* go to school on Mondays?

____

4. I don't go to school on Saturdays and Sundays.

____

5. Does your brother go to school on Wednesdays?

____

6. My brother goes to school on Tuesdays.

____

7. Does your sister go to school on Thursdays?

____

8. My sister goes to school on Fridays.

----

9. Tomorrow is Sunday.

----

10. Yesterday was Tuesday.

----

11. What day was yesterday?

----

12. What day is tomorrow?

D. Notice that, unlike English, the Spanish names for the days of the week are *not* capitalized. Can you write them down from memory, in the correct order? Use this line:

Check to make sure you have spelled all the names correctly.

E. *Conversación*. Use Topic Questions 9A, 9B, and 9C on page 46 to ask your classmate (1) what day it is, (2) what day it will be tomorrow, and (3) what day it was yesterday. After your classmate answers (in Spanish, of course!), he or she will turn to another student, asking the same questions but in a different order. A fourth student, after answering the questions, will ask them of a fifth, and so on. Vary the game by asking questions like "Si hoy es jueves, ¿qué día es mañana?" (or ". . . ¿qué día fue ayer?").

La columna personal de Anita Gómez (4)

el 5 de abril

Querida Anita Gómez:

Yo tengo mucho dinero. Yo soy guapo. Yo tengo un coche grande. Yo tengo un problema. Yo no tengo novia.

Roberto Oro y Plata

Vocabulario

dinero, money
soy, I am
guapo, handsome
grande, big
oro, gold
plata, silver
debe, ought
bailes, dances
para conocer, in order to meet
en casa, at home
todas las noches, every night
según, according to

el 25 de abril

Querido Roberto Oro y Plata:

Ud. no tiene problema. Ud. debe ir a los bailes para conocer a las muchachas.

Anita Gómez

P.D. Mi teléfono es 01-12-36. Yo estoy en casa todas las noches.

F. Complete the sentences:

1. Roberto se llama Oro y Plata porque ________________

2. Roberto dice que él es ________ y tiene ________________

3. El problema de Roberto es que ________________

4. Según Anita Gómez, Roberto debe ir a los bailes para ________________ ________________

5. Anita Gómez dice que ella está ________________

Crucigrama (1)

(Crossword Puzzle)

Across

3. *Spanish*
6. Tengo un coche pero no tengo _____ para manejar.
7. Yo me _____ Isabel.
8. ¿Cómo se dice *boy* en español?
10. "¿Está Ud. enfermo hoy?" "Sí, yo no estoy _____."
11. ¿_____ está su padre?
14. *I don't drive* = yo no _____.
17. _____ quiere decir *father*.
20. "La señorita Smith" = _____ Smith en inglés.
21. *but*
24. _____ se llaman Carlos y Rebeca.
26. María _____ mi hermana.
27. This fruit is called a _____ both in Spanish and in English.

Down

1. ¿ _____ sus hermanos un coche?
2. *because*
4. Diego es mi amigo _____.
5. Mis hermanos se _____ Juan y José.
9. Yo tengo un _____ usado.
12. *we don't drive* = no _____
13. Me llamo Ernesto, _____ servirle.
15. ¿Cómo se dice *Henry* en español?
16. "La Sra. Marín" = _____ Marín en inglés.
18. ¿Cómo se dice *de* en italiano?
19. Nosotros _____ así así.
21. iniciales de Pablo López
22. *Helen* = _____ en español.
23. *Rose* = _____ en español.
25. ¿Adónde _____ Ud.? = *Where are you going?*

Lesson 15

nadar, *to swim*

TOPIC QUESTION 10

¿Nada Ud.?
Do you swim?

present tense of ***nadar***			
yo **nado**	I swim	nosotros **nadamos**	we swim
Ud. **nada**	you swim	Uds. **nadan**	you swim
él **nada**	he swims	ellos } **nadan**	they swim
ella **nada**	she swims	ellas }	

A. *Preguntas y respuestas*

Practice reading aloud the following questions and answers:

1. ¿Nada Ud. bien?
No, yo no nado bien.

2. ¿Nadan Uds. mucho?
Sí, nosotros nadamos mucho.

3. ¿Nada él bien?
Sí, él nada bien.

4. ¿Nada ella bien?
Sí, ella nada bien.

5. ¿Nadan ellos mucho?
Sí, ellos nadan mucho.

Vocabulario

la piscina, the swimming pool
el océano, the ocean
la playa, the beach
¿adónde? (to) where?

Learn to ask and answer these questions without looking at the page.

For questions 6 to 11, write the missing parts of the answers:

6. ¿Nada Ud.?
Sí, yo ____________________

7. ¿Nadan Uds.?
No, nosotros no ____________________

8. ¿Nada su padre?
Sí, mi padre ____________________

Teodoro no nada bien.

9. ¿Nada su madre?
   No, mi madre ____________________

10. ¿Nadan sus hermanos?
    Sí, ______________________________________

11. ¿Nada su amiga favorita?
    Sí, ______________________________________

Ask a classmate these questions about a boy and a girl in your class:

	RELAYED ANSWER
12. ¿Nada él?	______________________________
13. ¿Nada ella?	______________________________

B. *Lectura*

Yo me llamo Enrique. Yo nado en la piscina de la escuela. No nado bien.

Mi amigo Pepe nada bien. Mi hermano Ignacio nada bien. Ignacio nada en Acapulco. Acapulco está en México. Está en el Océano Pacífico. Tiene una playa bonita.

Preguntas

1. ¿Cómo se llama el muchacho? ____
2. ¿Dónde nada Enrique? ____
3. ¿Nada bien Enrique? ____
4. ¿Nada bien Pepe? ____
5. ¿Cómo se dice *Pepe* en inglés?______________________________________
6. ¿Dónde nada Ignacio?____
7. ¿Dónde está Acapulco? ____

C. *Preguntas personales*

1. ¿Nada Ud. los domingos?
   ____
2. ¿Tiene su escuela una piscina?
   ____
3. ¿Nadan Ud. y su amigo (amiga)?
   ____
4. ¿Nadan bien sus hermanos?
   ____
5. ¿Qué quiere decir *piscina* en inglés?
   ____

D. *Tema.* Write a composition in Spanish entitled *¿Nada Ud.?* Mention the names of people you know and tell whether each person swims well or not. Prepare to give your *tema* orally.

____

____

____

____

E. *Traduzca Ud. al español:*

1. We don't swim much. ______________________
2. Does your brother swim in the ocean? ______________________
3. They swim in the pool. ______________________
4. He doesn't swim well. ______________________
5. Do your brothers swim well? ______________________

F. *Diálogo.* In the following dialogue, play the roles of Inés and Laura. Write their responses in the blanks.

JUANITA: (speaking to Inés and Laura): ¿Adónde van ustedes para nadar?

INÉS: ____

JUANITA: Yo no voy a la playa para nadar. Yo nado en la piscina de mi escuela. ¿Nadan ustedes mucho?

LAURA: ____

JUANITA: Inés, ¿va usted a nadar mañana?

INÉS: ____

Lesson 16

THE POSSESSIVE ADJECTIVES mi AND nuestro

A. *My* is **mi** in Spanish: **mi** amigo, *my friend*. It is **mis** before a noun in the plural: **mis** amigos, *my friends*.

Change the phrase from singular to plural or vice versa:

1. mis clases ______________________
2. mi hermana ______________________
3. mi padre ______________________
4. mis libros ______________________

B. *Our* is **nuestro** in Spanish. This adjective has four possible endings, depending on whether the noun it is used with is masculine or feminine, singular or plural:

nuestr**o** libr**o**	nuestr**a** cas**a**
nuestr**os** libr**os**	nuestr**as** cas**as**

Write the correct form of *nuestro*.

EXAMPLE: __*nuestras*__ amigas

1. ____________________ casa
2. ____________________ coche
3. ____________________ libros
4. ____________________ escuela
5. ____________________ hermanas
6. ____________________ amigo

C. Complete the sentences with the names of your friends. Read the sentences aloud for practice, and be ready to repeat them orally in class without looking at your paper.

Mi amigo se llama __________________.
Mis amigos se llaman __________________ y __________________.

Nuestro amigo se llama __________________.
Nuestros amigos se llaman __________________ y __________________.

Nuestra amiga se llama __________________.
Nuestras amigas se llaman __________________ y __________________.

D. *Traduzca Ud. al español:*

1. Our mother has a car. ____
2. Our brothers drive. ____
3. Our father doesn't swim. ____
4. Our mothers go to school. ____

E. *Repaso* (Review). Translate these phrases in two ways as shown in the example.

EXAMPLE: his friend *a. su amigo*
b. el amigo de él

1. his car
a. ______________________________
b. ______________________________

2. your house *(Ud.)*
a. ______________________________
b. ______________________________

3. your house *(Uds.)*
a. ______________________________
b. ______________________________

4. her friends *(f.)*
a. ______________________________
b. ______________________________

5. their sister
a. ______________________________
b. ______________________________

6. your books *(Ud.)*
a. ______________________________
b. ______________________________

Lesson 17

los números once a veinte, *numbers eleven to twenty*

A. Learn the Spanish words for numbers 11 to 20:

11 **once**	16 **diez y seis**
12 **doce**	17 **diez y siete**
13 **trece**	18 **diez y ocho**
14 **catorce**	19 **diez y nueve**
15 **quince**	20 **veinte**

B. Read these sentences aloud, and write them as equations in arithmetic.

EXAMPLE: (Read aloud) Once menos tres son ocho.

(Write) 11 − 3 = 8

1. Once y tres son catorce. ________________
2. Quince y cuatro son diez y nueve. ________________
3. Doce y seis son diez y ocho. ________________
4. Trece y dos son quince. ________________
5. Catorce menos siete son siete. ________________
6. Diez y diez son veinte. ________________
7. Diez y seis menos siete son nueve. ________________

C. Answer with a complete sentence in Spanish. Write out all numbers as words.

EXAMPLE: ¿Cuántos son cinco y seis?
Cinco y seis son once.

¿Cuántos son . . . ?

1. quince y cinco ________________
2. nueve y cuatro ________________
3. diez y ocho menos catorce ________________
4. siete y doce ________________
5. siete y siete ________________
6. veinte menos diez ________________
7. seis y seis ________________

D. 1. Cuente Ud. desde once hasta quince.

---

2. Cuente Ud. desde diez y seis hasta veinte.

E. *Traduzca Ud. al español:*

1. Eight and nine is seventeen.

2. Six and five is eleven.

3. Eleven and seven equals eighteen.

4. Four plus eight is twelve.

5. Thirteen minus two is eleven.

6. Twelve and seven is nineteen.

7. Eleven and nine is twenty.

8. Ten and four is fourteen.

9. Eight and seven is fifteen.

10. Nineteen and one is twenty.

11. How much is ten and three?

12. How much is fifteen minus thirteen?

Lesson 18

jugar, *to play*

TOPIC QUESTION 11

¿A qué deportes juega Ud.? What sports do you play?

present tense of ***jugar (ue)***			
yo **juego**	I play	nosotros **jugamos**	we play
Ud. **juega**	you play	Uds. **juegan**	you play
él / ella } **juega**	he / she } plays	ellos / ellas } **juegan**	they play

A. *Preguntas y respuestas*

Practice reading aloud the following questions and answers:

1. ¿Juega Ud. al fútbol?
Sí, yo juego al fútbol.

2. ¿Juegan Uds. al jai alai?
No, nosotros no jugamos al jai alai.

3. ¿Juega él al tenis?
Sí, él juega al tenis.

4. ¿Juega ella al boliche?
Sí, ella juega al boliche.

5. ¿Juegan ellos al béisbol?
No, ellos no juegan al béisbol.

Mis padres juegan al boliche.

Learn to ask and answer these questions without looking at the page.

Here are some more questions to learn. Write the missing parts of the answers:

6. ¿A qué deportes juega Ud.?
Yo juego al ____________________ y al ____________________

7. ¿A qué deportes juegan Uds.?
Nosotros jugamos al ____

8. ¿A qué deportes juega su padre?
Mi padre ____

9. ¿A qué deportes juega su madre?
   Mi madre ______________________________

10. ¿A qué deportes juegan sus hermanos?
    Mis hermanos ______________________________

11. ¿A qué deportes juega su amigo favorito (amiga favorita)?
    Mi ______________________________

12. ¿A qué deportes juega él? ¿A qué deportes juega ella?
    Él ________________; ella ________________

Vocabulario

el **deporte,** sport
norteamericanos, Americans (= citizens of the U.S.A.)
juegan al béisbol, they play baseball
otros deportes, other sports
juega al boliche, he bowls (goes bowling)
esquían, they ski
españoles, Spaniards
latinoamericanos, Latin Americans
jai alai, a game similar to handball but played off four walls
el **mundo,** world
el **país,** country
hispánico, Spanish-speaking
los Estados Unidos, the United States
la **corrida de toros,** bullfight
la **liga,** league
el **beisbolero,** baseball player

B. *Lectura*

Los norteamericanos juegan al béisbol, al fútbol y al básquetbol. Ellos juegan a otros deportes también. Juegan al tenis, al golf, y al boliche. Muchos norteamericanos esquían también.

Los españoles y los latinoamericanos juegan al jai alai. El fútbol es popular en el mundo hispánico. El fútbol de los latinoamericanos se llama "soccer" en los Estados Unidos.

La corrida de toros es muy popular en muchos países hispánicos. . . . Muchos norteamericanos hispánicos juegan al béisbol profesional en los Estados Unidos. Juegan en las Ligas Americana y Nacional.

La corrida de toros es popular en España y México.

Preguntas

1. ¿A qué deportes juegan los norteamericanos?
   ____

2. ¿Qué deporte es popular en el mundo hispánico?
   ____

3. ¿Cómo se llama "soccer" en español?

---

4. ¿Qué deporte es popular en España y en otros países hispánicos?

---

5. En los Estados Unidos, ¿son hispánicos muchos beisboleros?

C. *Preguntas personales*

1. ¿Juega Ud. al boliche?

---

2. ¿A qué deporte juega su padre?

---

3. ¿Juega su madre al fútbol?

---

4. ¿Juega al boliche su amigo favorito?

---

5. ¿A qué deportes juegan sus hermanos?

D. *Tema.* Write a composition entitled *¿A qué deportes juega Ud.*? Tell which games you play (or do *not* play), which games are played by persons you know, etc. Be ready to repeat your *tema* orally in class.

E. *Traduzca Ud. al español:*

1. We don't play tennis.

---

2. What sport do the Latin Americans play?

---

3. They play jai alai.

---

4. Many Spanish-speaking Americans play baseball in the United States.

---

5. Latin American *fútbol* is called "soccer" in the United States.

---

6. I don't play golf.

----

7. He plays in the American League.

----

8. Do you *(Ud.)* bowl (go bowling)?

----

9. They don't bowl.

F. Ask your classmates questions 6 to 12 on pages 59–60, using one question per student. They should reply without looking at their papers.

Review of Preguntas y Respuestas

(Lessons 8–18)

G. Here are some answers. What are the questions?

EXAMPLE: Nosotros estamos bien. *¿Cómo están Uds.?*

1. Hoy es martes. --
2. No, mi hermano no nada. --
3. No, yo no voy mucho al cine. --
4. Se dice *tener* en español. --
5. *Manejar* quiere decir *to drive*. --
6. Mi madre juega al boliche. --
7. Cinco y cinco son diez. --

Lesson 19

los números veinte y uno a ciento, *numbers twenty-one to one hundred*

A. Learn to count by tens in Spanish:

10	**diez**	60	**sesenta**
20	**veinte**	70	**setenta**
30	**treinta**	80	**ochenta**
40	**cuarenta**	90	**noventa**
50	**cincuenta**	100	**ciento**

Complete these sentences, writing all numbers as words:

1. Veinte y ochenta son ______________________________

2. Noventa menos sesenta son ______________________________

3. Cuarenta y diez son ______________________________

4. Ciento menos treinta son ______________________________

5. Cincuenta y cuarenta son ______________________________

B. Learn the Spanish words for 21 to 100:

21	**veinte y uno**	31	**treinta y uno**
22	**veinte y dos**	32	**treinta y dos**
23	**veinte y tres**	33	**treinta y tres**
24	**veinte y cuatro**	34	**treinta y cuatro**
25	**veinte y cinco**	35	**treinta y cinco**
	etc.		etc.

Read these sentences aloud, and write them as equations in arithmetic.

EXAMPLE: (Read aloud) Cuarenta y dos y veinte y uno son sesenta y tres.

(Write) 42 + 21 = 63

1. Ciento menos ochenta y tres son diez y siete. ____________

2. Sesenta y cinco y veinte y cuatro son ochenta y nueve. ____________

3. Veinte y cinco y veinte y cinco son cincuenta. ____________

4. Veinte y uno y cincuenta son setenta y uno. ____________

5. Noventa menos cincuenta son cuarenta. ____________

6. Cincuenta y tres y veinte y nueve son ochenta y dos. ____________

7. Noventa y tres menos diez y siete son setenta y seis. ____________

C. Answer with a complete sentence in Spanish:
¿Cuántos son . . . ?

1. cincuenta menos cuarenta ____________________
2. treinta y treinta ____________________
3. ciento menos noventa ____________________
4. sesenta y cuarenta ____________________
5. veinte y dos y treinta y cinco ____________________
6. noventa menos sesenta y nueve ____________________
7. setenta y cinco y diez y ocho ____________________

D. **Ciento** is shortened to **cien** before a noun: **cien libros,** *a hundred books.*

Write the correct form of *ciento*:

1. ____________ páginas **2.** ____________ coches **3.** ____________ muchachos

E. Cuente Ud. por dieces *(by tens)* desde diez hasta ciento.

____

____

F. *Traduzca Ud. al español:*

1. Forty and thirty is seventy.

____

2. Twenty-five and fifteen is forty.

____

3. Eighty minus fifty equals thirty.

____

4. Count by tens from ten to one hundred.

____

5. How much is ninety minus twenty?

____

6. How much is sixty-five minus thirty-three?

____

7. Fifty plus forty-six equals ninety-six.

____

8. Sixty and thirty is ninety.

____

9. Seventy-eight minus sixty is eighteen.

____

10. The book has a hundred pages.

____

La columna personal de Anita Gómez (5)

Vocabulario

siempre, always
sufre, suffers
dar, to give
posible, possible
entrar, to enter
sin, without
todos los días, every day

el 7 de mayo

Querida Anita Gómez:

Mi hija María siempre va al cine. Va al cine los lunes, los martes, los jueves, los viernes y los domingos.
¿Qué debo yo hacer?

Madre Que Sufre

María va mucho al cine.

el 8 de mayo

Querida Madre Que Sufre:

Ud. no debe dar dinero a su hija. No es posible entrar en el cine sin dinero. ¿Por qué no va María al cine los miércoles y los sábados?

Anita Gómez

G. Complete the sentences:

1. La hija de la madre se llama ____________________
2. Ella va al cine todos los días excepto ____________________
3. Anita Gómez dice que la madre no debe ______________ a su hija porque ____________________

Lesson 20

hablar, *to speak, to talk*

TOPIC QUESTION 12A	**¿Habla Ud. español?** Do you speak Spanish?

present tense of ***hablar***			
yo **hablo**	I speak	nosotros **hablamos**	we speak
Ud. **habla**	you speak	Uds. **hablan**	you speak
él / ella } **habla**	he / she } speaks	ellos / ellas } **hablan**	they speak

A. *Preguntas y respuestas*

Practice reading aloud the following questions and answers:

1. ¿Habla Ud. español?
Sí, yo hablo español.

2. ¿Hablan Uds. inglés?
Sí, nosotros hablamos inglés.

3. ¿Habla él español?
No, él no habla español.

4. ¿Habla ella inglés?
Sí, ella habla inglés.

5. ¿Hablan ellos español?
Sí, ellos hablan español.

Mi padre habla mucho.

B. *Preguntas personales*

1. ¿Habla Ud. español o inglés en casa?

---

2. ¿Hablan Uds. español en la clase?

---

3. ¿Hablan español sus amigos?

---

4. ¿Quién habla español en su familia?

---

5. ¿Qué lengua *(language)* hablan sus amigos?

TOPIC QUESTION 12B

¿Habla Ud. mucho al teléfono?
Do you talk a lot on the telephone?

C. *Preguntas personales*

1. ¿Habla Ud. mucho al teléfono?

____

2. ¿Habla su padre mucho al teléfono?

____

3. ¿Habla su madre mucho al teléfono?

____

4. ¿Hablan sus hermanos mucho al teléfono?

____

5. ¿Habla mucho al teléfono su amigo favorito?

____

Mi madre habla mucho al teléfono.

D. *Lectura*

Yo me llamo Diego. Diego en inglés es *James*. Yo no hablo mucho.

Mi padre habla mucho. Mi madre habla mucho también. Ella habla mucho al teléfono.

Mis hermanos Juanito y Rosita no hablan mucho. Mi hermana Margarita habla mucho. Ella habla mucho al teléfono.

Preguntas

1. ¿Cómo se llama el muchacho? ______________________________
2. ¿Cómo se dice *Diego* en inglés? ______________________________
3. ¿Habla mucho el padre de Diego? ______________________________
4. ¿Habla mucho la madre de Diego? ______________________________
5. ¿Habla ella mucho al teléfono? ______________________________
6. ¿Hablan mucho Juanito y Rosita? ______________________________
7. ¿Habla mucho Margarita? ______________________________

E. *Tema*. Write a composition entitled *¿Habla Ud. mucho al teléfono*?

____

____

____

____

____

____

F. *Traduzca Ud. al español:*

1. I don't talk much.

---

2. My father doesn't talk a lot.

---

3. Do you *(Ud.)* talk much on the phone?

---

4. His mother talks a lot on the phone.

---

5. Does your sister talk much?

---

6. Do your brothers and sisters talk much?

---

7. We talk a lot on the phone.

G. *Conversación.* Ask your classmates five questions in Spanish chosen from the *Preguntas personales* in parts B and C. They should reply without looking at their papers.

Review of Topic Questions 1–12

(Lessons 1–20)

H. Translate these Topic Questions into Spanish:

1 What is your name? ____________________

2 How are you? ____________________

3 Do you have a car? ____________________

4 Do you drive? ____________________

5 What does *manejar* mean? ____________________

6 How do you say "thank you"? ____________________

7 How much is five and twelve? ____________________

8 Do you go to the movies much? ____________________

9 What day is today? ____________________

10 Do you swim? ____________________

11 What sports do you play? ____________________

12 Do you talk a lot on the phone? ____________________

13 Are you in good health? ________________________________

14 Do you speak English? ________________________________

Vocabulary Review

I. Complete in Spanish:

1. ____________________ es *Mr.* en español.

2. ____________________ es *Mrs.* en español.

3. "Buenos ____________________, Alberto."

4. "Buenas ____________________, Srta. Mendoza."

5. "¡Hola! ¿Qué ____________________?"

6. "Gracias." "De ____________________."

7. "Adiós. Hasta la ____________________."

8. Me llamo José, para ____________________le.

9. "¿Cómo se llaman sus padres?"
"Mi padre se llama José, y mi ____________________ se llama María."

10. "¿Cómo se llaman sus hermanos?"
"Mi hermano se llama Tomás, y mi ____________________ se llama Enriqueta."

11. María maneja, pero ____________________ amiga no maneja.
(her)

12. Roberto maneja, pero ____________________ amigos no manejan.
(his)

COGNATES (3)

COGNATE TYPE 3

Spanish words ending in **-oso** or **-osa** have English cognates ending in *-ous*. Example: **famoso,** *famous*.

J. Pronounce and translate the following words:

1. furioso ____________________

2. monstruoso ____________________

3. supersticioso ____________________

4. maravilloso ____________________

5. ansioso ____________________

6. estudioso ____________________

Write these words in Spanish:

7. mysterious ____________________

8. precious ____________________

9. generous ____________________

10. numerous ____________________

11. delicious ____________________

12. industrious ____________________

K. *Diálogo*. In the following dialogue, play the role of Ramón. Write his responses in the blanks.

CLARA: Su amigo Raúl tiene un coche nuevo, ¿verdad? ¿Qué marca es?

RAMÓN: ____

CLARA: ¿Tiene usted coche?

RAMÓN: ____

CLARA: No tengo coche tampoco pero tengo una licencia para manejar.

RAMÓN: ____

CLARA: ¿Por qué no aprende usted a manejar?

RAMÓN: ____

La columna personal de Anita Gómez (6)

el 10 de junio

Querida Anita Gómez:

Mi esposo dice que yo siempre canto en el sueño. Por eso, él no puede dormir. ¿Qué debo yo hacer?

Señora Musical

el 20 de junio

Querida Señora Musical:

Ud. debe cantar canciones de cuna.

Anita Gómez

Vocabulario

dice, says
cantar, to sing
en el sueño, in (my) sleep
no puede dormir, can't sleep
canción de cuna, lullaby, cradle song

Mi esposa canta en el sueño.

L. Complete the sentences:

1. El esposo de la señora no puede dormir porque ______________________
2. Anita Gómez dice que la señora debe ____________________________

Lesson 21

preferir, *to prefer*

TOPIC QUESTION 13 — **¿Prefiere Ud. café, té o leche?**
Do you prefer coffee, tea or milk?

present tense of ***preferir (ie)***			
yo **prefiero**	I prefer	nosotros **preferimos**	we prefer
Ud. **prefiere**	you prefer	Uds. **prefieren**	you prefer
él / ella **prefiere**	he / she prefers	ellos / ellas **prefieren**	they prefer

A. *Preguntas y respuestas*

Practice reading aloud the following questions and answers:

1. ¿Prefiere Ud. café o té?
Yo prefiero café.

2. ¿Prefieren Uds. tocino o jamón?
Nosotros preferimos tocino.

3. ¿Prefiere él panecillos o pan tostado?
Él prefiere panecillos.

4. ¿Prefiere ella jugo de naranja o jugo de tomate?
Ella prefiere jugo de naranja.

5. ¿Prefieren ellos jugo o café?
Ellos prefieren jugo.

Write the missing parts of the answers:

6. ¿Prefiere Ud. café, té o leche?
Yo ____________________ leche.

7. ¿Prefieren Uds. café, té o leche?
Nosotros ________________________ café.

8. ¿Prefiere su madre café, té o leche?
Mi madre ____

9. ¿Prefieren sus hermanos café, té o leche?
Mis hermanos ____

10. ¿Prefiere su amiga favorita café, té o leche?
Mi amiga favorita ____________________

11. ¿Prefiere ella café, té o leche?
Ella ____________________

Vocabulario

para el desayuno, for breakfast
café, coffee
té, tea
leche, milk
un vaso de leche, a glass of milk
él pide, he orders, asks for
él quiere, he wants
con, with
pero, but
jugo de naranja, orange juice
jugo de tomate, tomato juice
huevos fritos, fried eggs
huevos revueltos, scrambled eggs
tocino, bacon
jamón, ham
pan tostado, toast
pan dulce, sweet roll
panecillo, roll
mantequilla, butter
mermelada, marmalade
tomar, to take, to have (= eat)

B. *Lectura*

Antonio prefiere jugo de naranja para el desayuno. Él prefiere huevos fritos con tocino. No quiere* pan tostado. Prefiere* pan dulce o panecillos. Él pide mantequilla y mermelada. También pide café.

Su hermano Jesús prefiere jugo de tomate para el desayuno. No quiere huevos fritos. Prefiere huevos revueltos con jamón. Pide pan tostado. Quiere mantequilla pero no quiere mermelada. Pide un vaso de leche.

Preguntas

1. ¿Qué prefiere Antonio para el desayuno?
____

2. ¿Qué pide Antonio?
____

3. ¿Cómo se llama el hermano de Antonio?
____

4. ¿Quiere el hermano huevos fritos?
____

5. ¿Qué pide?
____

*Notice that the subject pronoun (**yo, Ud., él,** etc.) may be omitted if the subject of the verb is obvious or does not need emphasis.

C. *Preguntas personales*

1. ¿Prefiere Ud. jugo de naranja o jugo de tomate?

   ----

2. ¿Prefieren Uds. café o té?

   ----

3. ¿Prefiere su padre huevos fritos o huevos revueltos?

   ----

4. ¿Prefiere su madre café o leche?

   ----

5. ¿Cómo se dice *scrambled eggs* en español?

   ----

6. ¿Prefiere Ud. tocino o jamón?

   ----

7. ¿Cómo se dice *toast*?

D. *Tema.* Write a composition entitled *¿Qué prefiere Ud. para el desayuno*? Tell what you prefer for breakfast, and also mention the breakfast preferences of some people you know.

E. *Traduzca Ud. al español:*

1. He prefers scrambled eggs and bacon.

   ----

2. What do your friends prefer?

   ----

3. We prefer rolls.

   ----

4. John prefers fried eggs and ham.

   ----

5. Do you *(Uds.)* prefer a sweet roll?

   ----

6. He wants butter and marmalade.

   ----

7. He asks for a glass of milk.

F. *Conversación.* Ask a classmate, "¿Prefiere Ud. jugo de naranja o jugo de tomate?" He or she answers in Spanish, then turns to another classmate and asks, "¿Prefiere Ud. huevos fritos o huevos revueltos?" After the answer is given, the student turns to a fourth classmate to ask a different question of preference, and so on, till everyone has had a turn asking or replying to the following questions:

1. ¿Prefiere Ud. jugo de naranja o jugo de tomate?
2. ¿Prefiere Ud. huevos fritos o huevos revueltos?
3. ¿Prefiere Ud. tocino o jamón?
4. ¿Prefiere Ud. pan tostado or pan dulce?
5. ¿Prefiere Ud. café, té o leche?

G. *¿Qué prefiere Juan para el desayuno?* To find out, print the Spanish words suggested by these pictures, subtracting the letters following the minus signs. Then print the remaining letters in the boxes.

 – IJA +  –ESCLA+ 

–AS+  –ANCA +  –TADO

ANSWER: ☐☐☐☐☐☐ ☐☐☐☐☐☐

Lesson 22

estudiar, *to study*

TOPIC QUESTION 14A

¿Qué lengua estudia Ud.? What language are you studying?*

present tense of ***estudiar***	
yo **estudio**	nosotros **estudiamos**
Ud. / él / ella **estudia**	Uds. / ellos / ellas **estudian**

A. *Preguntas y respuestas*

Practice reading aloud the following questions and answers:

1. ¿Qué lengua estudia Ud.?
   Yo estudio español.
2. ¿Qué lengua estudian Uds.?
   Nosotros estudiamos alemán.
3. ¿Qué lengua estudia él?
   Él estudia francés.
4. ¿Qué lengua estudia ella?
   Ella no estudia una lengua.
5. ¿Qué lengua estudian ellos?
   Ellos estudian inglés.

Vocabulario
lengua, language
inglés, English
francés, French
alemán, German
Paco, Frank (nickname)

---

*Notice that a Spanish verb in the present tense can be translated in two ways:

ella **estudia** { she studies / she is studying

ella **no estudia** { she doesn't study / she isn't studying

¿estudia ella? { Does she study? / Is she studying?

Learn these questions too. Write the missing parts of the answers:

6. ¿Estudia Ud. español?

   Sí, yo ______________________________

7. ¿Qué lengua estudia su madre?

   Mi madre ______________________________

8. ¿Qué lengua estudia su padre?

   Mi padre ______________________________

9. ¿Qué lengua estudian sus hermanos?

   Mis hermanos ______________________________

10. ¿Qué lengua estudia su amigo favorito?

    Mi amigo favorito ______________________________

B. *Lectura*

Roberto estudia español. Su hermano Enrique no estudia una lengua.

El amigo favorito de Roberto se llama Paco. Estudia francés. Paco en inglés es *Frank*.

La amiga favorita de Roberto se llama Inés. Estudia alemán. Los hermanos de Inés se llaman Tomás y Margarita. Ellos estudian inglés.

Preguntas

1. ¿Qué lengua estudia Roberto?

   ____

2. ¿Estudia Enrique una lengua?

   ____

3. ¿Cómo se llama el amigo favorito de Roberto?

   ____

4. ¿Cómo se dice *Paco* en inglés?

   ____

5. ¿Qué lengua estudia Inés?

   ____

6. ¿Cómo se llaman los hermanos de Inés?

   ____

7. ¿Qué lengua estudian Tomás y Margarita?

   ____

C. *Tema*. Write a composition entitled *¿Estudia Ud. una lengua?* Include the following information: (1) the language you are studying; (2) a language that you *want* to study ("I want" = *yo quiero*); (3) the languages that your friends or members of your family are studying.

D. *Traduzca Ud. al español:*

1. I am studying Spanish.

---

2. What language do you *(Ud.)* study?

---

3. We don't study German.

---

4. You *(Uds.)* study French.

---

5. Do your brothers and sisters study Spanish?

---

6. Is Margaret studying French?

TOPIC QUESTION 14B	**¿Qué asignaturas estudia Ud.?** What subjects are you studying?

TOPIC QUESTION 14C	**¿Qué asignaturas toma Ud.?** What courses are you taking?

present tense of ***tomar***	
yo **tomo**	nosotros **tomamos**
Ud. / él / ella **toma**	Uds. / ellos / ellas **toman**

E. *Preguntas y respuestas*

Vocabulario
tomar, to take
asignatura, subject, course
matemáticas, mathematics
aritmética, arithmetic
ciencia, science
educación física, physical education ("gym")
artes industriales, industrial arts ("shop")
historia, history
geografía, geography
arte, art
música, music

1. ¿Qué asignaturas estudia Ud.?
   Yo estudio historia, español, matemáticas y ciencia.
2. ¿Qué asignaturas estudian Uds.?
   Nosotros estudiamos aritmética, inglés, historia norteamericana y francés.
3. ¿Qué asignaturas estudia su hermana?
   Ella estudia arte, música, álgebra y geografía.
4. ¿Qué asignaturas toma Ud.?
   Yo tomo ciencia, matemáticas, educación física y artes industriales.
5. ¿Qué asignaturas toman Uds.?
   Nosotros ______________________________
6. ¿Qué asignaturas toman sus hermanos?
   Mis hermanos ______________________________
7. ¿Qué asignaturas toma su amiga favorita?
   Ella ______________________________

F. *Preguntas personales*

1. ¿Cuál es su asignatura favorita? ______________________________
2. ¿Cuántas asignaturas toma Ud.? ______________________________
3. ¿Toma Ud. educación física? ______________________________
4. ¿Qué asignaturas estudian sus hermanos? ______________________________
   ____
5. ¿Toman Uds. artes industriales? ______________________________

G. *Traduzca Ud. al español:*

1. I'm taking five subjects this term *(este semestre)*.
   ____
2. We study Spanish, English, art and mathematics.
   ____
3. They are not studying music this term.
   ____
4. Do you *(Uds.)* take shop?
   ____
5. Which courses are they taking?
   ____

Vocabulary Review

H. How many of the words listed below can you express in Spanish without looking them up? Write the Spanish words in the blanks. (With nouns, include the definite article.)

1. to go ____________________________
2. movies __________________________
3. elementary school _______________
4. university ______________________
5. city ____________________________
6. high school ____________________
7. Matthew ________________________
8. their ___________________________
9. what? __________________________
10. today __________________________
11. tomorrow ______________________
12. yesterday ______________________
13. to swim ________________________
14. swimming pool _________________
15. Pacific Ocean ___________________
16. Henry __________________________
17. our _____________________________
18. my ______________________________
19. to play ________________________
20. sports __________________________
21. bowling ________________________
22. also ____________________________
23. world ___________________________
24. leagues ________________________
25. the United States ______________
26. baseball player ________________
27. to speak, talk __________________
28. English ________________________
29. to prefer ______________________
30. orange juice ____________________
31. toast __________________________
32. fried eggs ______________________
33. scrambled eggs _________________
34. roll ____________________________

35. sweet roll ______________________
36. butter ______________________
37. ham ______________________
38. bacon ______________________
39. a glass ______________________
40. milk ______________________
41. coffee ______________________
42. breakfast ______________________

I. Write the Spanish names for the days of the week:

____

Write the Spanish words for:

J. the numbers 1 to 10

____

____

K. the numbers 11 to 20

____

____

L. the numbers 10 to 100 *by tens*

____

____

M. *Frases revueltas*. Unscramble the sentences:

1. mi favorito amigo Antonio es .

   ____

2. tostado prefiero pan yo .

   ____

3. cuatro Ud. cuente nueve desde hasta .

   ____

4. diez ¿ son cuántos ? menos uno

   ____

5. uno seis son y cinco .

   ____

6. dos siete menos cinco son .

____

7. hermana tengo yo dos hermanos una y .

____

8. a Enrique universidad va la .

____

9. escuela Mateo y ? qué Carlota a van ¿

____

10. va él cine mucho al .

____

11. México , padre D.F. mi está en .

____

12. es ? qué mañana día ¿

____

13. ¿ la Uds. los a van escuela sábados ?

____

14. piscina nado la yo en la escuela de .

____

15. Pacífico Acapulco Océano en el está .

____

16. dos catorce menos doce son .

____

17. el hispánico fútbol mundo popular es en el .

____

18. cincuenta noventa son menos cuarenta .

____

19. habla teléfono ella al mucho .

____

20. huevos tocino prefiere con él fritos .

____

N. *Conteste Ud. en español* (Answer in Spanish):

1. ¿Manejan Uds.? ________________________________
2. ¿Qué días no va Ud. a la escuela? ________________________________

____

3. ¿Va su padre a la escuela? ________________________________

4. ¿Qué día es hoy? ______________________________

5. ¿Qué día es mañana? ______________________________

6. ¿Qué día fue ayer? ______________________________

7. ¿Nada Ud.? ______________________________

8. ¿Juegan Uds. al béisbol? ______________________________

9. ¿Habla mucho al teléfono su madre? ______________________________

10. ¿Prefieren Uds. café, té o leche? ______________________________

Lesson 23

la familia y los parientes,
the family and relatives

esposo — esposa

A. El esposo de mi madre es mi padre. La esposa de mi padre es mi madre.

El plural de *padre* es *padres*. *Padres* quiere decir *parents*.

1. ¿Qué quiere decir *esposo*? ________________________

2. ¿Qué quiere decir *esposa*? ________________________

3. ¿Cómo se dice *parents* en español? ________________________

tío — tía

B. El hermano de mi padre o de mi madre es mi tío. La hermana de mi padre o de mi madre es mi tía.

4. ¿Qué quiere decir *tío*? ________________________

5. ¿Cómo se dice *aunt* en español? ________________________

hijo — hija

C. El hijo de mis padres es mi hermano. La hija de mis padres es mi hermana.

6. ¿Qué quiere decir *hijo*? ________________________

7. ¿Qué quiere decir *hija*? ________________________

primo — prima

D. El hijo de mi tío o de mi tía es mi primo. La hija de mi tío o de mi tía es mi prima.

8. ¿Qué quiere decir *primo*? ________________________

sobrino — sobrina

E. El hijo de mi hermano o de mi hermana es mi sobrino. La hija de mi hermano o de mi hermana es mi sobrina.

9. ¿Qué quiere decir *sobrino*? ______________________

10. ¿Cómo se dice *niece*? ______________________

abuelo — abuela

F. El padre de mi padre o de mi madre es mi abuelo. La madre de mi padre o de mi madre es mi abuela.

11. ¿Qué quiere decir *abuelo*? ______________________

12. ¿Qué quiere decir *abuela*? ______________________

13. ¿Cómo se dice *grandparents*? ______________________

Adivinanzas (Riddles)

14. María es mi sobrina, pero yo no soy el tío de ella. ¿Quién soy yo? ____________________

15. Me llamo Juan. El padre de José es mi abuelo, y la hija de José es mi prima. ¿Quién soy yo? ____________________

Vocabulario

la **familia,** family	el **primo,** cousin (boy)
los **parientes,** relatives	la **prima,** cousin (girl)
el **esposo,** husband	el **sobrino,** nephew
la **esposa,** wife	la **sobrina,** niece
el **tío,** uncle	el **abuelo,** grandfather
la **tía,** aunt	la **abuela,** grandmother
el **hijo,** son	**yo soy,** I am
la **hija,** daughter	

El padre de mi padre es mi abuelo.

COGNATES (4)

G. You would have no trouble finding English cognates for *these* words. Pronounce each word and write its meaning in English:

1. fonógrafo ______________________
2. fotografía ______________________
3. teléfono ______________________
4. filosofía ______________________
5. catedral ______________________
6. admirar ______________________
7. observar ______________________
8. completar ______________________
9. sistema ______________________
10. imaginar ______________________
11. micrófono ______________________
12. conservar ______________________

La columna personal de Anita Gómez (7)

Vocabulario

cheques, checks
malos, bad
bastante, enough
comprar, to buy
vestidos, dresses
sombreros, hats
zapatos, shoes
blusas, (woman's) jackets, blouses
faldas, skirts
medias, stockings
buscar empleo, to look for a job
necesitar, to need

el 10 de agosto

Querida Anita Gómez:

Mi esposa siempre escribe cheques malos porque ella no tiene bastante dinero en el banco. Ella compra muchos vestidos, sombreros, zapatos, y muchas blusas, faldas y medias.
. . . ¿Qué debo yo hacer?

Pobre Esposo

el 23 de agosto

Querido Pobre Esposo:

Usted no debe hacer nada. *Ella* debe buscar empleo.

Anita Gómez

H. Complete the sentences:

1. La esposa escribe cheques malos porque ________________________________
2. Ella necesita dinero para comprar ____________________________________
3. Anita Gómez dice que la esposa debe __________________________________

***Preguntas personales* (a review)**

I. Answer each question with a complete sentence in Spanish:

1. ¿Cómo se llama Ud.? ____
2. ¿Cómo está Ud.? ____
3. ¿Tiene Ud. un coche? _______________________________________
4. ¿Maneja Ud.? ____
5. ¿Tiene Ud. una licencia para manejar? __________________________

6. ¿A qué escuela va Ud.? ____

7. ¿Nada Ud.? ¿Dónde nada Ud.? ¿Nada Ud. bien? ____________________________

____

8. ¿A qué deportes juega Ud.? _______________________________________

9. ¿Habla Ud. mucho? ____

10. ¿Qué lengua habla Ud.? ____

11. ¿Qué prefiere Ud. para el desayuno? (Start with ''Prefiero'' and list breakfast items.)

____

12. ¿Qué familia y parientes tiene Ud.? ____________________________________

____

Lesson 24

aprender, *to learn*

TOPIC QUESTION 15

> **¿Qué aprende Ud.?**
> What are you learning?

present tense of ***aprender***	
yo **aprendo**	nosotros **aprendemos**
Ud. / él / ella } **aprende**	Uds. / ellos / ellas } **aprenden**

A. *Preguntas y respuestas*

Practice reading aloud the following questions and answers:

1. ¿Qué aprende Ud.?
Yo aprendo química.

2. ¿Qué aprenden Uds.?
Nosotros aprendemos biología.

3. ¿Qué aprende él?
Él aprende física.

4. ¿Qué aprende ella?
Ella aprende química.

5. ¿Aprenden ellos biología?
Sí, ellos aprenden biología.

Vocabulario

la **química,** chemistry
la **física,** physics
la **biología,** biology
el **Instituto Politécnico,** Polytechnical Institute

Learn these questions too. Write the missing parts of the answers:

6. ¿Aprende Ud. química?
No, yo no _______________ química.

7. ¿Aprenden Uds. química?
Sí, nosotros ____________________________________

8. ¿Aprende su padre biología?
Sí, mi padre ____________________________________

Andrés aprende química.

9. ¿Aprende su madre biología?
   No, ella ___________________________________

10. ¿Aprenden sus hermanos física?
    Sí, ellos ___________________________________

11. ¿Aprende física su amigo favorito?
    No, él ______________________________________

12. ¿Qué ciencias aprenden Ud. y sus amigos?
    Nosotros ____________________ física y biología.

B. *Lectura*

Andrés, Tomás y Enrique van al Instituto Politécnico en Monterrey, México. Andrés aprende química. Tomás y Enrique aprenden física. La novia de Andrés se llama Anita. Ella aprende biología.

Preguntas

1. ¿A qué escuela van los muchachos? _______________________________________
2. ¿Qué aprende Andrés? ____
3. ¿Quiénes aprenden física? ____
4. ¿Cómo se llama la novia de Andrés? _____________________________________
5. ¿Qué aprende ella? ____

C. *Preguntas personales*

1. ¿Aprende Ud. una ciencia?
   ____

2. ¿Aprenden sus hermanos una ciencia?
   ____

3. ¿Qué ciencia aprenden Uds.?
   ____

4. ¿Aprende su madre una lengua?
   ____

5. ¿Qué lenguas aprenden sus padres?
   ____

D. *Traduzca Ud. al español:*

1. I'm learning chemistry. ________________
2. They learn physics. ________________
3. What science are your friends learning? ________________
4. Why doesn't William *(Guillermo)* learn chemistry? ________________
____
5. We learn biology. ________________

E. *Conversación.* You and your classmates can take turns asking one another "¿Qué aprende Ud.?" As each student answers, he or she turns to another classmate and asks the same question. (The answers do not have to be limited to the sciences.)

Vocabulary Review

F. Complete the sentences:

1. Tres y ________________ son diez.
2. Siete menos ________________ son cinco.
3. Ricardo y Tomás van a la escuela. ________________ (Their) hermana no va a la escuela.
4. Hoy es lunes. ________________ es martes. ________________ fue domingo.
5. Yo ________________ en la piscina.
6. Nosotros nadamos en el ________________ Pacífico.
7. Mi hermano Enrique y yo ________________ a la escuela superior. Mi hermano Tomás ________________ a la escuela superior también.
8. Ricardo no ________________ al tenis.
9. ¿________________ Ud. al boliche?
10. Yo hablo inglés. Ellos ________________ español.
11. Tomasina prefiere ________________ de naranja.
12. Yo prefiero ________________ fritos.
13. Anita prefiere ________________ tostado.
14. Yo no prefiero tocino. Yo prefiero ________________.

Crucigrama (2)

Across

1. *Paul*
5. ¿Cómo se dice *Ana* en inglés?
6. iniciales de Dolores Trevino
7. Ud. es = *you* _____.
9. Ella _____ español.
10. forma plural del artículo definido
13. Estar = *to* _____.
16. Diego en inglés es _____.
18. ¿Qué quiere decir *prima*?
20. apellido español
22. iniciales de Raúl Espinosa Torre
25. Ella habla mucho al _____.
26. *to sing*
27. *Oh!*
29. ¿Cuántos son treinta y dos menos uno?
30. ¿Qué quiere decir *vestido*?
33. Yo _____ llamo Andrés.
34. Yo no manejo = *I do* _____ *drive*.
35. iniciales de Carlos Nóguez Olivera
36. El fútbol es popular en el mundo _____.
39. ¿Cómo _____ llama su amiga?
40. ¿Qué quiere decir *americanos*?
41. *to go*
42. _____ preferimos leche.

Down

1. *parents*
2. *before*
3. iniciales de Berta Nogales
4. *language*
8. *to speak, talk*
11. "Omitir" quiere decir *to* _____.
12. ¿Qué quiere decir *setenta*?
13. *Good evening* = _____ noches.
14. No voy a la escuela hoy porque _____ enfermo.
15. En Inglaterra hablan _____.
17. *salt*
19. *gold*
21. *I know* = yo _____.
23. *butter*
24. Paco en inglés es _____.
28. *science*
31. ¿Cómo se dice *hijos* en inglés?
32. "¡Alto!" quiere decir _____!
37. El fútbol de los latinoamericanos se llama _____ en los Estados Unidos.
38. *dog*
39. ¿Cuántos son dos y cuatro?
43. ¿Cuántos son diez menos dos?

Lesson 25

escribir, *to write*

TOPIC QUESTION 16

¿Qué escribe Ud.?
What are you writing?

present tense of ***escribir***	
yo **escribo**	nosotros **escribimos**
Ud. / él / ella } **escribe**	Uds. / ellos / ellas } **escriben**

A. *Preguntas y respuestas*

Practice reading aloud the following questions and answers:

1. ¿Qué escribe Ùd.?
Yo escribo una carta.

2. ¿Qué escriben Uds.?
Nosotros escribimos nuestras lecciones.

3. ¿Qué escribe él?
Él escribe cartas a su novia.

4. ¿Qué escribe ella?
Ella escribe su lección.

5. ¿Escribe Ud. una carta?
No, yo escribo un tema.

6. ¿Escriben Uds. mucho?
No, no escribimos mucho.

7. ¿Escriben ellos bien?
Sí, ellos escriben bien.

Vocabulario

la **carta,** letter
la **lección,** lesson
(no accent in the plural)
menor, younger, youngest
mayor, older, oldest
el **ejército,** army
el **liceo,** high school
(in some Hispanic countries)
la **carta de amor,** love letter

Learn these questions too. Write the missing parts of the answers:

8. ¿Escribe Ud. cartas?
Sí, yo ______________________________

9. ¿Escriben Uds. sus lecciones?
No, nosotros no ______________________________

10. ¿Escribe su padre cheques?
Sí, mi padre ______________________________

11. ¿Escribe su madre cheques?

Sí, ella también ______________________

12. ¿Escribe bien el español?

Sí, ella ______________________ el español.

13. ¿Escribe cartas su hermana menor?

No, mi hermana menor ______________________

B. *Lectura*

Teresa va a un liceo en Buenos Aires, capital de la Argentina. Ella escribe mucho. Escribe mucho en casa y en la escuela.

La madre de Teresa escribe muchas cartas a Guillermo que está en el ejército. Guillermo es el hermano mayor de Teresa.

El padre de Teresa no escribe muchas cartas. Escribe cheques buenos. No escribe cheques malos.

El señor Cárdenas escribe cheques malos.

Preguntas

1. ¿Dónde está la escuela de Teresa?

____

2. ¿Dónde escribe Teresa?

____

3. ¿Qué escribe la madre de Teresa?

____

4. ¿Quién es Guillermo?

____

5. ¿Escribe muchas cartas el padre de Teresa?

____

Catalina escribe una carta de amor.

C. *Preguntas personales*

1. ¿Escribe Ud. sus lecciones?

____

2. ¿Escriben Uds. en español?

____

3. ¿Escribe su padre muchas cartas?

____

4. ¿Qué escribe su madre?

____

5. ¿Escriben sus hermanos cheques?

____

D. *Tema.* Write a composition entitled *¿Qué escribe Ud.?* Tell whether you write a lot, what or to whom you write, etc. Give similar information about people you know.

____

____

____

____

____

E. *Traduzca Ud. al español:*

1. I don't write much. ______________________________

2. Does Juan write a lot? ______________________________

3. They write letters. ______________________________

4. His brother is in the army. ______________________________

5. Do you *(Uds.)* write well? ______________________________

6. You *(Ud.)* write Spanish well. ______________________________

7. Do Mary and Henry write well? ______________________________

8. We don't write bad checks. ______________________________

F. *Conversación.* Ask a classmate "¿Qué escribe Ud.?" He or she answers and then turns to another student, asking "¿Escribe Ud. mucho?" The student who answers then asks another classmate "¿Escribe Ud. muchas cartas?"—and so on, till everyone has had the chance to ask or reply to questions like those of the *Preguntas y respuestas* on page 92.

G. *¿Por qué no quiere Juan aprender a manejar?* To find out why, print the Spanish words suggested by these pictures, subtracting the letters following the minus signs. Then print the remaining letters in the boxes.

 − DIER +  − RRA + 

____

−OCH +  − ASA +  − BLI

____

ANSWER: [ ][ ] [ ][ ][ ][ ][ ] [ ][ ][ ][ ][ ]

Lesson 26

comer, *to eat;* **tomar el desayuno,** *to have breakfast*

TOPIC QUESTION 17A	**¿Come Ud. mucho?** Do you eat a lot?

present tense of ***comer***	
yo **como**	nosotros **comemos**
Ud. / él / ella } **come**	Uds. / ellos / ellas } **comen**

A. *Preguntas y respuestas*

Practice reading aloud the following questions and answers:

1. ¿Come Ud. mucho?
Sí, yo como mucho.

2. ¿Comen Uds. mucho?
No, no comemos mucho.

3. ¿Come mucho su padre?
No, mi padre no come mucho.

4. ¿Comen mucho sus hermanos?
Sí, mis hermanos comen mucho.

5. ¿Come mucho su amigo favorito?
No, él no come mucho.

6. ¿Come mucho ella?
Sí, ella come mucho.

Nosotros comemos en la cafetería de la escuela.

Learn these questions too. Write the missing parts of the answers:

7. ¿Come Ud. en la cafetería?
Sí, yo ______________________________

8. ¿Comen Uds. en casa?
Sí, ______________________________ en casa.

9. ¿Comen ellos en la cafetería?
No, ellos ______________________________

10. ¿Come su familia en la cocina?
Sí, mi familia ______________________________

TOPIC QUESTION 17B

¿Dónde toma Ud. el desayuno?
Where do you have breakfast?

B. *Preguntas y respuestas*

Vocabulario
la cocina, kitchen
el **almuerzo,** lunch
algunas veces, sometimes
gordo, -a, fat
flaco, -a, thin, skinny
cerca de, near
o, or

1. ¿Dónde toma Ud. el desayuno?
Yo tomo el desayuno en casa.

2. ¿Dónde toman Uds. el desayuno?
Tomamos el desayuno en la cocina.

3. ¿Dónde toma Ud. el almuerzo?
Tomo el almuerzo en un restaurante.

4. ¿Toma ella el almuerzo en la cafetería?
Sí, algunas veces ella toma el almuerzo en la cafetería.

5. ¿Toma Ud. el desayuno?
Sí, yo ______________________________

6. ¿Toman Uds. el desayuno?
No, ______________________________ el desayuno.

7. ¿Toman sus padres el desayuno?
Sí, mis padres ______________________________

8. ¿Toman ellos el desayuno?
Sí, ______________________________

9. ¿Dónde toma su madre el desayuno?
Mi madre ______________________________ en la cocina.

10. ¿Dónde toman Uds. el almuerzo?
______________________________ en la cafetería.

C. *Lectura*

Pablo y Luis son amigos. Pablo come mucho. Come mucho en casa y come mucho en la cafetería de su escuela. Por eso es muy gordo.

Luis no come mucho. Por eso es muy flaco. Luis va a la universidad. Toma el desayuno en casa. Toma el almuerzo en la cafetería de la universidad. Algunas veces come con sus amigos en un restaurante cerca de la universidad.

Luis toma el desayuno en casa.

Preguntas

1. ¿Por qué es gordo Pablo? ________________
2. ¿Por qué es flaco Luis? ________________
3. ¿Dónde toma Luis el desayuno? ________________
4. ¿Dónde toma el almuerzo? ________________
5. ¿Dónde come Luis algunas veces? ________________
6. ¿Dónde está el restaurante? ________________
7. ¿Cómo se dice *near* en español? ________________

D. *Preguntas personales*

1. ¿Come Ud. panecillos para el desayuno?

____

2. ¿Comen Uds. en la cafetería de su escuela?

____

3. ¿Comen mucho sus padres?

____

4. ¿Es gorda su amiga favorita?

____

5. ¿Prefiere Ud. comer en la cafetería de la escuela o en un restaurante?

____

6. ¿Dónde toma Ud. el desayuno?

____

7. ¿Dónde toman Uds. el almuerzo?

____

E. *Traduzca Ud. al español:*

1. You *(Ud.)* eat at home. ________________
2. Do you *(Uds.)* have lunch in school? ________________
3. We don't eat much. ________________
4. Does Paco eat a lot? ________________
5. Do your brothers and sisters have breakfast in the kitchen? ________________

____

6. Sometimes they don't have breakfast. ________________
7. We have lunch at home. ________________

F. *Tema*. Write a composition entitled *¿Dónde come Ud.?* Tell where you have breakfast, what you eat for breakfast, where you have lunch, where some people you know have *their* breakfast or lunch, etc.

____

____

____

____

COGNATES (5)

G. Pronounce the words listed below. Can you guess their meanings? In each blank, write an English cognate for the Spanish word.

1. abandonar ____________
2. abril ____________
3. absurdo ____________
4. abundancia ____________
5. adjetivo ____________
6. administración ____________
7. admirar ____________
8. adolescente ____________
9. agencia ____________
10. agosto ____________
11. aire ____________
12. alarma ____________
13. artículo ____________
14. artificial ____________
15. artista ____________
16. atleta ____________
17. automático ____________
18. autor ____________
19. bomba ____________
20. boxear ____________
21. cadáver ____________
22. calendario ____________
23. camello ____________
24. cigarrillo ____________
25. cine ____________
26. cliente ____________
27. combate ____________
28. compañero ____________
29. dama ____________
30. declarar ____________
31. ejecutivo ____________
32. enemigo ____________
33. femenino ____________
34. Francia ____________
35. general ____________
36. guardia ____________
37. húngaro ____________
38. inglés ____________
39. isla ____________
40. Italia ____________
41. lámpara ____________
42. latinoamericano ____________
43. liberación ____________
44. mar ____________
45. masculino ____________
46. nación ____________
47. Naciones Unidas ____________
48. naturalista ____________
49. octubre ____________
50. olímpico ____________
51. pianista ____________
52. piloto ____________

53. poema________________________ **57.** sacrificio ______________________
54. poético ______________________ **58.** tecnológico______________________
55. psicología ____________________ **59.** veterano _______________________
56. resurrección __________________ **60.** zona __________________________

H. *Verdad o Mentira* (True or False). In the blank on the left, write *V* (for *Verdad*) if the statement is true, *M* (for *Mentira*) if the statement is false.

____ **1.** El presidente de los Estados Unidos se llama Ronald Reagan.
____ **2.** Tres y cuatro son siete.
____ **3.** Diez menos dos son seis.
____ **4.** Nosotros vamos a la primaria.
____ **5.** Si hoy es miércoles, mañana es jueves.
____ **6.** Si hoy es viernes, ayer fue martes.
____ **7.** Si mañana es domingo, hoy es sábado.
____ **8.** Nosotros nadamos en el desierto.
____ **9.** Once y ocho son diez y ocho.
____ **10.** Veinte menos nueve son once.
____ **11.** Nosotros no hablamos japonés en la escuela.
____ **12.** Los estudiantes buenos estudian.
____ **13.** El jai alai es popular en España.
____ **14.** Treinta y cincuenta son noventa.
____ **15.** Ciento menos sententa son cuarenta.
____ **16.** Nosotros no tomamos el desayuno en la escuela.
____ **17.** Los niños de ocho años no manejan.
____ **18.** Jugamos al béisbol en los Estados Unidos.
____ **19.** Estudiamos español.
____ **20.** El padre de mi padre es mi tío.
____ **21.** La hermana de mi madre es mi tía.
____ **22.** El abuelo de mi padre es mi hijo.
____ **23.** No escribimos en la escuela.
____ **24.** Quien mucho duerme poco aprende.
____ **25.** Los gordos no comen mucho.

Vocabulario
desierto, desert
japonés, Japanese
niños, children
años, years
los gordos, fat people

I. *Lectura*

LA VIRGEN DE GUADALUPE

Los países de Latinoamérica son católicos. Muchos países católicos tienen un santo patrón o una santa patrona. Por ejemplo, el santo patrón de Irlanda es San Patricio (Saint Patrick) y el de Puerto Rico es San Juan.

La santa patrona de México es la Virgen de Guadalupe. La iglesia dedicada a la Virgen se llama la Basílica de Guadalupe. Está situada en el pueblo de Guadalupe. El pueblo de Guadalupe está a tres millas al norte de la ciudad de México. El sitio de la Basílica es el más sagrado de México.

Preguntas

1. ¿Qué tienen muchos países católicos?

---

2. ¿Quién es el santo patrón de Puerto Rico?

---

3. ¿Quién es la santa patrona de México?

---

4. ¿Qué iglesia está dedicada a la Virgen de Guadalupe?

---

5. ¿Dónde está el pueblo de Guadalupe?

---

6. ¿Cuál es el sitio más sagrado de México?

---

7. ¿Qué país de habla inglesa tiene un santo patrón? Quién es?

Vocabulario

el **país,** country
católico, -a, Catholic
el **santo patrón** / la **santa patrona** } patron saint
la **Virgen,** Virgin
la **iglesia,** church
dedicado, -a, dedicated
situado, -a, situated, located
el **pueblo,** town
la **milla,** mile
al norte de, north of
el **sitio,** site, place
el más sagrado, the most sacred

la **basílica,** basilica, a title given by the Pope to certain churches as a special honor

Lesson 27

dormir, *to sleep*

TOPIC QUESTION 18

¿Cuántas horas duerme Ud.? How many hours do you sleep?

present tense of ***dormir (ue)***	
yo **duermo**	nosotros **dormimos**
Ud. / él / ella } **duerme**	Uds. / ellos / ellas } **duermen**

A. *Preguntas y respuestas*

Practice reading aloud the following questions and answers:

1. ¿Cuántas horas duerme Ud.?
Yo duermo ocho horas.

2. ¿Duermen Uds. en sus clases?
No, nosotros no dormimos en nuestras clases.

3. ¿Duerme él ocho horas?
Sí, él duerme ocho horas.

4. ¿En qué clase duerme ella?
Ella duerme en su clase de inglés.

5. ¿Cuántas horas duermen ellos?
Ellos duermen ocho horas.

6. ¿Cuántas horas prefiere dormir su hermano?
Él prefiere dormir diez horas.

Vocabulario
¿cuántos, -as? how many?
la **hora,** hour

El señor Gutiérrez duerme bien.

Learn these questions too. Write the missing parts of the answers.

7. ¿Cuántas horas duerme Ud.?
Yo ___________________ siete horas.

8. ¿Cuántas horas duermen Uds.?
Nosotros ___________________ ocho horas.

9. ¿Cuántas horas duerme su padre?

   Mi padre ______________________________ horas.

10. ¿Cuántas horas duerme su madre?

    Mi madre ______________________________ horas.

11. ¿Cuántas horas prefiere Ud. dormir?

    Yo prefiero ______________________________ horas.

B. *Lectura*

Andrés no duerme mucho. Duerme cinco o seis horas. Sus hermanos menores duermen ocho horas.

La madre de Andrés duerme siete horas. El padre de Andrés no duerme mucho. Duerme cinco o seis horas.

Preguntas

1. ¿Cuántas horas duerme Andrés?

   ____

2. ¿Cómo se dice *younger brothers and sisters* en español?

   ____

3. ¿Cuántas horas duermen los hermanos menores de Andrés?

   ____

4. ¿Cuántas horas duerme la madre de Andrés?

   ____

5. ¿Quién duerme cinco o seis horas?

   ____

C. *Preguntas personales*

1. ¿Duermen Uds. ocho horas? ____
2. ¿Cuántas horas duermen sus hermanos? ________________________________
3. ¿Duerme mucho su amiga favorita? ____________________________________
4. ¿Dónde duerme Ud.? ____
5. ¿Dónde prefiere Ud. dormir? ____

D. *Tema*. Write a composition entitled *¿Cuántas horas duerme Ud.?*

____

____

____

____

____

E. *Traduzca Ud. al español:*

1. Does Andrew sleep a lot?

____

2. I don't sleep much.

____

3. You *(Uds.)* sleep eight hours.

____

4. We sleep eight hours.

____

5. Do you *(Ud.)* sleep in your classes?

____

6. Your brothers and sisters sleep eight hours.

____

7. How many hours do you *(Uds.)* prefer to sleep?

____

8. We prefer to sleep seven hours.

____

F. *Conversación.* You and your classmates take turns asking one another the questions in part A on pages 101–102.

Lesson 28

beber, *to drink*

TOPIC QUESTION 19

¿Qué bebe Ud.? What do you drink?

present tense of ***beber***	
yo **bebo**	nosotros **bebemos**
Ud. / él / ella } **bebe**	Uds. / ellos / ellas } **beben**

A. *Preguntas y respuestas*

Practice reading aloud the following questions and answers:

1. ¿Qué bebe Ud.?
Yo bebo leche.

2. ¿Qué beben Uds.?
Bebemos café.

3. ¿Qué bebe ella?
Ella bebe un refresco.

4. ¿Qué bebe él?
Él bebe agua.

5. ¿Bebe él leche?
No, él no bebe leche.

6. ¿Bebe Ud. cerveza?
No, yo no bebo cerveza.

7. ¿Beben ellos café?
Sí, ellos beben café.

Vocabulario

el **agua** *(f),* water
el **refresco,** soft drink
(with or without carbonation)
la **gaseosa,** soda
la **cerveza,** beer
el **vino,** wine
la **tequila,** a Mexican liquor
todo, everything
¿quiere Ud.? do you want?
yo quiero, I want

Learn these questions too. Write the missing parts of the answers:

8. ¿Qué beben sus padres?
Mis padres ____________________

9. ¿Qué beben sus hermanos?
Ellos ____________________

10. ¿Qué bebe su amigo favorito?

Mi amigo favorito ____

11. ¿Beben Uds. vino?

No, ____ vino.

12. ¿Qué quiere Ud. beber?

Yo quiero ____ una gaseosa.

B. *Lectura*

Adelita bebe leche o un refresco. No bebe café.

El padre de Adelita bebe café. Algunas veces bebe té. También bebe cerveza.

Los hermanos de Adelita beben leche. No beben café.

El amigo favorito de Adelita se llama Guillermo. Guillermo bebe todo: café, té, leche, agua, cerveza, vino y tequila.

Guillermo bebe un refresco.

Preguntas

1. ¿Bebe Adelita café? ____

2. ¿Qué bebe Adelita? ____

3. ¿Qué bebe el padre de Adelita? ____

4. ¿Quién bebe café, té y vino? ____

5. ¿Qué beben los hermanos de Adelita? ____

6. ¿Cómo se llama el amigo favorito de Adelita? ____

____

7. ¿Qué bebe Guillermo? ____

C. *Preguntas personales*

1. ¿Bebe Ud. cerveza? ____

2. ¿Qué beben Uds.? ____

3. ¿Qué bebe su padre? ____

4. ¿Beben cerveza sus hermanos menores? ____

____

5. ¿Qué refresco prefiere Ud.? ____

6. ¿Qué prefiere Ud. beber para el desayuno? ____

____

7. ¿Bebe Ud. una gaseosa algunas veces? ____

D. *Tema.* Write a composition entitled *¿Qué bebe Ud.?*

E. *Traduzca Ud. al español:*

1. You *(Ud.)* drink milk. ____________
2. Do you *(Uds.)* drink soda? ____________
3. We don't drink beer. ____________
4. Does your mother drink wine? ____________
5. They drink water. ____________
6. What do your friends drink? ____________
7. What do you want to drink? ____________

F. *Conversación.* You and your classmates take turns asking one another the questions in part A on pages 104–105.

Review Exercises

(Lessons 21–28)

G. *Frases revueltas.* Unscramble the sentences:

1. no su lengua hermano estudia una .

   ____

2. ¿ lengua Roberto qué estudia ?

   ____

3. hijo sobrino el mi de es mi hermano .

   ____

4. padre padre abuelo mi de el es mi .

   ____

5. ¿ escuela qué los a ? muchachos van .

   ____

6. Andrés Guillermo mayor es hermano el de .

   ____

7. el ella casa en desayuno toma .

   ____

8. restaurante prefieren en comer un .

____

9. toman ellos desayuno no el .

____

10. patrón tienen un muchos santo países .

____

11. México la la de Guadalupe de santa es Virgen patrona .

____

12. Basílica el sagrado sitio México la más es de .

____

13. ocho menores duermen sus horas hermanos .

____

14. ¿ Ud. cuántas duerme ? horas

____

15. bebe de la café madre Adelita .

____

16. ¿ Adelita hermanos qué de los beben ?

____

Vocabulary Review

H. Write these words in Spanish. (With nouns, include the definite article.)

1. to study ____________	**15.** biology ____________
2. language ____________	**16.** science ____________
3. French ____________	**17.** to write ____________
4. Frank ____________	**18.** army ____________
5. German ____________	**19.** older ____________
6. husband ____________	**20.** letters ____________
7. aunt ____________	**21.** checks ____________
8. daughter ____________	**22.** good ____________
9. cousin ____________	**23.** bad ____________
10. nephew ____________	**24.** lesson ____________
11. grandfather ____________	**25.** to eat ____________
12. to learn ____________	**26.** sometimes ____________
13. chemistry ____________	**27.** near ____________
14. physics ____________	**28.** younger ____________

29. lunch ____________________________
30. restaurant ____________________________
31. country ____________________________
32. soda ____________________________
33. church ____________________________
34. town ____________________________
35. north ____________________________
36. mathematics ____________________________
37. to sleep ____________________________
38. How many hours? ____________________________
39. to drink ____________________________
40. beer ____________________________
41. wine ____________________________
42. water ____________________________
43. history ____________________________
44. soft drink ____________________________

I. Write the opposites of the following:

1. señor ____________________________
2. ¡Buenos días! ____________________________
3. ¡Hola! ____________________________
4. Gracias. ____________________________
5. Adiós. ____________________________
6. Hasta la vista. ____________________________
7. madre ____________________________
8. hermano ____________________________
9. él ____________________________
10. ellas ____________________________
11. ayer ____________________________
12. esposa ____________________________
13. malo ____________________________
14. día ____________________________

J. Here are some answers. What are the questions?

EXAMPLE: Yo no voy mucho al cine. *¿Va Ud. mucho al cine?*

1. Juan aprende química. ____________________________
2. No, yo no como mucho. ____________________________
3. María no escribe cheques. ____________________________
4. Mi padre prefiere café. ____________________________
5. No, mi amigo favorito no aprende química. ____________________________
6. Sí, mi madre habla mucho al teléfono. ____________________________
7. Mis hermanos duermen ocho horas. ____________________________
8. Mi hermana no estudia una lengua. ____________________________

Lesson 29

leer, *to read*

TOPIC QUESTION 20

¿Qué lee Ud.? What do you read?

present tense of ***leer***	
yo **leo**	nosotros **leemos**
Ud. / él / ella } **lee**	Uds. / ellos / ellas } **leen**

A. *Preguntas y respuestas*

Practice reading aloud the following questions and answers:

Vocabulario
el **periódico,** newspaper
la **revista,** magazine
los **libros escolares,** schoolbooks

1. ¿Qué lee Ud.?
   Yo leo un periódico.
2. ¿Qué leen Uds.?
   Nosotros leemos revistas.
3. ¿Lee Ud. mucho?
   Sí, yo leo mucho.
4. ¿Lee él periódicos?
   No, él no lee periódicos.
5. ¿Leen ellos sus libros escolares?
   Algunas veces ellos leen sus libros escolares.

El señor López lee el periódico.

In questions 6 to 11, write the missing parts of the answers:

6. ¿Qué lee Ud.?
   Yo _______________ un periódico.
7. ¿Qué lee su padre?
   Mi padre _______________ una revista.
8. ¿Qué lee su madre?
   Ella____

9. ¿Qué leen sus hermanos?
   Mis hermanos ____

10. ¿Qué lee su amiga favorita?
    Ella ____

11. ¿Qué leen Uds.?
    ______________________________ revistas.

B. *Lectura*

El señor López no lee mucho. Lee los periódicos.

La señora de López lee mucho. Lee periódicos, revistas y libros.

Los hijos de los señores López se llaman Ricardo y Emilia. Leen mucho. Leen periódicos, revistas y libros escolares.

Antonia estudia sus libros escolares.

Preguntas

1. ¿Lee mucho el señor López? ______________________________
2. ¿Qué lee el señor López? ______________________________
3. ¿Qué lee la señora de López?______________________________
4. ¿Cómo se llaman los hijos? ______________________________
5. ¿Qué quiere decir *revista*? ______________________________
6. ¿Qué leen los hijos? ______________________________
7. ¿Cómo se dice *newspaper* en español? ______________________________

C. *Preguntas personales*

1. ¿Lee Ud. periódicos? ______________________________
2. ¿Leen Uds. libros escolares? ______________________________
3. ¿Qué periódico lee su madre? ______________________________
4. ¿Qué revistas lee Ud.? ______________________________
5. ¿Qué prefiere Ud. leer? ______________________________
6. ¿Qué prefieren leer sus hermanos?______________________________

D. *Tema.* Write a composition entitled *¿Qué lee Ud.?*

____

____

____

____

E. *Traduzca Ud. al español:*

1. I don't read much. ______________________

2. Does your father read the newspapers? ______________________

3. What does your mother read? ______________________

4. We read a lot in school (en *la* escuela). ______________________

5. Your brothers and sisters read their schoolbooks. ______________________

____

6. You *(Uds.)* read magazines. ______________________

7. She wants to read the newspaper. ______________________

F. *Conversación.* You and your classmates take turns asking one another the questions in part A on pages 109–110.

La columna personal de Anita Gómez (8)

Vocabulario
yo puedo, I can
el profesor / **la profesora** } teacher
aburrido, -a, bored
tonto, -a, silly

el 15 de octubre

Querida Anita Gómez:

Yo no puedo dormir en la clase de español porque mi profesor siempre habla.
¿Qué debo yo hacer?

Antonio Aburrido

el 25 de octubre

Querido Antonio Aburrido:

Ud. no debe dormir en la clase de español. ¡Ud. debe dormir en casa, tonto!

Anita Gómez

G. Complete the sentences:

1. Antonio no puede dormir en la clase porque ______________________

2. Según Anita Gómez, Antonio debe dormir ______________________

Preguntas personales (a review)

H. Answer each question with a complete sentence in Spanish:

1. ¿Qué lengua estudia Ud.?______________________________

2. ¿Cuántos hijos tienen sus padres? ______________________________

3. ¿Aprende su padre español?______________________________

4. ¿Escribe Ud. cheques? ______________________________

5. ¿Dónde toma Ud. el almuerzo? ______________________________

6. ¿Quién es la santa patrona de México? ______________________________

7. ¿Cuántas horas duerme Ud.? ______________________________

8. ¿Qué bebe su madre? ______________________________

9. ¿Qué bebe Ud.?______________________________

10. ¿Lee Ud. mucho? ______________________________

11. ¿Qué leen sus hermanos?______________________________

12. ¿Cómo se dice *grandparents* en español? ______________________________

Mis padres tienen cuatro hijos.

Lesson 30

Gender and Plural of Nouns; Articles; Adjectives; Expressing Possession

Here is a summary of some basic rules of Spanish grammar that you learned in earlier lessons:

A. *Gender and Plural of Nouns*

1. All Spanish nouns have *gender*; that is, they are either masculine or feminine.

Nouns ending in **-o** are usually masculine.
Nouns ending in **-a, -d,** or **-ión** are usually feminine.

There are some exceptions. If you are not sure of the gender of a noun, consult the Vocabulary on pages 307–318. In the Vocabulary, gender is indicated by the definite article preceding the noun.

If the noun is masculine, write *el*; if it is feminine, write *la*:

1. __________ amigo	**4.** __________ ciudad	**7.** __________ nación
2. __________ café	**5.** __________ coche	**8.** __________ salud
3. __________ muchacha	**6.** __________ madre	**9.** __________ casa

2. The plural is formed as follows:
If the noun ends in a vowel, add **-s**; if it ends in a consonant, add **-es**.

EXAMPLES:	hermano	hermano**s**
	restaurante	restaurante**s**
	universidad	universidad**es**
	país	país**es**

A noun ending in **-ión** drops the accent mark in the plural:

nac**ión** naciones

Write the plural form:

10. amiga __________________	**13.** café ______________________
11. comunidad __________________	**14.** lección ______________________
12. español __________________	**15.** chico ______________________

B. *Articles*

The definite article in English is the word *the*. The definite article in Spanish has four forms:

el muchacho	the boy	**la** muchacha	the girl
los muchachos	the boys	**las** muchachas	the girls

Write the correct form of the definite article:

1. __________ casas	**3.** __________ padres	**5.** __________ hermanas
2. __________ coche	**4.** __________ madre	**6.** __________ sombreros

The indefinite article in English is *a* or *an*. The indefinite article in Spanish has four forms:

un muchacho	a boy	**unos** muchachos	some (a few) boys
una muchacha	a girl	**unas** muchachas	some (a few) girls

Write the correct form of the indefinite article:

7. __________ libro	**9.** __________ carta	**11.** __________ café
8. __________ semanas	**10.** __________ amigos	**12.** __________ licencia

C. *Adjectives*

1. Descriptive adjectives usually *follow* the nouns they modify:

mi amigo **favorito**
un muchacho **inteligente**

Numerical and possessive adjectives *precede* the nouns they modify:

cinco periódicos
muchas casas
mis padres

Decide whether the adjective goes before or after the noun, and write it in the correct blank.

EXAMPLE: (grande) ______________ casa ___*grande*___

1. (guapa) ______________ muchacha ______________
2. (cuatro) ______________ horas ______________
3. (mucho) ______________ dinero ______________
4. (español) ______________ amigo ______________

2. An adjective has a plural ending if it modifies a noun in the plural:

mis amigos favorito**s**
nuestro**s** libros escolar**es**

3. Adjectives that end in **-o** in the masculine singular have four possible endings:

mal**o** . . . . .masculine singular
mal**a** . . . . .feminine singular
mal**os** . . . . . . .masculine plural
mal**as** . . . . . . .feminine plural

Translate into Spanish:

5. their new house ______________________________
6. an old car ______________________________

7. the sick girl ______________________

8. our Spanish friends *(m.)* ______________________

9. a lot of milk ______________________

10. the big swimming pool ______________________

11. some Spanish-speaking boys ______________________

D. *Expressing Possession*

The Spanish language does not use *'s* to express possession. *Mary's house* is expressed in Spanish as **la casa de María** ("the house of Mary"). Possession is expressed by using the word **de** *(of)*. Here are other examples:

los hermanos de Diego	Diego's brothers ("the brothers of Diego")
el coche de mis padres	my parents' car ("the car of my parents")

Translate into English, using apostrophes:

1. los libros de Anita ______________________

2. la amiga de mis hermanas ______________________

3. el coche del señor García ______________________

Translate into Spanish:

4. Mrs. Mendoza's house ______________________

5. her son's friends ______________________

6. their daughters' teachers ______________________

7. my brother's big car ______________________

Review Quiz

E. Complete the following:

1. (my) ____________ amigo

2. (your) ____________ cartas

3. (our) ____________ cheques

4. (our) ____________ casa

5. (the) ____________ revista

6. (the) ____________ océanos

7. (the) ____________ universidades

8. (the) ____________ desayuno

9. (a) ____________ madre

10. (a) ____________ estado

11. (some) ____________ pueblos

12. (some) ____________ muchachas

13. (our) ____________ amigo

14. (our) ____________ hermanas

F. *Traduzca Ud. al español:*

1. He has my brother's books. ____
2. Mary drives my mother's car. ______________________________________
3. They read John's letters.____
4. They are going to Mary's house. ____________________________________
5. Joseph's sweetheart is in Acapulco. _________________________________

La novia de José está en Acapulco.

G. *¿Qué quiere recibir Elena para su cumpleaños*? To find out, use the following clues to fill in the boxes of this puzzle. The answer will appear in one of the columns (reading down).

Vocabulario
recibir, to receive, get
Elena, Helen
el **cumpleaños,** birthday
primer día, first day

1. el primer día de escuela
2. "Henry" en español es ________.
3. Laura es gorda porque ________ mucho.
4. Vamos a la iglesia los ________.
5. Voy al cine hoy para ver a mis ________ favoritos.
6. Para el desayuno, Carlos pide dos ________.
7. No vamos a la ________ los sábados.

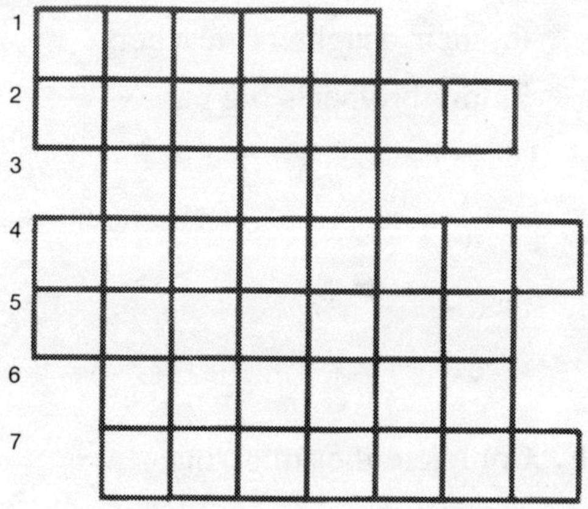

Lesson 31

a + el = al; de + el = del

The Spanish language has only two contractions: **al** and **del**. Unlike English contractions, which combine two words that may also be used separately (*doesn't* or *does not, won't* or *will not,* etc.), **al** and **del** are never replaced by the words that are combined in them. One cannot say "a el muchacho."

Al, *to the,* and **del**, *of the,* are used only before a masculine singular noun:

al muchacho	**del** muchacho

but otherwise:

a la muchacha	**de la** muchacha
a los muchachos	**de los** muchachos
a las muchachas	**de las** muchachas

Vocabulario

¿a quién? / **¿a quiénes?** to whom?
el **pie,** foot
pequeño, -a, small
más pequeños que, smaller than
el **autor** / la **autora** author

A. Read these sentences aloud, then answer in Spanish:

La muchacha escribe una carta al muchacho.

El muchacho escribe una carta a la muchacha.

1. ¿A quién escribe el muchacho? ____________________
2. ¿A quién escribe la muchacha? ____________________

El muchacho escribe una carta a las muchachas.

La muchacha escribe una carta a los muchachos.

3. ¿A quiénes escribe el muchacho? ____________________
4. ¿A quiénes escribe la muchacha? ____________________

B. Read these sentences aloud, then complete the sentences that follow:

Los pies del muchacho son grandes.

Los pies de la muchacha son pequeños.

El autor del libro es Raúl Méndez.

La autora de los libros es María Salas.

1. Los pies__________ son más grandes que los pies __________
2. Los pies__________ son más pequeños que los pies __________
3. María Salas es la autora ____________________
4. Raúl Méndez es el autor ____________________

Lesson 32

tú, *you, familiar singular*

As we learned, *you* in Spanish can be either **Ud.** or **Uds.** It can also be translated by a third Spanish pronoun: **tú**. The pronoun **tú** is used when speaking to a parent, a brother or sister, a relative, a friend, a classmate, a child, or an animal. For that reason, **tú** is called the *familiar* singular. (**Ud.** is called the *formal* or "polite" singular.)

The **tú** form of the verb is obtained by adding **-s** to the **Ud.** form:

Ud. habla	Ud. aprende
tú hablas	**tú** aprendes

Tú has a corresponding plural form, **vosotros**, but it is used only in Spain. (See Lesson 40.) In Latin America, the plural of **tú** is expressed by **Uds.**

In the *Preguntas* of the lessons that follow, you will sometimes be addressed as **tú** rather than **Ud.**, to give you practice in recognizing the verb forms used with that pronoun.

A. Write the indicated forms of the verb:

	tú	*Ud.*	*Uds.*
1. escribir	________	________	________
2. comer	________	________	________
3. beber	________	________	________
4. estar	________	________	________
5. tener	________	________	________
6. manejar	________	________	________
7. ir	________	________	________
8. jugar (ue)	________	________	________
9. nadar	________	________	________
10. preferir (ie)	________	________	________
11. estudiar	________	________	________
12. dormir (ue)	________	________	________

B. As you have learned, it is not always necessary to express the pronoun subject of a verb:

tú hablas
or simply } you speak
hablas

Translate the questions into Spanish, using the *tú* form of the verb. Omit the pronoun *tú*. On the second line, write an answer in Spanish, omitting the pronoun *yo*.

1. What are you studying? ________________________

____

2. What is your name? ________________________

(Replace *se* with *te*.) ________________________

3. Are you going to the movies? ________________________

____

4. Do you sleep in class? ________________________

____

5. Where are you? ________________________

____

6. Do you have lunch at home? ________________________

____

7. Do you eat in the cafeteria? ________________________

____

8. Do you have a new car? ________________________

____

9. How are you? ________________________

____

10. Are you writing a letter? ________________________

____

Lesson 33

COMMANDS

Spanish verbs are of three types, called *ar, er,* and *ir* verbs. The letters refer to the ending of the infinitive:

hablar	comer	escribir
to speak	*to eat*	*to write*

*1. To form a command in Spanish, change the **-o** ending of the first person singular to the opposite vowel. For *ar* verbs, the opposite vowel is **e**; for *er* and *ir* verbs, the opposite vowel is **a**:

ar VERBS
yo habl**o** Change **-o** to **-e**: ¡habl**e** Ud.! *speak*!

er AND *ir* VERBS	
yo com**o**	yo escrib**o**
Change **-o** to **-a**:	
¡com**a** Ud.! *eat*!	¡escrib**a** Ud.! *write*!

2. If the command is directed at two or more persons, the plural form is used. To form the plural, simply add **-n** to the singular:

¿hable**n** Uds.! ¡coma**n** Uds.! ¡escriba**n** Uds.!

Commands may also be negative:

¡**no** hablen Uds.!	¡**no** coman Uds.!	¡**no** escriban Uds.!
don't speak!	*don't eat!*	*don't write!*

3. The pronoun **Ud.** or **Uds.** may be expressed or omitted. For example, *speak!* = **¡hable Ud.!** or simply **¡hable!**

4. The verb **ir** has irregular command forms that must be learned separately:

¡**vaya** Ud.! ¡**vayan** Uds.!	go!	¡no **vaya** Ud.! ¡no **vayan** Uds.!	don't go!

*These rules apply only to *formal* commands, that is, to those addressed to **Ud.** or **Uds.** The informal or "familiar" commands are not taught in this book.

A. Write three command forms for each verb, as shown in the following example:

EXAMPLE: hablar: *¡hable Ud.! ¡hablen Uds.! ¡no hable Ud.!*

1. tomar: ____________________
2. aprender: ____________________
3. dormir: ____________________
4. leer: ____________________
5. nadar: ____________________
6. estudiar: ____________________
7. beber: ____________________
8. pedir (yo *pido*): ____________________
9. cantar: ____________________
10. ir: ____________________

B. Complete the sentences with the command form of the verb.

EXAMPLE: (hablar) No __*hable*__ Ud. en la clase.

1. (manejar) ____________________ Ud. con cuidado.
2. (estudiar) ____________________ Uds. sus lecciones.
3. (aprender) ____________________ Uds. la lección.
4. (beber) ____________________ Ud. un poco de leche.
5. (leer) ____________________ Uds. sus libros.
6. (escribir) ____________________ Ud. una carta.
7. (cantar) No ____________________ Uds. en la clase.
8. (fumar) No ____________________ Uds.
9. (traducir [*yo traduzco*]) ____________________ Uds. la frase al español.
10. (ir) ____________________ Ud. al cine mañana.
11. (dormir) ____________________ Ud. ocho horas.
12. (tomar) ____________________ Ud. el almuerzo en casa.

Vocabulario

en la clase, in class
con cuidado, carefully
un poco de, a little
la **frase,** sentence
en casa, at home

Crucigrama (3)

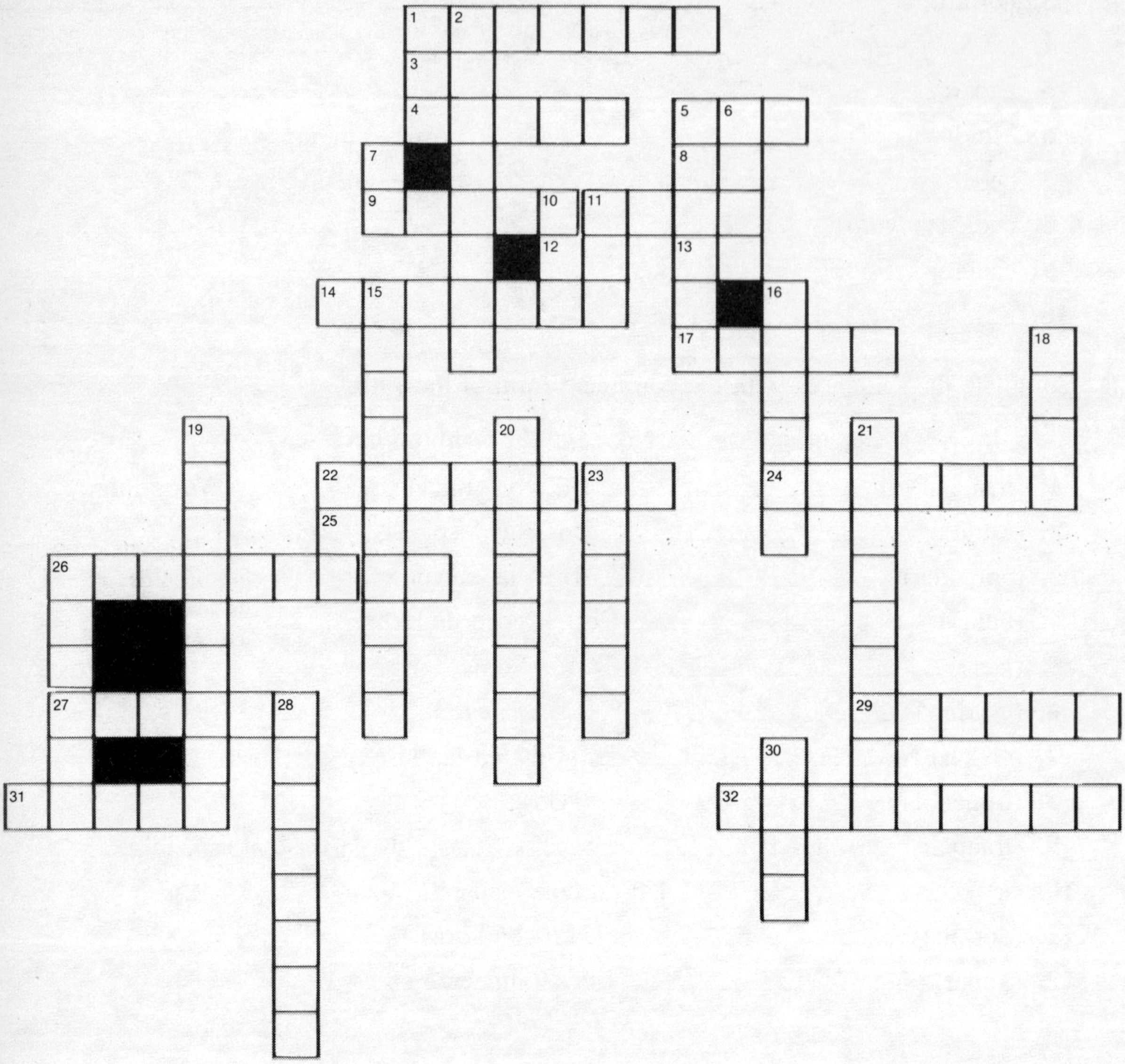

(Each blank represents one word.)

Across

1. una bebida alcohólica mexicana
3. iniciales de Enrique Jiménez
4. *airmail* = correo _____.
5. ¿Qué quiere decir *hombre*?
8. Estoy = *I* _____.
9. Mi amigo Dionisio bebe _____ _____, y por eso no puede estudiar mucho.
12. abreviatura de "Artistas Unidos" en inglés
13. iniciales de Urías Rafferty
14. ¿Qué quiere decir *cartas*?
17. Yo me _____ Cristina.
22. La santa patrona de México es la _____ _____ Guadalupe.
24. ¿Cómo se dice *ejemplo* en inglés?
25. las primeras dos letras del alfabeto
26. Si Uds. no quieren ir al cine, ¿adónde _____ _____?
27. Nosotros _____ revistas.
29. ¿Qué quiere decir *iglesia*?
31. Yo duermo ocho _____.
32. ¿Cómo se dice *periódico* en inglés?

Down

1. ¿Cómo se dice *té* en inglés?
2. ¿Cómo se dice *army* en español?
5. nombre de muchacho
6. *love*
7. abreviatura inglesa de *in the afternoon* o *in the evening*
10. ¿Cómo se dice *nuestro* en inglés?
11. Si tú _____ al cine esta noche, yo voy también.
15. Nosotros _____ muchas cartas.
16. *countries*
18. ¿Qué quiere decir *vino*?
19. ¿Qué quiere decir *algunas veces*?
20. *soft drink*
21. En Latinoamérica, hay más _____ que protestantes.
22. Ellos no _____ a la escuela hoy.
23. Duerma Ud. en casa; ¡no debe _____ en la clase!
26. *What am I reading?* = ¿_____ _____?
28. Yo me llamo Tim, para _____.
30. ¿Quieres _____ mi revista?

Lesson 34

EXPRESSING "TO LIKE" BY USING **gustar,** *to please*

TOPIC QUESTION 21	**¿Le gusta a Ud. el café?** Do you like coffee?

A. *Preguntas y respuestas*

Practice reading aloud the following questions and answers:

1. ¿Le gusta a Ud. el café?
Sí, me gusta el café.

2. ¿Te gusta el té?
No, no me gusta el té.

3. ¿Les gusta a Uds. el café?
No, no nos gusta el café.

4. ¿Le gusta a su padre el café?
Sí, a mi padre le gusta el café.

5. ¿Les gusta a sus hermanos el café?
Sí, a mis hermanos les gusta el café.

6. ¿Le gusta a su amigo favorito el café?
No, a mi amigo favorito no le gusta el café.

7. ¿Le gusta a él el café?
No, a él no le gusta el café.

8. ¿Le gusta a ella el café?
Sí, a ella le gusta el café.

Vocabulario

me gusta, I like
te gusta, you like
le gusta { you like / he, she } likes
nos gusta, we like
les gusta { you *(pl.)* like / they like
¿Le gusta a Ud.? Do you like it?
Sí, me gusta. Yes, I like it.
No me gusta. I don't like it.
la **bebida,** beverage, drink

Learn these questions too. Write the missing parts of the answers:

9. ¿Le gusta a Ud. la leche?
Sí, me _______________ la leche.

10. ¿Te gusta el refresco?
No, no me _______________ el refresco.

11. ¿Les gusta a Uds. el café?

No, no nos _______________ el café.

12. ¿Les gusta a ellos?

Sí, a ellos ____

13. ¿Le gusta a su padre la cerveza?

Sí, a mi padre ____

14. ¿Le gusta a su madre el té?

Sí, a ella ____

15. ¿Les gusta a sus hermanas jugar al tenis?

Sí, a mis hermanas les ____

B. *Lectura*

Me llamo Margarita. Mi hermano se llama Paco. A Paco le gusta el café, pero a mí me gusta la leche. No me gusta el café.

Al señor Fernández le gusta el café. No le gusta la leche.

A la señora Fernández le gusta el té. No le gusta el café.

A los hermanos de Elena les gusta la leche. No les gusta a ellos el café.

A Diego le gusta el café.

Preguntas

1. ¿Qué bebida le gusta a Margarita?

____

2. ¿Qué bebida no le gusta a ella?

____

3. ¿Qué prefiere Paco?

____

4. ¿Qué bebida le gusta al señor Fernández?

____

5. ¿Qué bebida no le gusta a él?

____

6. ¿Qué le gusta a la señora Fernández?

____

7. ¿Qué bebida no le gusta a ella?

____

8. ¿Qué bebida les gusta a los hermanos de Elena?

____

9. ¿Qué no les gusta a ellos?

____

10. ¿A quién le gusta el té?

____

C. *To like* is expressed in Spanish in a way that is completely different from English. In Spanish, "we like coffee" becomes *coffee pleases us* or *coffee is pleasing to us*. The verb **gustar** means *to please*.

1. To translate "I like," "you like," "we like," etc., first change the sentence to the form in which the thought would be expressed in Spanish:

we like coffee = *the coffee pleases us*

pleases = **gusta**
us = **nos**
pleases us = **nos gusta**

The subject of **gusta** is **el café,** which *follows* the verb:

Nos gusta el café.

2. Similarly, "we like it" becomes *it pleases us*:

it pleases = **gusta**
us = **nos**
Hence, "we like it" = **Nos gusta.**

Another example: "they don't like it" becomes *it does not please them*:

it does not please = **no gusta**
them = **les**
Hence, "they don't like it" = **No les gusta.**

Translate into English:

1. Nos gusta el coche. ______________________
2. No me gusta la cerveza. ______________________
3. Le gusta el refresco. You ______________________
4. Le gusta la revista. She ______________________
5. Les gusta el libro. They______________________

Traduzca Ud. al español:

6. I don't like coffee. ______________________
7. We like the magazine. ______________________
8. They like it. ______________________

3. The object pronoun **le** may mean either *(to) you, (to) him,* or *(to) her*:

le gusta { it pleases you *(you like it)*
it pleases him *(he likes it)*
it pleases her *(she likes it)*

To make it very clear which of the meanings of **le** is the *intended* meaning, we can add a clarifying phrase:

le gusta **a Ud.**	you like it
le gusta **a él**	he likes it
le gusta **a ella**	she likes it
Le gusta **a ella** el coche.	She likes the car.

The phrase may also *begin* the sentence: **A Ud.** le gusta. **A él** le gusta. **A ella** le gusta. **A ella** le gusta el coche.

Translate into English:

9. A él le gusta la gaseosa. ________________

10. ¿Le gusta a ella la leche? ________________

11. A Ud. no le gusta la revista. ________________

Translate into Spanish, using a clarifying phrase (*a Ud., a él,* etc.):

12. Does he like the house? ________________

13. Do you *(sing.)* like the pool? ________________

14. She doesn't like the book. ________________

4. The object pronoun **les** may mean *(to) you* (plural), *(to) them* (masculine), or *(to) them* (feminine):

les gusta { you *(pl.)* like it
they *(m.)* like it
they *(f.)* like it

To avoid confusion, we can add a clarifying phrase:

les gusta **a Uds.**	you *(pl.)* like it
les gusta **a ellos**	they *(m.)* like it
les gusta **a ellas**	they *(f.)* like it

Translate into English:

15. No les gusta a ellos la escuela. ________________

16. A Uds. les gusta la clase. ________________

17. No les gusta a ellas. ________________

Translate into Spanish, using a clarifying phrase (*a Uds., a ellos,* etc.):

18. They *(f.)* like the book. ______________________

19. Don't you *(pl.)* like the house? ______________________

20. They *(m.)* like beer. ______________________

D. *Summary of object pronouns used with* **gustar**

me, (to) me
te, (to) you *(familiar)*
le, (to) you, (to) him, (to) her
nos, (to) us
les, (to) you *(pl.),* (to) them

When using **me, te,** and **nos,** the phrases **a mí, a ti,** and **a nosotros** may be added for emphasis:

Te gusta.	You like it.
Te gusta **a ti,** pero no me gusta **a mí.**	*You* like it but *I* don't. ("It is pleasing *to you* but not *to me.*")
Nos gusta la leche.	We like milk.
A nosotros nos gusta la leche; **a él** le gusta el café.	*We* like milk; *he* likes coffee.

E. *Traduzca Ud. al español:*

1. I like milk. ______________________

2. *I* like milk; what do *you* like? (*you,* familiar) ______________________

____

3. My father likes coffee. ______________________

4. My mother doesn't like coffee. ______________________

5. They like milk. ______________________

6. Do your brothers and sisters like wine? ______________________

____

7. Our friends like baseball, but *we* like soccer. ______________________

____

8. We like to play baseball. ______________________

F. *Conversación.* You and your classmates take turns asking one another the questions in part A on pages 124–125.

La columna personal de Anita Gómez (9)

el 2 de noviembre

Querida Anita Gómez:

Yo fumo mucho. Yo fumo tres cajetillas de cigarrillos al día. ¿Qué debo yo hacer?

Isabel Fumamucho

Vocabulario

fumar, to smoke
la **cajetilla,** (cigarette) pack
el **cigarrillo,** cigarette
al día, per day
el **médico,** doctor
dicen, say
el fumar, smoking
malo, bad
el **corazón,** heart
los **pulmones,** lungs
en vez de, instead of
masticar chicle, to chew gum
cuando, when, whenever

el 16 de noviembre

Querida Isabel Fumamucho:

Ud. no debe fumar más. Los médicos dicen que el fumar es malo para el corazón y los pulmones. En vez de fumar, ¿por qué no mastica Ud. chicle?

Anita Gómez

P.D. Yo no fumo más. Cuando quiero fumar, mastico chicle. Ahora tengo seis cavidades nuevas.

G. Complete the sentences:

1. Isabel dice que fuma mucho porque ella fuma ______________________________
2. Isabel no debe fumar más porque el fumar ______________________________
3. En vez de fumar, Anita Gómez ______________________________

Lesson 35

USING **gustar** *(continued)*

TOPIC QUESTION 22 | **¿Qué deportes le gustan a Ud.?** Which sports do you like?

A. *Preguntas y respuestas*

Practice reading aloud the following questions and answers:

1. ¿Qué deportes le gustan a Ud.?
Me gustan el fútbol y el béisbol.

2. ¿Qué deportes les gustan a Uds.?
Nos gustan el fútbol y el tenis.

3. ¿Qué deportes les gustan a Ud. y a su hermano?
A mí me gusta el tenis, y a él le gusta el golf.

4. ¿Le gustan a Ud. el fútbol y el béisbol?
Sí, me gustan.

5. ¿Les gustan a Uds. los deportes?
Sí, nos gustan.

6. ¿Le gustan a su madre el fútbol y el béisbol?
No, a ella no le gustan.

7. ¿Qué deportes les gustan a sus hermanos?
A mis hermanos les gustan el fútbol y el béisbol.

8. ¿Les gustan también a sus amigos?
Sí, a ellos les gustan también.

9. ¿Le gustan a Ud. el fútbol y el béisbol?
Sí, me ____

10. ¿Les gustan a Uds. el fútbol y el béisbol?
Sí, nos ____

11. ¿Qué deportes le gustan a su padre?
A él le ____

Vocabulario

Me gustan. I like them.
les gusta más {you *(pl.)* / they} like best
Dorotea, Dorothy
todos los deportes, all sports, every sport

12. ¿Qué deportes le gustan a su madre?

A ella ______________________________

13. ¿Le gustan a su hermana el fútbol y el béisbol?

No, a mi hermana no ______________________________

14. ¿Qué deportes le gustan a ella?

A ella ______________________________

15. ¿Te gustan el tenis y el golf?

No, ______________________________

B. *Lectura*

A Dorotea le gusta el tenis. No le gustan a ella el fútbol y el jai alai.

A los hermanos de Dorotea les gusta más el fútbol. Les gustan a ellos todos los deportes.

A la madre de Dorotea le gusta el boliche. No le gustan a ella los otros deportes.

Al padre de Dorotea le gusta mucho la corrida de toros. También le gustan a él el fútbol y el golf.

A Dorotea le gustan el tenis y el golf.

Preguntas

1. ¿Qué deporte le gusta a Dorotea?

____

2. ¿Qué deportes no le gustan a ella?

____

3. ¿Qué deporte les gusta más a los hermanos de Dorotea?

____

4. ¿Les gustan a ellos todos los deportes?

____

5. ¿Qué deporte le gusta a la madre?

____

6. ¿Le gustan a ella los otros deportes?

____

7. ¿Qué deporte le gusta mucho al padre de Dorotea?

____

8. ¿Qué otros deportes le gustan a él?

____

C. **Gusta** and **gustan**

1. In Lesson 34, we learned to use the form **gusta,** which is the third person singular. It is used when the subject of the verb—the thing liked—is in the singular:

Me **gusta el libro.**	I like the book.
Les **gusta** a ellos **el café.**	They like coffee.

When the subject is in the plural, the form **gustan** is used:

Me **gustan los libros.**	I like the books.
Les **gustan** a ellos **el café y la leche.**	They like coffee and milk. ("Coffee and milk please them.")

2. The singular form **gusta** is also used if the subject is an infinitive:

Me **gusta nadar.**	I like to swim.

Complete the sentence by writing either *gusta* or *gustan*:

1. A ellos les ____________________ el coche.
2. ¿Le ____________________ a Ud. las revistas?
3. No me ____________________ los huevos.
4. Nos ____________________ la casa.
5. ¿Qué deportes les ____________________ a Uds.?
6. ¿Te ____________________ las bebidas?
7. A mis amigos no les ____________________ el café y el té.
8. ¿Qué te ____________________ hacer?

D. *Preguntas personales*

1. ¿Qué deporte le gusta más a Ud.?

____

2. ¿Le gustan a Ud. todos los deportes?

____

3. ¿Qué deporte le gusta más a su padre?

____

4. ¿Le gustan a él todos los deportes?

____

5. ¿Les gusta a sus amigos el fútbol?

____

6. ¿Les gustan a ellos todos los deportes?

____

7. ¿Qué deporte le gusta más a su amigo favorito?

---

8. ¿Le gusta a Ud. jugar al béisbol?

E. *Traduzca Ud. al español:*

1. I like tennis. ______________

2. I like tennis and golf. ______________

3. Do you *(Uds.)* like all sports? ______________

4. Yes, we like them. ______________

5. We don't like jai alai. ______________

6. My brothers like football. ______________

A nuestros padres les gustan todos los deportes.

7. My brothers like to play football. ______________

8. My father likes all sports. ______________

9. *I* like tennis; what do *you* like? (*you,* familiar) ______________

10. My sister doesn't like football and bullfighting. ______________

F. *Conversación.* You and your classmates take turns asking one another the questions in part A on pages 130–131.

La columna personal de Anita Gómez (10)

el 9 de marzo

Querida Anita Gómez:

A mí me gusta ir al cine, pero mi novio prefiere ver programas de deportes en la televisión. ¿Qué debo hacer?

Chica Frustrada

Vocabulario

el **novio,** boyfriend, fiancé
ver, to see, watch
mirar, to watch, look at
la **chica,** girl
frustrado, -a, frustrated
no hay problema, there's no problem
mientras, while
puede, can

el 11 de marzo

Querida Chica Frustrada:

No hay problema. Vaya Ud. al cine mientras su novio mira la televisión.

Anita Gómez

G. Complete the sentences:

1. Le gusta al novio ______________________________

2. La chica prefiere ______________________________

3. Anita Gómez dice que no hay problema porque la chica puede ______________ ______________________ mientras su novio ______________________

Review Exercises

H. Commands (Lesson 33)

Can you translate these horoscopes into English? They were cast by Professor Caramba, an astrologer who likes to flavor his morning coffee with a bit of tequila. Perhaps he added a little too much flavor on the morning he wrote *these*.

On the blank line below #12, write the infinitive forms of the verbs used in the first six horoscopes.

1. Acuario ....No hablen Uds. a sus padres hoy. Hablen a sus amigos.
2. Piscis ....Manejen Uds. el coche de su padre a la escuela hoy.

3. Aries . . . . .No naden Uds. hoy en el océano. Naden Uds. en la piscina.
4. Tauro . . . . .Estudien Uds. ocho horas esta noche.
5. Géminis . . . . .No aprendan Uds. sus lecciones hoy.
6. Cáncer . . . . .Escriban Uds. una carta al presidente de los Estados Unidos.
7. Leo . . . . .No hablen Uds. a sus profesores hoy.
8. Virgo . . . . .No estudien Uds. hoy.
9. Libra . . . . .Escriban Uds. una carta a Castro en Cuba.
10. Escorpio . . . . .No hablen Uds. hoy.
11. Sagitario . . . . .Estudien Uds. cinco minutos hoy.
12. Capricornio . . . . . . .No manejen Uds. hoy.

I. Vocabulary (Lessons 23–28)

Complete the following sentences:

1. Yo estudio español. Mi hermano no estudia una ________________.
2. Mi padre es el ________________ de mi madre.
3. Mi ________________ es la hermana de mi madre.
4. Mi hermana es la ________________ de mis padres.
5. Mi ________________ es el hijo de mis tíos.
6. La hija de mi hermano es mi ________________.
7. La madre de mi madre es mi ________________.
8. Yo ________________________________ mis lecciones. (Write three verbs that can be used in this blank.)
9. Mi padre escribe ________________ buenos.
10. Nosotros vamos a la ________________ los domingos.
11. Muchos países hispánicos tienen un ________________ patrón.
12. María ________________ ocho horas.
13. Ellos ________________ cerveza.
14. La cerveza es la ________________ favorita de mi padre.
15. Mis padres ________________ el periódico.

Lesson 36

querer, *to want*

TOPIC QUESTION 23

¿Quiere Ud. un coche nuevo? Do you want a new car?

present tense of ***querer (ie)***			
yo	**quiero**	nosotros	**queremos**
tú	**quieres**		
Ud. / él / ella	**quiere**	Uds. / ellos / ellas	**quieren**

A. *Preguntas y respuestas*

Practice reading aloud the following questions and answers:

1. ¿Quiere Ud. un coche nuevo?
Sí, yo quiero un coche nuevo.

2. ¿Quieren Uds. un coche nuevo?
No, no queremos un coche nuevo.

3. ¿Quiere su padre un coche nuevo?
Sí, mi padre quiere un coche nuevo.

4. ¿Quiere su madre un coche nuevo?
No, mi madre no quiere un coche nuevo.

5. ¿Quieres tú comprar un coche?
Sí, yo quiero comprar un coche.

6. ¿Quiere tu hermano comprar un coche?
No, mi hermano quiere comprar una motocicleta.

7. ¿Quieren Uds. comprar un coche?
No, no queremos comprar un coche.

8. ¿Quiere comprar un coche tu hermana menor?
No, ella quiere comprar una bicicleta.

Vocabulario

comprar, to buy
tu(-s), your, *familiar*
la **motocicleta,** motorcycle
la **bicicleta,** bicycle

Enrique quiere un coche nuevo.

9. ¿Quiere Ud. comprar un coche?
¿Quieres tú comprar un coche?
Sí, yo ______________________________ un coche.

10. ¿Quieren Uds. comprar un coche?
No, no __________________________________ un coche.

11. ¿Qué quieres comprar?
______________________________ una bicicleta.

12. ¿Qué quieren comprar tus padres?
Mis padres _________________________________ un coche usado.

13. ¿Quieren ellos una motocicleta?
No, ellos ____________________ un coche.

14. ¿Quieres tú un coche?
No, ________________________ una motocicleta.

B. *Lectura*

Miguel quiere comprar un coche usado. Sus amigos Manuel y Rafael no quieren comprar un coche. Quieren comprar una motocicleta. El hermano menor de Miguel quiere comprar una bicicleta.

Preguntas

1. ¿Qué quiere comprar Miguel? ____
2. ¿Cómo se llaman sus amigos? ____
3. ¿Quieren comprar un coche Manuel y Rafael? ____________________________
4. ¿Qué quiere comprar el hermano de Miguel? ______________________________

C. *Preguntas personales*

1. ¿Quiere Ud. comprar un coche? ____
2. ¿Quieren Uds. comprar una motocicleta? ___________________________________
3. ¿Quiere su padre comprar un coche? ______________________________________
4. ¿Qué marca quiere comprar? ____
5. ¿Quiere su madre un coche? ____

D. *Traduzca Ud. al español:*

1. Do your parents want to buy a new car? ___________________________________
____
2. Yes, they want a new car. ____
3. What does your mother want? ____

4. Do you *(tú)* want a car? ______________________________

5. You *(Uds.)* want to buy a used car. ______________________________

6. No, we want a new motorcycle. ______________________________

E. *Conversación*. You and your classmates take turns asking one another the questions in part A on pages 136–137.

Manuel y Rafael quieren comprar una motocicleta.

La columna personal de Anita Gómez (11)

Vocabulario

no . . . más, not . . . anymore
amar, to love
el **perro,** dog
nadie, no one
sin, without
el **amor,** love
bañarse, to take a bath
de vez en cuando, once in a while

el 10 de diciembre

Querida Anita Gómez:

Yo no quiero vivir más. Mis padres no me aman. Mis hermanos no me aman. Mi amigo favorito no me ama. Mis profesores no me aman. Mi perro no me ama. Nadie me ama.

¿Qué debo yo hacer?

Pilar Sin Amor

Nadie me ama.

el 20 de diciembre

Querida Pilar Sin Amor:

Ud. debe bañarse de vez en cuando. ¿Tiene Ud. un desodorante bueno?

Anita Gómez

F. Complete the sentences:

1. Pilar dice: "No quiero vivir más porque ________________ me ama."
2. Anita Gómez dice que Pilar debe ____

Lesson 37

fumar, *to smoke*

TOPIC QUESTION 24

¿Fuma Ud.? Do you smoke?

present tense of ***fumar***	
yo **fumo**	nosotros **fumamos**
tú **fumas**	
Ud. / él / ella } **fuma**	Uds. / ellos / ellas } **fuman**

A. *Preguntas y respuestas*

Practice reading aloud the following questions and answers:

1. ¿Fuma Ud.?
Sí, yo fumo.

2. ¿Fuman Uds.?
No, no fumamos.

3. ¿Fuma él?
No, él no fuma.

4. ¿Fuma ella?
Sí, ella fuma.

5. ¿Fuman ellos?
No, ellos no fuman.

6. ¿Fumas tú?
Sí, yo fumo.

7. ¿Fuma Ud.?
No, yo no ______________________________________

8. ¿Fuman Uds.?
No, no ______________________________________

9. ¿Fuma su padre?
Sí, ______________________________________

Vocabulario

el fumar, smoking
la **salud,** health
los médicos dicen, doctors say
los **pulmones,** lungs
el **corazón,** heart
¿quiénes? *(pl.)* who?

10. ¿Fuma su madre?
No, ella ______________________________

11. ¿Fuman sus hermanos?
Sí, ellos ______________________________

12. ¿Fuma tu amigo favorito?
No, mi ______________________________ no fuma.

13. ¿Fuma ella?
Sí, de vez en cuando ______________________________

B. *Lectura*

El fumar no es bueno para la salud. Los médicos dicen que el fumar es malo para los pulmones y para el corazón.

Pablo no fuma. Su padre fuma. Su madre no fuma. Sus hermanos Guillermo y Antonia fuman. Su hermano mayor Ernesto no fuma.

Preguntas

1. ¿Qué dicen los médicos? ______________________________
2. ¿Qué quiere decir *pulmones*? ______________________________
3. ¿Cómo se dice *heart* en español? ______________________________
4. ¿Fuma Pablo? ______________________________
5. ¿Fuma su padre? ______________________________
6. ¿Fuma su madre? ______________________________
7. ¿Fuman Guillermo y Antonia? ______________________________
8. ¿Cómo se llama el hermano mayor de Pablo? ______________________________
9. ¿Quiénes no fuman? ______________________________

C. *Preguntas personales*

1. ¿Fumas tú? ______________________________
2. ¿Fuman tus padres? ______________________________
3. ¿Fuman tus hermanos? ______________________________
4. ¿Fuma tu amigo favorito? ______________________________

D. *Traduzca Ud. al español:*

1. Do you *(Ud.)* smoke? ______________________________
2. No, I don't smoke. ______________________________
3. Does your brother smoke? ______________________________
4. My mother doesn't smoke. ______________________________
5. Do your friends smoke? ______________________________

6. You *(tú)* don't smoke. ______________________________

7. What do doctors say? ______________________________

8. Does Robert smoke? ______________________________

9. He doesn't smoke. ______________________________

10. We smoke. ______________________________

E. *Conversación.* You and your classmates take turns asking one another the questions in part A on pages 140–141.

F. The maze of letters, below, contains the names of eleven Spanish-speaking countries and two Spanish surnames. They run horizontally and vertically. Can you find them all? Draw a line around each name. Then, if you copy, from left to right, the letters that lie outside the circled names, you will read Anita Gómez's reply to the following letter:

> Querida Anita Gómez:
>
> No tengo dinero. Mis amigos dicen que debo buscar empleo, pero no me gusta trabajar.
>
> ¿Qué debo hacer?
>
> Juan Perezoso

> Querido Juan Perezoso:
>
> ______________________________
>
> Anita Gómez

U	S	A	R	G	E	N	T	I	N	A
S	Á	T	E	D	D	I	C	U	B	A
E	N	M	É	X	I	C	O	R	O	M
E	C	H	I	L	E	A	L	U	L	E
C	H	B	E	B	S	R	O	G	I	N
U	E	U	S	C	P	A	M	U	V	D
A	Z	A	R	U	A	G	B	A	I	O
D	N	A	N	O	Ñ	U	I	Y	A	Z
O	V	I	A	R	A	A	A	I	C	A
R	V	E	N	E	Z	U	E	L	A	A

Vocabulario

buscar, to look for, seek
perezoso, -a, lazy

Preguntas personales (a review)

G. Translate into Spanish:

1. Do you prefer coffee, tea or milk? ______________________________

2. Do you study a language? ______________________________

3. Are you learning chemistry? ______________________________

4. Do you write checks? ______________________________

5. Do you eat a lot? ______________________________

6. How many hours do you sleep? ______________________________

7. What do you drink? ______________________________

8. Do you read much? ______________________________

9. Do you like coffee? ______________________________

10. Do you like football and baseball? ______________________________

11. Do you want a car? ______________________________

12. Do you smoke? ______________________________

Lesson 38

vivir, *to live*

TOPIC QUESTION 25A

> **¿ Dónde vive Ud.?**
> Where do you live?

present tense of ***vivir***	
yo **vivo**	nosotros **vivimos**
tú **vives**	
Ud. / él / ella } **vive**	Uds. / ellos / ellas } **viven**

A. *Preguntas y respuestas*

Practice reading aloud the following questions and answers:

1. ¿Dónde vive Ud.?
Yo vivo en la ciudad.

2. ¿Dónde viven Uds.?
Vivimos en las afueras.

3. ¿Dónde vive su amigo?
Vive cerca de la escuela.

4. ¿Dónde viven sus tíos?
Viven en México.

5. ¿En qué ciudad viven ellos?
Viven en las afueras de Monterrey.

6. ¿En qué ciudad viven sus abuelos?
No viven en la ciudad; viven en el campo.

7. ¿Vive Ud. con sus padres?
Sí, yo ____________________

8. ¿Viven Uds. en el campo?
No, nosotros ____________ en la ciudad.

9. ¿En qué ciudad vive Ud.?
Yo ____________________

Vocabulario

el **barrio,** neighborhood
el **campo,** country (the opposite of "city")
rico, -a, rich, wealthy
la **calle,** street
el Pedregal, a wealthy district in Mexico City built on lava *(pedregal)*

10. ¿En qué ciudad viven sus amigos?

Ellos ________________

11. ¿Dónde viven sus primos?

Ellos ________________

12. ¿Vive su amiga favorita con los padres de ella?

Sí, mi amiga ________________ con sus padres.

B. *Lectura*

Miguel Sánchez vive en la ciudad de México. Vive en un barrio que se llama Satélite.

Miguel va a la Universidad Nacional. La Universidad está cerca de un barrio muy rico que se llama el Pedregal.

Preguntas

1. ¿Qué es Satélite? ________________
2. ¿Dónde vive Miguel? ________________
3. ¿A qué escuela va Miguel? ________________
4. ¿Qué es el Pedregal? ________________

C. *Preguntas personales*

1. ¿Vives tú con tus padres? ________________
2. ¿En qué ciudad viven Uds.? ________________
3. ¿Te gusta vivir en la ciudad? ________________
4. ¿Dónde quieres vivir? ________________
5. ¿En qué calle vives? ________________
6. ¿En qué estado vives? ________________

D. *Traduzca Ud. al español:*

1. I live with my parents. ________________
2. He wants to live in Acapulco. ________________
3. My sister and brother live in California. ________________
4. Do you *(tú)* live in San Miguel de Allende? ________________
____
5. He lives in the state of Michoacán. ________________
6. The National University is near the Pedregal. ________________
____
7. Satélite is a neighborhood in the suburbs of Mexico City. ________________
____

8. Do you *(Uds.)* live with your parents? ________________________________

9. Does Michael live in Mexico City? ________________________________

10. Do Pepe and Enriqueta live in the Pedregal? ________________________________

____

TOPIC QUESTION 25B

¿Vive Ud. para comer o come Ud. para vivir?
Do you live to eat or do you eat to live?

E. *Preguntas y respuestas*

Practice reading these questions aloud. Write the missing parts of the answers:

1. ¿Vive Ud. para comer o come Ud. para vivir?
   Yo como para vivir.
2. ¿Viven Uds. para comer or comen Uds. para vivir?
   Nosotros ____________________ para vivir.
3. ¿Vive su padre para comer o come su padre para vivir?
   Mi padre ____________________ para ____________________
4. ¿Vive su madre para comer o come ella para vivir?
   Mi madre ____________________ para ____________________
5. ¿Viven sus amigos para comer o comen ellos para vivir?
   Mi amigo Sancho es muy gordo porque él ______________ para ______________
   Mis amigas Laura y María son flacas; ellas ______________ para ______________

F. *Tema.* Write a composition entitled *¿Dónde vive Ud.?*

____

____

____

____

____

____

La columna personal de Anita Gómez (12)

el 3 de enero

Querida Anita Gómez:

Yo tengo veinte años. Estoy enamorada de un hombre que tiene sesenta años. Él es muy rico y está enamorado de mí. Yo quiero casarme con él. Mi madre dice que no. ¿Qué debo yo hacer?

Ramona Veinte

el 12 de enero

Querida Ramona Veinte:

¿Está Ud. enamorada del hombre o de su dinero? Su madre tiene razón. Ud. no debe casarse con él.

Anita Gómez

P.D. El hombre debe casarse con una dama más vieja. Tal vez yo puedo ayudarle. ¿Cómo se llama el hombre? ¿Cuál es su dirección? ¿Cuál es su número de teléfono?

Vocabulario

tengo 20 años, I'm 20 years old
enamorado(-a) de, in love with
el **hombre,** man
casarse con, to marry
dice que no, says "no"
tener razón, to be right
la **dama,** lady
más vieja, older
tal vez, maybe
puedo ayudarle, can help him
¿cuál? what? which?
la **dirección,** address
el **número de teléfono,** phone number
cree, believes, thinks
interesar, to interest

G. Complete the sentences:

1. Ramona ____________________ veinte años y está ____________________ de un hombre que ______________________________ años.
2. Ramona dice que el hombre es muy ____________ y que está __________________ de ella.
3. Anita Gómez cree que la muchacha quiere ____________________ con el hombre porque él tiene mucho ____________________
4. Anita Gómez dice que la madre de Ramona tiene ____________________________
5. El hombre interesa a Anita Gómez porque ______________________________

Lesson 39

trabajar, *to work*

TOPIC QUESTION 26

¿Trabaja Ud.?
Do you work?

present tense of ***trabajar***	
yo **trabajo**	
tú **trabajas**	nosotros **trabajamos**
Ud. / él / ella } **trabaja**	Uds. / ellos / ellas } **trabajan**

A. *Preguntas y respuestas*

Practice reading aloud the following questions and answers:

1. ¿Trabaja Ud.?
Sí, trabajo en una tienda.

2. ¿Trabajan Uds.?
Sí, trabajamos en una fábrica.

3. ¿Trabaja él?
Sí, él trabaja.

4. ¿Dónde trabaja María?
Ella trabaja en una oficina.

5. ¿Dónde trabajan ellos?
Ellos trabajan en un almacén.

6. ¿Trabajas tú?
No, yo no trabajo.

7. ¿Trabaja Ud.?
No, yo no ____

Vocabulario

la **tienda,** store, shop
la **fábrica,** factory
la **oficina,** office
el **almacén,** department store
asistir a, to attend
después de las clases, after school
el **botones,** bellhop
el (la) **dependiente,** clerk
*el **ama de casa,** housewife

---

*Although **ama** is feminine, it is used with **el** because "la ama" is hard to pronounce as two separate words. The plural, however, is normal: "**las** amas."

8. ¿Trabajan Uds.?
Sí, ____

9. ¿Dónde trabajan Uds.?
________________________ en una tienda.

10. ¿Trabaja él?
No, él ____

11. ¿Dónde trabaja su padre?
Mi padre ____________________________________

12. ¿Trabaja su madre en una oficina?
No, mi madre ________________________________

13. ¿Trabajan sus hermanos?
Sí, mis hermanos _____________________________

14. ¿Dónde trabajan ellos?
Ellos ______________________________________

La madre de Felipe es ama de casa.

B. *Lectura*

Felipe Martínez asiste a la universidad. Él trabaja después de las clases. Trabaja en un hotel. Es botones.*

El padre de Felipe trabaja en una tienda. Es dependiente. La madre de Felipe trabaja en casa. Es ama de casa.

Felipe tiene dos hermanos y una hermana. Los hermanos no trabajan. Van a la escuela superior. La hermana se llama Beatriz. Trabaja en una oficina. Es secretaria.

Preguntas

1. ¿Quién asiste a la universidad? ______________________________

2. ¿Dónde trabaja Felipe? ______________________________

3. ¿Dónde trabaja su padre? ______________________________

4. ¿Dónde trabaja su madre? ______________________________

5. ¿Cómo se dice *housewife* en español? ______________________________

6. ¿Quiénes van a la escuela superior? ______________________________

7. ¿Cómo se llama la hermana de Felipe? ______________________________

8. ¿Quién es secretaria? ______________________________

---

*The article is not used in stating someone's trade or profession: **es médica,** she's a doctor; **es abogado,** he's a lawyer.

C. *Preguntas personales*

1. ¿Dónde trabaja su padre? ______________________________
2. ¿Trabajan sus hermanos? ______________________________
3. ¿Le gusta a Ud. trabajar? ______________________________
4. ¿Trabaja su amigo favorito? ______________________________
5. ¿A su padre le gusta trabajar? ______________________________

D. *Tema.* Write a composition entitled *¿Trabaja Ud.?*

____

____

____

____

____

____

E. *Traduzca Ud. al español:*

1. My mother doesn't work in an office. ______________________________
2. She is a housewife. ______________________________
3. Does your brother work? ______________________________
4. They work. ______________________________
5. Do you *(tú)* work? ______________________________
6. Yes, I work. ______________________________
7. No, I don't work. ______________________________
8. Does he work? ______________________________
9. My father likes to work. ______________________________
10. He is a clerk in a store. ______________________________
11. Does your father like to work? ______________________________
12. Do you *(pl.)* like to work? ______________________________

F. *Conversación.* You and your classmates take turns asking one another the questions in part A on pages 148–149.

Review Exercises

(Lessons 28–39)

G. Here are some answers. What are the questions?

1. Mi amigo favorito quiere un coche nuevo. ______________________________
2. Sí, a mi madre le gusta el café. ______________________________
3. María no fuma. ______________________________
4. Yo no trabajo. ______________________________
5. Mi padre bebe cerveza. ______________________________
6. A mi hermano le gustan el fútbol y el béisbol. ______________________________
7. Mis hermanos viven en la ciudad de Guadalajara. ______________________________

H. Translate the following words into Spanish:

1. to read ______________________
2. the newspaper ______________________
3. the magazine ______________________
4. the book ______________________
5. the schoolbook ______________________
6. I like it. ______________________
7. to want ______________________
8. to buy ______________________
9. to smoke ______________________
10. the doctor ______________________
11. the lungs ______________________
12. the heart ______________________
13. to live ______________________
14. the suburbs ______________________
15. near ______________________
16. rich ______________________
17. the neighborhood ______________________
18. to work ______________________
19. after ______________________
20. to attend ______________________
21. the bellhop ______________________
22. the housewife ______________________
23. the clerk ______________________
24. the store ______________________
25. the office ______________________

Crucigrama (4)

Across

3. *motorcycle*
5. *to want*
7. Miguel _____ en las afueras de la ciudad.
8. Descriptive adjectives usually _____ the noun.
10. The Spanish definite article has _____ forms.
11. ¿Cómo se dice *higo* en inglés?
13. iniciales de Elena López Ugarte
15. ¿Cómo se dice *enfermo* en inglés?
18. Nouns ending in *-o* are usually _____ in gender.
19. *I make*
21. vamos = *we* _____
22. *the heart*
23. This word shows possession in Spanish.

Down

1. No quiero _____ porque es malo para los pulmones.
2. *the street*
4. ¿Qué quiere decir *la corrida de toros?*
6. ¿Qué quiere decir *barrio?*
9. Su apellido es Pérez y su nombre de _____ es Carlos.
11. Nouns ending in *-a, -d,* or *-ión* are usually _____.
12. *To like* is expressed by using the verb _____.
14. If "you" = *tú,* then "your house" = _____ *casa.*
16. Yo _____ el periódico todas las mañanas.
17. *word*
19. *él* en inglés
20. iniciales de Guido Calderón

Lesson 40

vosotros / vosotras — *you, familiar plural*

Lesson 32 introduced the pronoun **tú,** which is used when speaking to a friend, a child, a classmate, or a member of one's family. The plural of **tú** is **vosotros.** If the persons addressed are all female, the feminine form **vosotras** is used.

Vosotros and its verb forms are heard only in Spain. In the rest of the Hispanic world, the plural of **tú** is **ustedes.**

A. To obtain the **vosotros** form of the verb, drop the infinitive ending (**-ar, -er,** or **-ir**) and add as follows:

ar VERBS	*er* VERBS	*ir* VERBS
hablar	**beb**er	**escrib**ir
habl-	**beb-**	**escrib-**
Add **-áis:**	Add **-éis:**	Add **-ís:**
vosotros **habláis**	vosotros **bebéis**	vosotros **escribís**

Write the *vosotros* form of the verb:

1. nadar ____________________________ **4.** leer ____________________________

2. comer ____________________________ **5.** preferir ____________________________

3. vivir ____________________________ **6.** trabajar ____________________________

B. In some of the verbs you have learned, a vowel in the infinitive stem changes when the verb is conjugated. For example:

		But:
j**u**gar:	yo j**ue**go, tú j**ue**gas, etc.	nosotros j**u**gamos vosotros j**u**gáis
pref**e**rir:	yo pref**ie**ro, tú pref**ie**res, etc.	nosotros pref**e**rimos vosotros pref**e**rís

Notice that the two exceptions are the **nosotros** and **vosotros** forms, which do not change the stem vowel.

In this book, stem-changing verbs are indicated as such by showing the type of stem-vowel change in parentheses: **jugar (ue), preferir (ie), pedir (i),** etc.

Write the *tú* and *vosotros* forms of each verb.

EXAMPLE: preferir (ie) *tú prefieres*; *vosotros preferís*

1. dormir (ue) ____________________

2. querer (ie) ____________________

3. pedir (i) ____________________

4. contar (ue) ____________________

The verb **ir,** *to go,* has an irregular *vosotros* form that must be learned separately: **vais.**

5. ir ____________________

C. Write the indicated forms of the verbs:

	tú	*vosotros*	*usted*	*ustedes*
1. poder (ue)	______	______	______	______
2. estudiar	______	______	______	______
3. estar	______	______	______	______
4. pedir (i)	______	______	______	______
5. tener (ie)	______	______	______	______
6. querer (ie)	______	______	______	______
7. manejar	______	______	______	______
8. dormir (ue)	______	______	______	______
9. ir	______	______	______	______
10. vivir	______	______	______	______
11. comer	______	______	______	______
12. mostrar (ue)	______	______	______	______

Astrology

Do you want to find out what the stars reveal about your personality? The following descriptions were supplied by Professor Caramba, the famous astrologer. He assures us that they are accurate, but you may disagree. (Well, nobody is perfect.)

ACUARIO *del 20 de enero al 18 de febrero*

Al acuario le gusta manejar un coche. Maneja bien. Por desgracia muchos acuarios no tienen coche.

PISCIS *del 19 de febrero al 20 de marzo*

A los piscis les gusta nadar. Algunos piscis nadan bien. Algunos piscis no nadan bien. No les gusta beber agua. Los piscis toman mucha cerveza.

Vocabulario

por desgracia, unfortunately
algunos, -as, some, a few
palomitas, popcorn
toreros, bullfighters
hablar en el sueño, to talk in one's sleep
pasar, to spend *(time)*
la cárcel, jail
amantes, lovers
relajar, to relax

ARIES *del 21 de marzo al 19 de abril*

Los aries van mucho al cine. Ellos comen muchas palomitas en el cine. Los aries miran mucho la televisión y comen mucho. Comen día y noche. Los aries son muy gordos.

TAURO *del 20 de abril al 20 de mayo*

A los tauros les gustan los deportes. Su deporte favorito es el boliche. También les gusta la corrida de toros. Ellos son buenos toreros.

GÉMINIS *del 21 de mayo al 21 de junio*

Los géminis hablan mucho. Hablan, hablan y hablan. Hablan en la escuela, en casa, en el coche, en la calle y en el sueño.

CÁNCER *del 22 de junio al 22 de julio*

Los cáncer no toman el desayuno. No les gusta comer mucho. Son muy flacos. También son muy inteligentes. Les gusta estudiar. No les gusta mirar la televisión.

LEO *del 23 de julio al 22 de agosto*

Los leos escriben muchos cheques. Escriben cheques malos. Muchos leos son criminales. Pasan mucho tiempo en la cárcel.

VIRGO *del 23 de agosto al 22 de septiembre*

A los virgos les gusta dormir. Duermen en casa, en la escuela, en el coche y en la calle.

LIBRA *del 23 de septiembre al 23 de octubre*

A los libras les gusta leer. Leen libros, periódicos y revistas. No leen libros escolares. A los libras les gusta la astrología.

ESCORPIO *del 24 de octubre al 21 de noviembre*

Los escorpios son muy románticos y tienen muchos amantes.

SAGITARIO *del 22 de noviembre al 21 de diciembre*

A los sagitarios no les gusta trabajar. Les gusta relajar. Van mucho al cine, al teatro y al restaurante. Beben mucho y comen mucho. No trabajan.

CAPRICORNIO *del 22 de diciembre al 19 de enero*

A los capricornios les gusta estudiar español. Estudian español cinco o seis horas cada día. Los capricornios trabajan mucho. Les gusta el dinero.

D. El profesor Caramba dice que:

1. Los acuarios manejan bien. Por ____________________, no tienen coche.
2. Los piscis toman mucha ____________________
3. Los aries ________________ muchas palomitas en ____________________
4. El deporte favorito de los tauros es el ____________________
5. Los géminis ____________________ en el sueño.
6. Los cáncer no son gordos. Son ____________________
7. Los leos ________________ mucho tiempo en la cárcel porque ________________ malos.
8. A los virgos les ____________________ dormir.
9. Los libras no leen libros ____________________
10. Los ____________________ son amantes.
11. A los sagitarios no ________________ gusta trabajar.
12. Los ____________________ trabajan mucho.

E. How did Anita Gómez answer the following letter? To find out, use the eight clues listed on the next page, and fill the boxes on the right.

Querida Anita Gómez:

Mi amiga Gertrudis es flaca pero bonita. Yo soy gordo pero guapo. Cuando tomo el almuerzo con ella en la escuela, siempre me recuerda que debo perder peso. No me gusta ser gordo pero detesto las dietas.

¿Qué debo hacer?

Pepe el Pesado

Vocabulario

siempre me recuerda, she always reminds me
perder peso, to lose weight
detestar, to hate, detest
pesado, -a, heavy
diga (Ud.), say

Querido Pepe el Pesado:

____

Anita Gómez

1. Si Ud. no quiere té, _______ Ud. café.
2. Cuando Ud. habla con su profesor, no diga "tú"; diga "_______."
3. El singular de *los* es _______.
4. Yo tomo el _______ en la cafetería.
5. Vamos al cine _______ Carlos.
6. Luisa es _______ muchacha inteligente.
7. Gertrudis es mi _______ favorita.
8. Tomasina debe perder peso porque es _______.

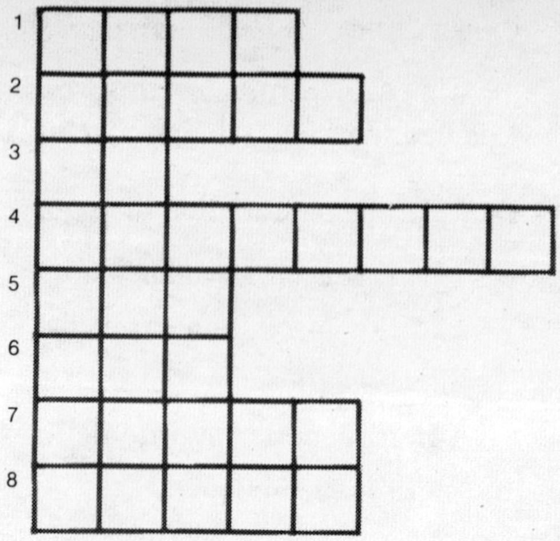

Lesson 41

tener...años, *to be...old,* AND OTHER IDIOMS WITH tener

TOPIC QUESTION 27

¿Cuántos años tiene Ud.? How old are you?

A. *Preguntas y respuestas*

Practice reading aloud the following questions and answers:

Vocabulario

tengo 14 años, I'm 14 years old
el **frío,** cold; el **calor,** heat
el **hambre** *(f.),* hunger
el **miedo,** fear
la **razón,** reason
la **sed,** thirst
el **sueño,** sleep
la **vergüenza,** shame

1. ¿Cuántos años tiene Ud.?
Yo tengo catorce años.

2. ¿Cuántos años tienen Uds.?
Yo tengo catorce años y ella tiene quince.

3. ¿Cuántos años tiene su padre?
Mi padre tiene cuarenta años.

4. ¿Cuántos años tiene su madre?
Mi madre tiene treinta y siete años.

5. ¿Cuántos años tienen sus hermanos?
Mi hermana tiene doce años y mi hermano tiene nueve.

6. ¿Cuántos años tiene su amigo favorito?
Él tiene trece años.

El señor Gutiérrez tiene cien años.

7. ¿Cuántos años tienes tú?
Yo ________________________________ años.

8. ¿Cuántos años tienen tus padres?
Mi madre ______________________ años y mi padre ______________________

9. ¿Cuántos años tenéis vosotros?
Yo ____________________________ y él (ella) ____________________________

10. ¿Cuántos años tiene el padre de tu amigo favorito?
El padre de mi amigo ____

B. *Lectura*

Felipe Martínez tiene veinte años. Su padre tiene cuarenta y cinco años. Su madre tiene cuarenta y tres años.

Felipe tiene dos hermanos. Su hermano Raúl tiene diez y siete años y su hermano Federico quince años.

Preguntas

1. ¿Cuántos años tiene Felipe? ____
2. ¿Cuántos años tienen sus padres? ____
3. ¿Quién tiene veinte años? ____
4. ¿Cuántos años tienen los dos hermanos de Felipe? ______________________________

____

C. A person's age is expressed in Spanish by using the verb **tener,** *to have.* Thus, "How old are you?" "I am 15 years old" is expressed as "How many years do you have?" "I have 15 years." Expressions like **tener . . . años** are called *idioms.* An idiom is an expression that cannot be translated word-for-word into English because the English language expresses the same idea in a different way.

D. *Traduzca Ud. al español:*

1. How old are you *(Ud.)*? ____
2. I am nineteen years old. ____
3. Felipe's father is forty-five years old. ______________________________

   ____
4. How old is she? ____
5. She is twelve years old. ____
6. How old is Philip? ____
7. How old is Philip's mother? ____
8. How old is your father? ____

E. Other Idioms With **tener**

tener frío, to be cold
tener calor, to be warm
tener hambre, to be hungry
tener miedo, to be afraid
tener razón, to be right
tener sed, to be thirsty
tener sueño, to be sleepy
tener vergüenza,* to be ashamed

*The two dots over the **u** show that the **u** must be pronounced. (It sounds like a *w*: "ver-GWEN-sa.")

Complete the sentences:

1. Mi madre tiene _______________ de los ratones *(mice)*.
2. Yo no tengo frío en Acapulco. Yo tengo _______________ en Acapulco.
3. Mis amigos toman un refresco cuando tienen _______________
4. Yo duermo cuando tengo _______________
5. Nosotros comemos cuando tenemos _______________
6. Roberto dice que cuarenta y treinta son sesenta. Diego dice que cuarenta y treinta son setenta. _______________ tiene razón.
7. Nosotros _______________ vergüenza cuando no estudiamos.

F. *Traduzca Ud. al español:*

1. I am thirsty. _______________
2. They are sleepy. _______________
3. We are cold. _______________
4. You *(Uds.)* are right. _______________
5. She is hungry. _______________
6. Are you *(tú)* afraid? _______________
7. He is not ashamed. _______________
8. I am warm. _______________

G. Notice that the word following **tener** is a *noun*. For example, *to be hungry* is expressed as "to have hunger." Therefore, to be *very* hungry becomes "to have *much* hunger": **tener mucha hambre.** Similarly, to be *very* sleepy is **tener mucho sueño,** to be hot (= *very* warm) is **tener mucho calor,** etc.

Traduzca Ud. al español:

1. We are very thirsty. _______________
2. The boys are very cold. _______________
3. I am not very hungry. _______________
4. Are you *(vosotros)* very sleepy? _______________
5. They are very warm. _______________

Lesson 42

los nombres españoles, *Spanish names*

En los países de habla española, todo el mundo tiene dos apellidos: el apellido del padre y el apellido de la madre.

Juan González y García es un muchacho de Colombia. El primer apellido, González, es el apellido de su padre. El segundo, García, es el apellido de su madre.

La hermana de Juan se llama María González y García. Al casarse con Antonio Moreno y Martínez, ella se llama María González de Moreno. Los hijos de María González de Moreno se llaman Moreno y González.

Vocabulario

de habla española, Spanish-speaking
todo el mundo, everybody
primer, primero, first
segundo, second; **el segundo,** the second one
al casarse, on getting married
¿cuál? what? which?
el **apellido,** last name, surname
¿de quién? whose?

A. *Preguntas*

1. ¿Cuántos apellidos tiene todo el mundo en los países de habla española?

____

2. ¿De quién es el primer apellido?

____

3. ¿Cómo se llama María González y García al casarse con Antonio Moreno?

____

4. ¿María tiene una hija que se llama Lupe. ¿Cómo se llama Lupe al casarse con Diego Sánchez y Seguro?

____

5. ¿Cuál es el apellido de Ud.?

____

COGNATES (6)

B. Pronounce the words listed below. Can you guess their meanings? In each blank, write the English cognate that means the same thing as the Spanish word.

1. adorar ____________	**5.** aristocrático ____________
2. adulto ____________	**6.** arqueología ____________
3. amoroso ____________	**7.** arrogante ____________
4. anticipar ____________	**8.** atribuir ____________

9. boxeador ______________________
10. brutalidad ______________________
11. capital ______________________
12. capitalismo ______________________
13. carácter ______________________
14. característica ______________________
15. católico ______________________
16. celebrar ______________________
17. cementerio ______________________
18. centígrado ______________________
19. científico ______________________
20. civilización ______________________
21. clima ______________________
22. coincidencia ______________________
23. completo ______________________
24. concentración ______________________
25. cultura ______________________
26. decisión ______________________
27. delicado ______________________
28. democrático ______________________
29. destrucción ______________________
30. dinamita ______________________
31. divorcio ______________________
32. ecuador ______________________
33. Europa ______________________
34. hipocresía ______________________
35. Inglaterra ______________________
36. lunático ______________________
37. Londres ______________________
38. monarquía ______________________
39. monstruo ______________________
40. polo norte ______________________
41. política ______________________
42. popular ______________________
43. popularidad ______________________
44. primitivo ______________________
45. profesión ______________________
46. profesional ______________________
47. publicación ______________________
48. religioso ______________________
49. revelación ______________________
50. ridículo ______________________
51. ritmo ______________________
52. robar ______________________
53. roca ______________________
54. romántico ______________________
55. sagrado ______________________
56. saliva ______________________
57. saxófono ______________________
58. secreto ______________________
59. tentación ______________________
60. termonuclear ______________________

La columna personal de Anita Gómez (13)

el 4 de julio

Querida Anita Gómez:

Yo bebo mucha tequila y mi esposo bebe mucha tequila. Somos alcohólicos.

¿Qué debemos hacer?

Margarita Borracha

Vocabulario

somos, we are
borracho, -a, drunk, drunkard
buena suerte, good luck

el 12 de julio

Querida Margarita Borracha:

Uds. deben ir a la organización que se llama Alcohólicos Anónimos. ¡Buena suerte!

Anita Gómez

P.D. Yo prefiero cerveza y vino.

C. Complete the sentences:

1. Margarita y su esposo son alcohólicos porque ______________________________

2. Anita Gómez les recomienda una organización que se llama en *inglés* ____________
____

3. Anita Gómez prefiere beber ____

Review Exercises

Commands (Lesson 33)

D. Here are Professor Caramba's horoscopes for next Tuesday. On the line below #12, write the infinitive forms of the verbs used in the horoscopes (four infinitives in all).

1. ACUARIO . . . . .No coman Uds. hoy.
2. PISCIS . . . . .Duerman Uds. ocho horas esta noche.
3. ARIES . . . . .No beban Uds. café hoy.
4. TAURO . . . . .Coman Uds. todo el día.
5. GÉMINIS . . . . .Lean Uds. dos libros hoy.
6. CÁNCER . . . . .Duerman Uds. en la clase de español.
7. LEO . . . . .No duerman Uds. esta noche.
8. VIRGO . . . . .Coman Uds. en la casa de su profesor de español esta noche.
9. LIBRA . . . . .No lean Uds. nada hoy.
10. ESCORPIO . . . . .Coman Uds. toda la noche.
11. SAGITARIO . . . . . . .Duerman Uds. en la calle esta noche.
12. CAPRICORNIO . . . . .Beban Uds. leche hoy.

Vocabulario
esta noche, tonight
todo el día, all day
no . . . nada, nothing, not . . . anything

Verbs (Lessons 1–42)

E. Write the form of the verb that goes with the indicated subject.

1. dormir: yo ____________________
2. dormir: nosotros ____________________
3. dormir: tú ____________________
4. aprender: nosotros ____________________
5. estar: yo ____________________
6. preferir: nosotros ____________________
7. preferir: Ud. ____________________
8. llamarse: yo ____________________
9. llamarse: nosotros ____________________
10. manejar: vosotros ____________________
11. ir: Uds. ____________________
12. tener: ellos ____________________
13. escribir: tú ____________________
14. vivir: Uds. ____________________
15. leer: ellas ____________________
16. querer: ella ____________________

17. querer: nosotros ________________________________
18. comer: yo ________________________________
19. comer: Uds. ________________________________
20. jugar: tú ________________________________

Articles and adjectives (Lesson 30)

F. Write the correct form of the Spanish word that translates the word in parentheses:

1. (the) __________ escuela
2. (the) __________ cheques
3. (the) __________ ciudad
4. (the) __________ sobrinos
5. (the) __________ iglesias
6. (a) __________ coche
7. (a) __________ universidad
8. (my) __________ hermanas
9. (my) __________ madre
10. (his) __________ libros
11. (her) __________ libros
12. (your) __________ libro
13. (our) __________ lección
14. (our) __________ lecciones
15. (their) __________ sobrina
16. (their) __________ abuelos
17. (favorite) amiga __________________
18. (bad) cheques __________________
19. (older) hermanos __________________
20. (many) ______________ casas

Contractions (Lesson 31)

G. **1.** (to the) __________ muchacho
2. (to the) __________ muchachos
3. (to the) __________ ciudad
4. (to the) __________ ciudades
5. (of the) __________________ tío
6. (of the) __________________ tía
7. (of the) __________________ sobrinos
8. (of the) __________________ sobrinas

Possession (Lesson 30)

H. Translate into Spanish:

1. my brother's friend ____
2. my friend's car ____
3. Robert's books ____
4. Mr. Gómez's restaurant ____

Preguntas personales

I. Answer in Spanish:

1. ¿Le gusta a Ud. el café? ____
2. ¿Le gustan a Ud. los deportes? ____

3. ¿Le gustan a su madre los deportes? ______________________________

____

4. ¿Quiere Ud. un coche? ______________________________

5. ¿Quieren Uds. estudiar? ______________________________

6. ¿Fuma Ud.? ______________________________

7. ¿Fuman sus padres? ______________________________

8. ¿En qué ciudad vive Ud.? ______________________________

9. ¿Trabaja Ud.? ______________________________

10. ¿Cuántos años tiene Ud.? ______________________________

11. ¿Cuántos años tiene su amigo(-a) favorito(-a)? ______________________________

____

12. ¿Cuál es tu apellido? ______________________________

13. ¿Dónde tomas el almuerzo? ______________________________

14. ¿Tienes hambre ahora? ______________________________

Lesson 43

ser, to be (Part 1)

TOPIC QUESTION 28A — **¿Es Ud. alto(-a) o bajo(-a)?**
Are you tall or short?

present tense of ***ser***	
yo **soy**	nosotros **somos**
tú **eres**	vosotros **sois**
Ud. / él / ella } **es**	Uds. / ellos / ellas } **son**

A. *Preguntas y respuestas*

Practice reading aloud the following questions and answers:

1. Juan, ¿es Ud. alto o bajo?
Yo soy alto.

2. María, ¿es Ud. alta o baja?
No soy alta y no soy baja.

3. Juan y María, ¿son Uds. altos o bajos?
Nosotros somos bajos.

4. Anita y Clara, ¿son Uds. altas o bajas?
Nosotras somos altas.

5. ¿Es él bajo?
No, él no es bajo.

6. ¿Es ella baja?
Sí, ella es baja.

7. ¿Son ellos altos?
No, ellos no son altos.

8. ¿Eres tú alto(-a) o bajo(-a)?
Yo ______________________________

9. ¿Sois altos o bajos?
Nosotros ______________________________

10. ¿Son Uds. altas o bajas?
Nosotras ______________________________

11. ¿Es alto o bajo su padre?
Mi padre ______________________________

12. ¿Es alta o baja su madre?
Mi madre ______________________________

13. ¿Son altos o bajos sus hermanos?
Ellos ______________________________

Tomás es bajo. Su novia es alta.

14. ¿Es alto su amigo favorito?
No, él ______________________________

15. ¿Son altas sus hermanas?
No, ellas ______________________________

B. *Lectura*

Juanita Gutiérrez es una muchacha que vive en un rancho. Es mexicana. No es alta. No es baja.

El padre de Juanita no es alto y no es bajo. La madre de Juanita no es alta. Es baja.

Los hermanos de Juanita se llaman Roberto y Miguel. Ellos no son bajos. Son altos. La hermana de Juanita se llama Pilar. Es baja.

Preguntas

1. ¿Es Juanita una muchacha de la ciudad? ______________________________
2. ¿Es alta? ______________________________
3. ¿Cómo se dice *short* en español? ______________________________
4. ¿Es alto el padre de Juanita? ______________________________
5. ¿Quién es baja? ______________________________
6. ¿Quiénes son altos? ______________________________
7. ¿Cómo se llama la hermana de Juanita? ______________________________
8. ¿Es alta o baja? ______________________________

C. *Preguntas personales*

1. ¿Es Ud. alto(-a) o bajo(-a)?* ______________________________
2. ¿Son Uds. mexicanos(-as)? ______________________________
3. ¿Es su madre alta o baja? ______________________________
4. ¿Es su padre alto o bajo? ______________________________
5. ¿Son sus hermanos altos o bajos? ______________________________

TOPIC QUESTION 28B

¿Prefiere Ud. ser rico(-a) o inteligente?
Do you prefer to be rich or intelligent?

D. *Preguntas y respuestas*

1. ¿Prefiere Ud. ser rico(-a) o inteligente?
Yo prefiero ser rico.

---

*The "(-a)" means that girls must use the feminine forms **alta** and **baja** in their answers.

2. ¿Prefieren Uds. ser ricos(-as) o inteligentes?
   Preferimos ser inteligentes.
3. ¿Prefiere su madre ser rica o inteligente?
   Ella prefiere ser inteligente.
4. ¿Prefieren sus amigas ser ricas o inteligentes?
   Mis amigas prefieren ser ricas.
5. ¿Prefieren sus hermanos ser ricos o inteligentes?
   Mis hermanos ______________________________
6. ¿Prefiere su padre ser rico o inteligente?
   Mi padre ______________________________
7. María y Carlos, ¿preferís ser ricos o inteligentes?
   Nosotros ______________________________
8. ¿Eres norteamericano(-a) o mexicano(-a)?
   Yo ______________________________
9. ¿Son inteligentes tus padres?
   Sí, mis padres ______________________________
10. ¿Son Uds. norteamericanas o mexicanas?
    Nosotras ______________________________

E. *Traduzca Ud. al español:*

1. I *(f.)* am not tall. ______________________________
2. My brothers and sisters are not tall. ______________________________
3. You (Ud., *m.*) are tall. ______________________________
4. You (Uds., *f.*) are short. ______________________________
5. You (tú, *m.*) are not short and you are not tall. ______________________________
   ____
6. We *(f.)* aren't Americans. ______________________________
7. Are you (Ud., *m.*) tall or short? ______________________________
8. His sisters are very smart. ______________________________
9. Are your sisters short? ______________________________
10. Does your brother prefer to be rich or intelligent? ______________________________
    ____
11. We prefer to be rich and smart. ______________________________

Lesson 44

ser, to be (*Part 2*)

A. *Lectura*

Juan es un muchacho simpático. No es guapo y no es feo. No es gordo y no es delgado.

El padre de Juan es simpático. No es guapo y no es feo. Es gordo. No es delgado.

La madre de Juan es simpática. Es bonita y gorda. No es fea.

Los hermanos de Juan no son feos y no son guapos. La hermana de Juan no es bonita. Es fea y gorda. El amigo favorito de Juan es feo y gordo también.

Vocabulario

simpático, -a, nice, likeable
guapo, -a, handsome, pretty
feo, -a, ugly
delgado, -a, slim, slender

La madre de Juan es bonita y gorda.

Preguntas

1. ¿Qué quiere decir *simpático*? ______________________
2. ¿Es simpático Juan? ______________________
3. ¿Es guapo Juan? ______________________
4. ¿Cómo se dice *ugly* en español? ______________________
5. ¿Es gordo o delgado el padre de Juan? ______________________
6. ¿Es bonita la hermana de Juan? ______________________
7. ¿Es simpática la madre de Juan? ______________________
8. ¿Qué quiere decir *gordo*? ______________________
9. ¿Quién es feo y gordo? ______________________
10. ¿Quién es fea y gorda? ______________________

B. *Preguntas personales*

1. ¿Es simpática su madre? ______________________
2. ¿Es Ud. gordo(-a)? ______________________
3. ¿Son simpáticos sus amigos? ______________________
4. ¿Es su padre alto o bajo? ______________________
5. ¿Es Ud. alto(-a)? ______________________
6. ¿Son Uds. feos? ______________________

C. *Traduzca Ud. al español:*

1. Mary and John are nice. ________________
2. They aren't ugly. ________________
3. She isn't fat. ________________
4. She is pretty. ________________
5. We aren't fat. ________________
6. Is his father nice? ________________

Lesson 45

USES OF **ser** AND **estar**

A. Both **ser** and **estar** mean *to be,* but they are not used in the same ways. Here are some rules that will help you choose the right verb:

1. To express *identity* or *personal characteristics,* use **ser**:

Yo **soy** Alberto. **Somos** mexicanos. Ella **es** guapa.

2. To express (*a*) *location* or (*b*) *state of health,* use **estar**:

(*a*) **Estoy** en la clase. Madrid **está** en España.
(*b*) ¿Cómo **está** Juan? Él **está** enfermo.

B. *Lectura*

Yo soy Enrique. No soy alto y no soy bajo. Estoy bien de salud. Estoy en la escuela.

Mi padre no está en casa. Está en la fábrica donde trabaja. Es un hombre alto y delgado.

Mi madre está en casa. No está bien. Tiene un resfriado. No es gorda y no es delgada. Es baja. No es alta.

Mis hermanos Diego y Andrés están en la escuela. Están bien. Son altos y delgados.

Vocabulario

la **fábrica,** factory
tener un resfriado, to have a cold
¿Cómo es su padre? What is your father like?

Preguntas

1. ¿Es Enrique alto o bajo? ________________________________
2. ¿Cómo está? ________________________________
3. ¿Dónde está? ________________________________
4. ¿Dónde está el padre de Enrique? ________________________________
5. ¿Quién trabaja en una fábrica? ________________________________
6. ¿Cómo es el padre? ________________________________
7. ¿Quién está en casa? ________________________________
8. ¿Cómo está la madre? ________________________________
9. ¿Cómo es la madre? ________________________________

C. *Preguntas personales*

1. ¿Dónde está Ud.? ______________________________
2. ¿Cómo está Ud.? ______________________________
3. ¿Cómo es Ud.? ______________________________
4. ¿Es alto su padre? ______________________________
5. ¿Es baja su madre? ______________________________
6. ¿Tiene Ud. un resfriado? ______________________________
7. ¿Están Uds. bien? ______________________________

D. *Traduzca Ud. al español:*

1. She is tall. ______________________________
2. She is at home. ______________________________
3. She is not well. ______________________________
4. How is your mother? ______________________________
5. What is she like? ______________________________
6. Are you (Uds., *f.*) tall? ______________________________
7. We *(m.)* are not short. ______________________________

Review Exercises

E. Vocabulary (Lessons 29–39)

Complete the sentences:

1. Mi padre ________________ el periódico.
2. Mi madre lee la ______________________________
3. Yo leo mis ____________________ escolares.
4. Me ________________ el café.
5. Mi madre no tiene coche porque no ____________________ un coche.
6. El ____________________ no es bueno para los pulmones.
7. Vivimos en los ____________________ Unidos.
8. Satélite es un ________________ de la ciudad de México.
9. Mi primo vive ________________ de la escuela.
10. Mi hermana asiste ____________ la escuela.
11. Roberto trabaja en un ________________. Es botones.
12. Mi madre trabaja en casa. Es ________________ de casa.
13. El señor González trabaja en una tienda. Es ______________________________.
14. Me ____________________ el fútbol y el béisbol.

F. Verbs (Lessons 1–22)

Write the appropriate verb form:

1. *llamarse*
nosotros ________________________
tú ________________________
ellos ________________________
Uds. ________________________

2. *estar*
yo ________________________
vosotros ________________________
él ________________________
tú ________________________

3. *tener*
ellos ________________________
ella ________________________
yo ________________________
vosotras ________________________

4. *manejar*
Uds. ________________________
nosotros ________________________

5. *estudiar*
él ________________________
vosotros ________________________

6. *ir*
yo ________________________
ellos ________________________
vosotros ________________________
él ________________________

7. *nadar*
yo ________________________
vosotros ________________________

8. *jugar*
nosotros ________________________
ellos ________________________
tú ________________________
ella ________________________

9. *hablar*
Ud. ________________________
tú ________________________

10. *preferir*
tú ________________________
vosotros ________________________
yo ________________________
Uds. ________________________

Crucigrama (5)

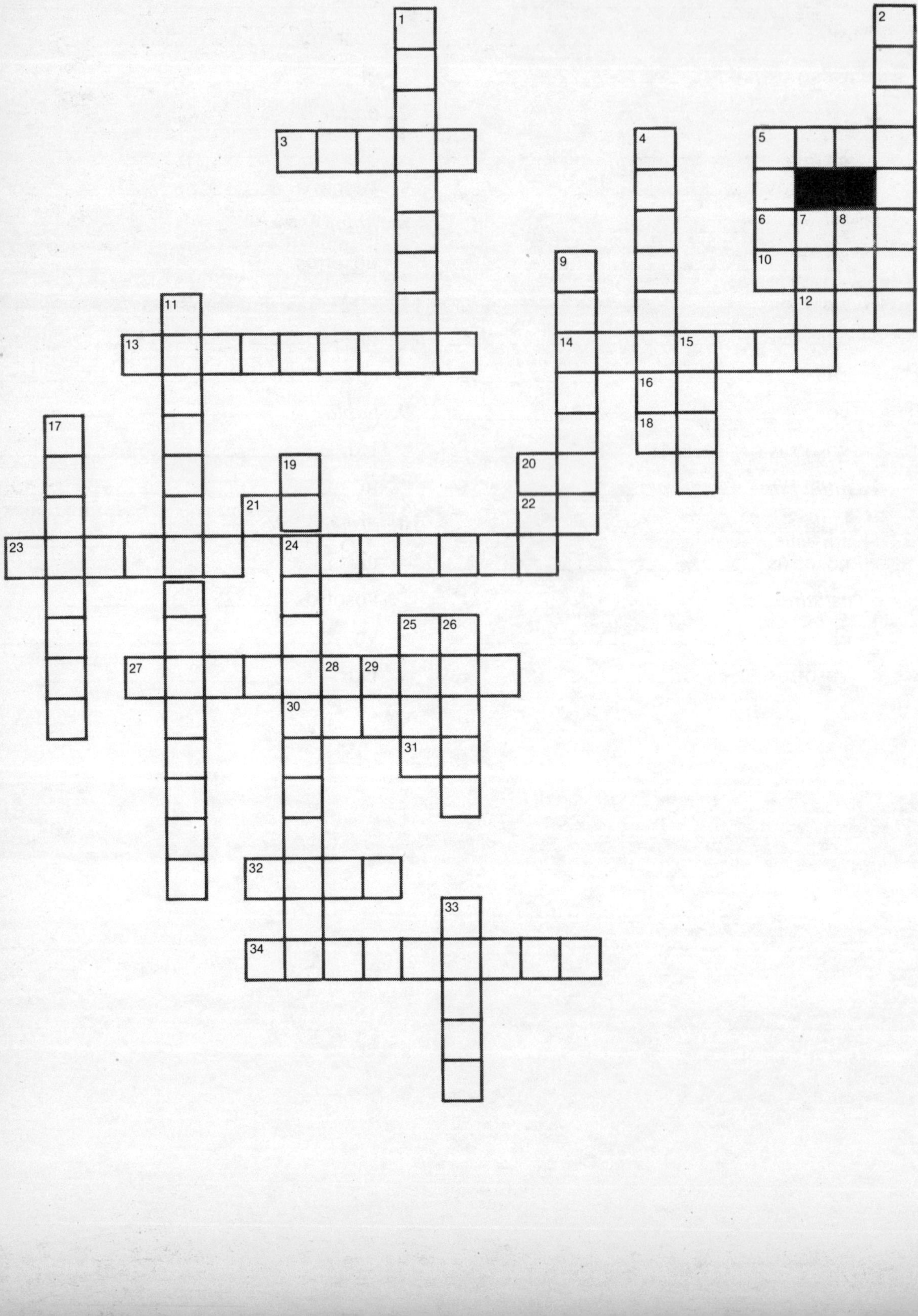

Across

3. Tim no es feo; es _____.
5. ¿Qué quiere decir *tarjeta?*
6. *short*
10. _____ quiere decir *delgado* en inglés.
12. artículo definido inglés
13. En los países hispánicos, todo el mundo tiene dos _____.
14. "¿Trabaja Ud.?" "No, yo no _____."
16. *neither time nor money* = ni tiempo _____ dinero
18. *to the*
20. "Clara, ¿_____ gusta mi falda nueva?" "Sí, me gusta mucho."
21. artículo definido
22. Mi hermana _____ muy alta.
23. *ranch*
24. Kathy no es gorda; es _____.
25. Está en casa = *He's* _____ *home.*
27. Ella trabaja en una oficina. Es _____.
30. México está al sur de los Estados Unidos; el Canadá está al _____.
31. *She's at school* = Está _____ la escuela.
32. *A few pencils* = _____ lápices.
34. Mi madre no está bien. Tiene un _____.

Down

1. *nice*
2. ¿Qué quiere decir *guapo?*
4. "María, ¿eres tú de México?" "Sí, yo soy _____."
5. sinónimo de *taxis* en inglés
7. Juan no es bajo; es _____.
8. iniciales de Jaime Ignacio Hernández
9. Él trabaja en un hotel. Es _____.
11. ¿Qué quiere decir *de habla española?*
15. apodo inglés de *Guillermo*
17. *Estar* is used to express health and _____.
19. *the clerk*
20. ¿Cómo se dice *té* en inglés?
25. *art*
26. Mi amigo favorito _____ quince años.
28. Voy a la escuela = *I'm going* _____ *school.*
29. infinitive ending
33. Nueve menos dos son _____.

Lesson 46

México, D. F.

En México, la ciudad de México se llama *México, D. F.,** porque está en el Distrito Federal. México, D. F., es la capital del país.

La plaza mayor de México, D. F., se llama *el Zócalo*. En el Zócalo, hay varios edificios importantes. Los más viejos son buenos ejemplos de la arquitectura colonial.

Uno de los edificios es la Catedral metropolitana. Otro edificio importante es el Palacio Nacional.

La Catedral es la iglesia más vieja de Norte América.

El Palacio Nacional tiene muchas oficinas federales. También tiene muchos murales de Diego Rivera.

Diego Rivera fue uno de los artistas más famosos de México. Sus murales ilustran la historia, los problemas y los sufrimientos de México.

Vocabulario

el **distrito,** district
la **plaza mayor,** main square
hay, there is, there are
varios, -as, several
el **edificio,** building
el **ejemplo,** example
la arquitectura colonial, Spanish architecture of the 17th and 18th centuries
el **Palacio Nacional,** the national capitol
la iglesia más vieja de, the oldest church in
el **mural,** wall painting
ilustrar, to illustrate
los **sufrimientos,** sufferings
el **gobierno,** government
la **pintura,** painting

Preguntas

1. ¿Qué quieren decir las letras "D. F."?

----

2. ¿Cuál es la capital de México?

----

3. ¿Qué es el Zócalo?

----

4. ¿Qué hay en el Zócalo?

----

5. ¿Cuáles son dos edificios importantes en el Zócalo?

----

6. ¿Por qué es famosa la Catedral?

----

*pronounced "DAY EFay"

7. ¿Qué edificio es el centro del gobierno nacional?

----

8. ¿Quién es Diego Rivera?

----

9. ¿Qué edificio tiene muchas pinturas murales de Diego Rivera?

Lesson 47

TELLING TIME

A. Note how the hour is expressed in Spanish:

la una	one o'clock	**a la una**	at one o'clock
las dos	two o'clock	**a las dos**	at two o'clock
las diez	ten o'clock	**a las diez**	at ten o'clock
		a mediodía	at noon
		a medianoche	at midnight

Traduzca Ud.:

1. five o'clock ____________________________

2. seven o'clock ____________________________

3. at four o'clock ____________________________

4. at one o'clock ____________________________

5. at noon ____________________________

B. y = *past the hour*

la una y cinco, five minutes after one
las tres y diez, ten minutes after three
las ocho y veinte, twenty minutes after eight
las cinco y cuarto, a quarter after five
las once y media, eleven thirty, half past eleven

Traduzca Ud.:

1. six minutes after two ____

2. twelve minutes after four ____

3. a quarter after one ____

4. at one thirty ____

5. at half past nine ____

C. menos = *approaching the hour*

la una menos cinco (''one o'clock minus five''), five minutes to one
las dos menos diez, ten minutes of two
las doce menos cuarto, a quarter to twelve

Traduzca Ud.:

1. seven minutes to nine ____

2. twenty minutes to one ____

3. nine minutes to seven ______________________
4. at a quarter to six ______________________
5. at eight minutes to eleven ______________________

D. ¿a qué hora? = *at what time?*

Preguntas y respuestas

1. ¿A qué hora tomas el desayuno?
   Tomo el desayuno a las siete y media.
2. ¿A qué hora toman Uds. el almuerzo?
   Tomamos el almuerzo a mediodía.
3. ¿A qué hora come Ud.?
   Como a las doce y media.
4. ¿A qué hora van Uds. a casa?
   Vamos a casa a las tres.

5. ¿A qué hora va Ud. a la escuela?
   Yo ______________________
6. ¿A qué hora estudia Ud.?
   Yo ______________________
7. ¿A qué hora jugáis al fútbol?
   Nosotros ______________________
8. ¿A qué hora toma su familia el almuerzo?
   Mi familia ______________________

E. *Traduzca Ud.:*

1. At what time do you *(Ud.)* eat? ______________________
2. I eat at noon. ______________________
3. At what time do you *(Uds.)* have breakfast? ______________________
4. We have breakfast at half past six. ______________________
5. At what time does your sister go to school? ______________________
6. She goes to school at 8:20. ______________________

F. ¿Qué hora es? = *What time is it?*

¿Qué hora es?

- **Es la una y cinco.** It's five minutes after one.
- **Es la una menos diez.** It's ten minutes to one.
- **Son las tres y media.** It's half past three.
- **Son las doce.** It's twelve o'clock.
- **Es mediodía.** It is noon.

It is (or *It's*) = **Es** if the time is one o'clock or begins with **la una (la una y . . . , la una menos . . .).**
It is = **Son** for all other times.

Traduzca Ud.:

1. What time is it? It's 3:15. ________________
2. It is half past one. ________________
3. It is nine o'clock. ________________
4. It is 8:22. ________________

G. de la mañana = A.M. or *in the morning*
de la tarde = P.M. or *in the afternoon*
de la noche = P.M. or *in the evening*

a las ocho de la mañana	at 8 A.M. (at eight o'clock in the morning)
Son las tres de la tarde.	It is 3 P.M. (It's three o'clock in the afternoon.)
Son las siete y media de la noche.	It's 7:30 P.M. (. . . in the evening.)

Traduzca Ud.:

1. one o'clock ________________
2. at one o'clock ________________
3. It is one o'clock. ________________
4. at two o'clock ________________
5. It is two o'clock. ________________
6. At what time? ________________
7. What time is it? ________________
8. It is ten minutes to eleven. ________________
9. It is ten minutes after eleven. ________________
10. It is midnight. ________________
11. It is twelve thirty. ________________
12. It's a quarter of nine in the evening (It's 8:45 P.M.).

    ____

13. It's ten minutes to ten in the morning (It's 9:50 A.M.).

    ____

14. It's eleven o'clock in the evening.

    ____

15. We're going to the movies at six o'clock in the afternoon.

    ____

La columna personal de Anita Gómez (14)

Vocabulario

bonito, -a, pretty
sólo, only
todavía, still
joven, young
esperar, to wait
amar, to love
  te ama, loves you
de veras, really, truly
esperará, will wait
lo, him

el 6 de febrero

Querida Anita Gómez:

Yo quiero casarme* con una muchacha. Se llama Catalina. Es muy bonita. Mi madre dice que no debo casarme porque tengo sólo once años.
¿Qué debo hacer?

Ignacio Onceaños

el 5 de mayo

Querido Ignacio:

Tu madre tiene razón. Todavía eres muy joven. Debes esperar unos años. Si la muchacha te ama de veras, ella esperará también.

Anita Gómez

H. Complete the sentences:

1. Ignacio quiere casarse con Catalina porque ella ______________________________
2. La madre de Ignacio dice que él no ________________________________ porque ____________________________________
3. Según Anita Gómez, la madre de Ignacio tiene ________________________ porque él ____
4. Anita Gómez dice que Catalina esperará si ella lo __________________________

*The **-se** ending of **casarse,** *to get married,* may change to **-me, -te,** or **-nos,** depending on the subject: ¿Quieres casar**te**? Do you want to get married?; Vamos a casar**nos**, We're going to get married.

Lesson 48

volver, *to return, come back;* **empezar,** *to begin;* **terminar,** *to end*

TOPIC QUESTION 29A

¿A qué hora vuelve Ud. a casa?
At what time do you return home?

present tense of ***volver (ue)***	
yo **vuelvo**	nosotros **volvemos**
tú **vuelves**	vosotros **volvéis**
Ud. / él / ella **vuelve**	Uds. / ellos / ellas **vuelven**

A. *Preguntas y respuestas*

El señor Ibáñez vuelve a casa a las seis.

1. ¿A qué hora vuelve Ud. a casa?
   Vuelvo a casa a las cuatro.
2. ¿A qué hora vuelven Uds. a casa?
   Volvemos a casa a las seis.
3. ¿A qué hora vuelve su madre a casa?
   Ella vuelve a casa a las cinco y media.
4. ¿A qué hora vuelve su padre a casa?
   Él vuelve a casa a las seis menos cuarto.
5. ¿A qué hora vuelven tus hermanos a casa?
   Mis hermanos ______________________________
6. ¿Vuelves a casa a las seis?
   No, yo ______________________________ de la tarde.
7. ¿A qué hora vuelve tu hermana?
   Ella ______________________________ de la tarde.
8. ¿Volvéis hoy?
   No, ______________________ mañana.

B. *Lectura*

Mi hermano Raúl va a la escuela a las ocho y media y vuelve a casa a las cuatro.

Mi padre va al trabajo a las ocho y vuelve a casa a las seis.

Mi madre va al mercado a la una y vuelve a casa a las dos y cuarto.

Yo voy a la nevera a las tres y vuelvo al televisor a las tres y veinte. A las cuatro vuelvo a la nevera porque todavía tengo hambre. A las cuatro y diez vuelvo al televisor.

A las siete menos cuarto todos tomamos la cena, y mi madre me pregunta por qué no tengo apetito.

Vocabulario

el **trabajo,** work, job
el **mercado,** market
la **nevera,** refrigerator
el **televisor,** TV set
tomar la cena, to have supper
me pregunta, asks me

Preguntas

1. ¿A qué hora va Raúl a la escuela?

____

2. ¿A qué hora vuelve su padre a casa?

____

3. ¿Adónde va su madre a la una?

____

4. ¿Por qué va a la nevera el hermano de Raúl?

____

5. ¿A qué hora toma la familia la cena?

____

TOPIC QUESTION 29B

¿A qué hora empieza la clase?
At what time does the class begin?

TOPIC QUESTION 29C

¿A qué hora termina?
At what time does it end?

present tense of:	
empezar (ie)	***terminar***
empiezo **empiezas** **empieza**	**termino** **terminas** **termina**
empezamos **empezáis** **empiezan**	**terminamos** **termináis** **terminan**

C. *Preguntas y respuestas*

1. ¿A qué hora empieza la clase de español?
La clase de español empieza a las nueve.
2. ¿A qué hora termina?
Termina a las diez menos cinco.
3. ¿A qué hora empieza la clase de biología?
Empieza a las diez.
4. ¿A qué hora termina?
Termina a las once menos cinco.
5. ¿A qué hora empieza su clase de matemáticas?
Mi clase de matemáticas ____________________
6. ¿A qué hora empieza su clase de historia?
Mi clase de historia ____________________
7. ¿A qué hora terminan sus clases?
Mis clases ____________________

D. *Lectura*

Marta Jiménez vive en San José, Costa Rica. Asiste a la escuela superior.

La primera clase de Marta es inglés. La clase empieza a las ocho y termina a las nueve menos cinco.

La segunda clase de Marta es biología. La clase empieza a las nueve y termina a las diez menos cinco.

Marta estudia la historia mundial. Es su tercera clase. Empieza a las diez y termina a las once menos cinco.

La cuarta clase de Marta es matemáticas. Empieza a las once y termina a las doce menos cinco.

Marta vuelve a casa a la una.

Vocabulario

asistir a, to attend
primero, -a,* first
segundo, -a, second
tercero, -a,* third
cuarto, -a, fourth
último, -a, last
el **horario,** schedule
la **historia mundial,** world history

Preguntas

1. ¿Dónde vive Marta? ____________________
2. ¿A cuántas clases asiste Marta? ____________________
3. ¿A qué hora empieza su primera clase? ____________________
4. ¿A qué hora termina su última clase? ____________________
5. ¿A qué hora vuelve Marta a casa? ____________________

---

*__Primero__ and **tercero** drop the final **-o** before a masculine singular noun: el **primer** hombre, the first man; el **tercer** libro, the third book.

E. *Tema*. Write a composition entitled *Mi Horario* in which you describe your school program in Spanish. (Consult the list of *asignaturas* on page 188.) Here is an example of how you might begin:

Mi Horario

Mi primera clase es química. La clase empieza a las ocho y termina a las nueve menos cinco.

Mi segunda clase es historia. Empieza a las nueve.

—and so forth.

F. *Conversación*. You and your classmates take turns asking one another the three Topic Questions of this lesson.

G. *Traduzca Ud. al español:*

1. His class in *(de)* world history begins at nine o'clock.

   ----

2. At what time does your biology class begin?

   ----

3. Her math class (''class of mathematics'') ends at five minutes to ten.

   ----

4. At what time do you *(tú)* return home?

   ----

5. I return home at 4 P.M.

   ----

6. Their classes end at three o'clock.

   ----

7. His first class is English.

Ordinal Numbers

primero, -a, first	**sexto, -a,** sixth
segundo, -a, second	**séptimo, -a,** seventh
tercero, -a, third	**octavo, -a,** eighth
cuarto, -a, fourth	**noveno, -a,** ninth
quinto, -a, fifth	**décimo, -a,** tenth

Clases y Asignaturas

la **banda,** band
la **orquesta,** orchestra
el **coro,** choir

la **teneduría,** bookkeeping
la **estenografía,** stenography
la **taquigrafía,** shorthand
la **mecanografía,** typewriting

el **manejo de la casa,** home economics
el **taller,** shop
el **dibujo mecánico,** mechanical drawing

el **arte,** art

las **matemáticas,** mathematics
la **trigonometría,** trigonometry
el **álgebra,** algebra

la **biología,** biology
la **química,** chemistry
la **física,** physics

la **historia mundial,** world history
la **economía,** economics
la **instrucción cívica,** civics

la **educación física,** physical education
el **gimnasio,** gymnasium
la **natación,** swimming

H. *Diálogo*. In the following dialogue, play the role of Steve. Write his responses in the blanks.

NANCY: ¿Qué asignaturas tomas este semestre?

STEVE: ____

NANCY: ¿Cuál es tu asignatura favorita?

STEVE: ____

NANCY: Mi primera clase es álgebra. La profesora es muy simpática pero no me gustan las matemáticas. ¿Te gustan a ti?

STEVE: ____

NANCY: Este semestre empiezo a estudiar español.

STEVE: ____

NANCY: Quiero aprender español porque es una lengua importante y me gusta mucho.

STEVE: ____

NANCY: Hoy Carolina y yo tomamos el almuerzo en la cafetería. ¿A qué hora comes tú?

STEVE: ____

NANCY: Nosotras comemos a la una también. ¿Por qué no comes con nosotras?

STEVE: ____

Review Exercises

(Lessons 42–48)

I. *Vocabulario*. Translate into Spanish:

1. a Spanish-speaking country *(two ways)* *a.* ______________________

b. ______________________

2. everybody ______________________

3. the surname (family name) ______________________

4. to get married ______________________

5. I want to get married. ______________________

6. The house is large. ______________________

7. The house is in the suburbs. ______________________

8. She is tall; he is short. ______________________

9. a nice girl ______________________

10. a handsome boy ______________________

11. an ugly man ______________________

12. They *(f.)* are fat; he is slim. ______________________

13. She is ill; she has a cold. ______________________

14. a famous doctor *a.* un doctor ______________________

b. una doctora ______________________

15. the words ______________________

16. there is, there are ______________________

17. the building ______________________

18. the problems ______________________

19. a quarter past three ______________________

20. at 6 A.M. ______________________

21. What time is it? ______________________

22. It's 8 P.M. ______________________

23. *a.* I begin ______________________

b. We begin ______________________

24. to end ______________________

25. *a.* we return ______________________

b. they return ______________________

26. tonight ______________________

27. all day ______________________________
28. Mexico City *(two ways)* *a.* ______________________________
b. ______________________________
29. the federal offices ______________________________
30. They attend the National University. ______________________________

J. *Frases revueltas*. Unscramble the sentences:

1. asiste Felipe la Martínez universidad a .
____
2. trabaja padre ¿dónde su ?
____
3. en tienda ellos trabajan una .
____
4. veinte y cinco Timoteo años tiene .
____
5. Ud. ¿ cuántos ? años tiene
____
6. Gutiérrez que rancho Juan muchacho un es vive en un .
____
7. son ellos bajos no .
____
8. ¿ casa esta en ellos están noche ?
____
9. soy , sí yo mexicana .
____
10. bajo padre es ¿ o ? tu alto
____
11. simpático es Juan un muchacho .
____
12. favorito y también amigo mi gordo es feo .
____
13. gordo es y flaco no es no .
____
14. salud bien estoy de .
____
15. está ¿ madre cómo ? la
____

16. capital México ¿ cuál es ? la de

---

17. tres la de tarde las son .

---

18. noche la de son media las diez y .

---

19. a la vuelve una Chavela a casa .

---

20. clase mi historia es segunda la de clase .

Lesson 49

las habitaciones de la casa,
the rooms of the house

Vocabulario

la **habitación** }
el **cuarto** } room
el **piso,** floor, story
abajo, downstairs
arriba, upstairs
la **cocina,** kitchen
el **comedor,** dining room
la **sala,** living room
el **cuarto de baño,** bathroom
el **dormitorio,** bedroom
construido, -a, built
al estilo español, in the Spanish style
dan a, face, open out to
la **fuente,** fountain
la **flor,** flower
el **árbol,** tree
pequeño, -a, small
se lava, washes herself

A. *Lectura*

La casa de los Mendoza tiene dos pisos.

La cocina, el comedor y la sala están abajo. Abajo hay un cuarto de baño también.

Arriba hay tres dormitorios y un cuarto de baño.

La casa de los Mendoza está construida al estilo español. Tiene un patio que está en el centro de la casa. Todas las habitaciones dan al patio. En el patio generalmente hay una fuente, muchas flores y unos árboles.

Preguntas

1. ¿Cuántos pisos tiene la casa de los Mendoza? ____________________
2. ¿Qué habitaciones están abajo? ____________________
3. ¿Qué habitaciones están arriba? ____________________
4. ¿A qué estilo está construida la casa de los Mendoza? ____________________
____
5. ¿Dónde está el patio? ____________________
____
6. ¿Qué hay en el patio? ____________________
____

B. *Preguntas personales*

1. ¿Es su cocina grande o pequeña?
____
2. ¿Cuántos pisos tiene su casa?
____
3. ¿Cuántos dormitorios tiene su casa?
____

El patio tiene árboles, flores y una fuente.

4. ¿Cuántos cuartos de baño tiene su casa?

---

5. ¿Tiene su casa un patio en el centro?

C. *Tema.* Write a composition in Spanish entitled *Nuestra Casa* in which you describe the house you live in. Here are two ways in which you might begin your *tema*:

Nuestra casa tiene dos pisos. La cocina, el comedor, la sala y un cuarto de baño están abajo. Arriba hay tres dormitorios y un cuarto de baño. . . .

Or:

Vivimos en un apartamento. El apartamento tiene cinco habitaciones* y dos cuartos de baño. Tenemos dos dormitorios grandes. La cocina es pequeña y la sala es grande. El comedor no es pequeña y no es grande. Comemos en el comedor, pero generalmente tomamos el desayuno en la cocina. . . .

María se lava en el cuarto de baño.

*Use **habitaciones** when answering the question "How many rooms does your house have?" (**¿Cuántas habitaciones tiene su casa?**)

La columna personal de Anita Gómez (15)

el 30 de septiembre

Querida Anita Gómez:

Estoy enamorada de un muchacho que se llama Ernesto. Mi madre también le tiene simpatía. Ella es una buena cocinera, y Ernesto viene muchas veces a mi casa para comer con nosotras. Él dice que me ama, pero en la escuela casi nunca me habla. Prefiere estar con sus amigos.

¿Qué debo hacer?

María Enamorada

Vocabulario

estar enamorado(-a) de, to be in love with
le tiene simpatía, likes him
viene, comes
muchas veces, often
el **cocinero** / la **cocinera** } cook
casi, almost
cocinar, to cook

el 2 de octubre

Querida María Enamorada:

Aprenda Ud. a cocinar.

Anita Gómez

D. Complete the sentences:

1. Ernesto viene muchas veces a comer en casa de María porque ____________________
____
2. Ernesto no habla con María en la escuela porque ______________________________
____
3. Anita Gómez dice que María debe ____

Lesson 50

el tiempo, *the weather;* **los meses del año,** *the months of the year*

TOPIC QUESTION 30	**¿En qué meses hace calor (frío)?** In what months is it warm (cold)?

A. *Preguntas y respuestas*

1. ¿En qué meses hace calor?
Hace calor en mayo, junio, julio y agosto.

2. ¿En qué meses hace frío?
Hace frío en diciembre, enero y febrero.

3. ¿En qué meses hace fresco?
Hace fresco en marzo y abril.

4. ¿En qué meses nieva?
Nieva en diciembre, enero y febrero.

5. ¿Hace buen tiempo hoy?
Sí, hoy ______________________________

6. ¿Llueve ahora?
No, ahora no llueve.

7. ¿Llueve mucho en agosto?
Sí, en agosto ______________________________

8. ¿Hace mal tiempo en julio?
No, en julio ______________________________

Vocabulario

el **mes,** month
hace calor, it is warm (weather)
hace mucho calor, it is hot
hace fresco, it is cool
hace frío, it is cold
¿qué tiempo hace? How is the weather?
hace buen tiempo, the weather is nice
hace mal tiempo, the weather is bad
llueve, it rains, is raining
nieva, it snows, is snowing
ahora, now

Hace buen tiempo en el mes de julio.

B. *Los meses*

Learn the Spanish names for the months:

enero (January)	**julio**
febrero	**agosto**
marzo	**septiembre***
abril	**octubre**
mayo	**noviembre**
junio	**diciembre**

*The *p* is silent: ''se-TIEM-brey.''

C. *Lectura*

Hace frío en los meses de diciembre, enero y febrero. Hace fresco en los meses de marzo y abril. Hace calor en los meses de mayo, junio, julio y agosto. Hace fresco en los meses de septiembre, octubre y noviembre.

Hace buen tiempo en los meses de mayo, junio, julio y agosto. Hace mal tiempo en enero, febrero y marzo.

Preguntas

1. ¿Cómo se dice *January* en español? ________________
2. ¿Hace frío en febrero? ________________
3. ¿Hace calor en diciembre? ________________
4. ¿Hace frío o calor en julio? ________________
5. ¿Qué tiempo hace en junio? ________________
6. ¿Qué tiempo hace en octubre? ________________
7. ¿Qué tiempo hace hoy? ________________
8. ¿En qué meses hace fresco? ________________
9. ¿En qué meses hace calor? ________________
10. ¿En qué meses hace frío? ________________
11. ¿Cuántos meses hay? ________________

D. *Traduzca Ud. al español:*

1. It rains a lot in April. ________________
2. It is cold in December. ________________
3. In what month is it hot? ________________
4. It is hot in the month of July. ________________
5. Does it snow a lot in January? ________________
6. The weather is nice in June. ________________
7. In what month is the weather bad? ________________
8. How is the weather today? ________________

Hace frío en el mes de diciembre.

COGNATES (7)

E. Pronounce the words listed below. Can you guess their meanings? In each blank, write the English cognate that means the same thing as the Spanish word.

1. acción ____________
2. acento ____________
3. actor ____________
4. actriz ____________
5. aeroplano ____________
6. aeropuerto ____________
7. alcohólico ____________
8. crimen ____________
9. cristianismo ____________
10. chófer ____________
11. dictador ____________
12. droga ____________
13. ejemplo ____________
14. ejercicio ____________
15. clcfante ____________
16. emplear ____________
17. geografía ____________
18. Gran Bretaña ____________
19. héroe ____________
20. humano ____________
21. inocente ____________
22. interpretación ____________
23. literatura ____________
24. medicina ____________
25. misterio ____________
26. misterioso ____________
27. norte ____________
28. nuevo ____________
29. oportunidad ____________
30. porcentaje ____________
31. poseer ____________
32. pronombre ____________
33. producción ____________
34. producir ____________
35. producto ____________
36. profundo ____________
37. prohibir ____________
38. prosperidad ____________
39. reciente ____________
40. reencarnación ____________
41. residencia ____________
42. respetable ____________
43. revelar ____________
44. revolución ____________
45. silencio ____________
46. símbolo ____________
47. sinceridad ____________
48. sinónimo ____________
49. substituto ____________
50. sudamericano ____________
51. suficiente ____________
52. testimonio ____________
53. tragedia ____________
54. traidor ____________
55. trofeo ____________
56. Turquía ____________
57. valle ____________
58. vegetación ____________
59. volcánico ____________
60. zoología ____________

Lesson 51

las estaciones, *the seasons*

TOPIC QUESTION 31

> **¿Qué tiempo hace?**
> How is the weather?

A. *Preguntas y respuestas*

1. ¿Qué tiempo hace hoy?
   Hoy hace fresco.
2. ¿Qué tiempo hace afuera?
   Hace buen tiempo afuera.
3. ¿Qué tiempo hace en el invierno?
   En el invierno hace frío.
4. ¿Qué tiempo hace en la primavera?
   En la primavera hace fresco y llueve mucho.
5. ¿Qué tiempo hace en el verano?
   En el verano ________________________
6. ¿Qué tiempo hace en el otoño?
   En el otoño ________________________
7. ¿Qué tiempo hace ahora?
   Ahora ___________________________________

Vocabulario

la **estación,*** season
hace viento, it's windy
hace mucho viento, it's very windy
hace sol, it's sunny
llover (ue), to rain
nevar (ie), to snow
afuera, outside

Nieva mucho en el invierno.

B. *Las estaciones*

Learn the Spanish names for the seasons:

la **primavera,** spring(time)
el **verano,** summer(time)
el **otoño,** autumn, fall
el **invierno,**† winter(time)

C. *Lectura*

Hace fresco en la primavera y llueve mucho.

Hace calor en el verano. Hace mucho sol y no llueve mucho. Generalmente hace buen tiempo.

Hace fresco en el otoño. También llueve mucho.

Hace mucho frío en el invierno. Nieva mucho y hace mucho viento. Hace mal tiempo en el invierno.

---

*The accent mark is dropped in the plural.

†pronounced "im-BIER-no"

Preguntas

1. ¿En qué estación llueve mucho? ________________
2. ¿Qué estación le gusta a Ud.? ________________
3. ¿En qué estación hace mucho sol? ________________
4. ¿En qué estación hace mucho frío? ________________
5. ¿Qué tiempo hace en el otoño? ________________
6. ¿Llueve hoy? ________________
7. ¿Nieva hoy? ________________

D. *Conversación.* You and your classmates take turns asking one another questions about the weather.

E. *Traduzca Ud. al español:*

1. How's the weather today? ________________
2. It's very warm in the summertime. ________________
3. It's cold today. ________________
4. It's not very cold in the fall. ________________
5. The weather is nice in the spring. ________________
6. It's cold and windy outside. ________________

Llueve mucho en la primavera.

Preguntas (a review)

F. Answer each question with a complete sentence in Spanish:

1. ¿Es Ud. alto(-a) o bajo(-a)? ________________
2. ¿Son Uds. mexicanos? ________________
3. ¿Es alto(-a) su profesor(-ra)? ________________
4. ¿Es simpática su madre? ________________

5. ¿Dónde está su madre? ______________________________

6. ¿Dónde está Ud.? ______________________________

7. ¿A qué hora vuelve Ud. a casa? ______________________________

8. ¿Cuántos dormitorios hay en su casa? ______________________________

9. ¿Cuál es su estación favorita? ______________________________

10. ¿A qué hora empieza la clase de español? ______________________________

____

11. En México, ¿qué palabras representan las letras *D.F.*? ______________________________

____

12. ¿Cómo se llama la plaza mayor de México, D. F.? ______________________________

____

13. ¿Cuáles son dos edificios importantes de la plaza mayor? ______________________________

____

14. ¿Quién fue Diego Rivera? ______________________________

15. ¿Dónde está el patio de una casa española? ______________________________

____

16. ¿En qué meses hace mucho frío? ______________________________

17. ¿En qué estación nieva mucho? ______________________________

18. ¿En qué estación hace mucho calor? ______________________________

19. ¿Cuántos meses hay? ______________________________

20. ¿Cuántas estaciones hay? ______________________________

*__lo bueno,__ the good news, the good part; **lo malo,** the bad news, the bad part (of it); **poder (ue),** to be able, can.

Lesson 52

hacer, *to do, to make*

TOPIC QUESTION 32

¿Qué hace Ud.? What do you do?

present tense of ***hacer***	
yo **hago**	nosotros **hacemos**
tú **haces**	vosotros **hacéis**
Ud. / él / ella } **hace**	Uds. / ellos / ellas } **hacen**

A. *Preguntas y respuestas*

1. ¿Qué hace Ud.?
Yo trabajo en una tienda.

2. ¿Qué haces tú?
Yo voy a la escuela.

3. ¿Qué hacen Uds.?
Vamos a la escuela.

4. ¿Qué hace ella?
Ella es ama de casa.

5. ¿Qué hacen ellos?
Ellos trabajan en una fábrica.

6. ¿Qué hace el dependiente?
El dependiente ____________________ en un almacén.

7. ¿Qué hace su amigo favorito?
Mi amigo favorito ____

8. ¿Qué hacéis los domingos?
Los domingos ____

B. *Lectura*

El padre de Juan trabaja en una fábrica. Juan no trabaja. Asiste a la Universidad de Puerto Rico. La madre de Juan es ama de casa. Trabaja en casa.

Preguntas

1. ¿Qué hace el padre de Juan? ____

2. ¿Cómo se dice *factory* en español? ________________________________

3. ¿Trabaja Juan? ____________________
4. ¿Qué hace Juan? ____________________
5. ¿Qué hace la madre de Juan? ____________________

C. *Preguntas personales*

1. ¿Qué hace Ud.? ____________________
2. ¿Qué hace su padre? ____________________
3. ¿Qué hacen sus hermanos? ____________________
4. ¿Qué hace Ud. los sábados? ____________________

D. *Conversación.* You and your classmates take turns asking one another such questions as **¿Qué hace Ud.?, ¿Qué hace Ud. por la noche?, ¿Qué hace Ud. los sábados (domingos)?** and **¿Qué hace Ud. después de las clases** (after school)?

E. *Traduzca Ud. al español:*

1. Robert's father works in a factory. ____________________
____
2. What do you *(tú)* do? ____________________
3. What does your mother do? ____________________
4. She is a housewife. ____________________
5. She works at home. ____________________
6. What do your brothers do after school? ____________________
____
7. What do you *(Uds.)* do on Sundays? ____________________
8. On Sundays we go to church. ____________________
9. When do you *(Ud.)* do your homework (tareas, *pl.*)? ____________________
____
10. I do my homework in the evening *(por la noche)*. ____________________
____

Vocabulary Review

F. Complete the sentences:

1. La Argentina es un país de habla ____________________
2. Todo el ______________ va a la escuela.
3. Mi ____________________ es Gómez.

4. Yo no soy alta; soy ______________________________

5. Ricardo no es feo; es muy ______________________________

6. Inés no es delgada; es muy ______________________________

7. Linda no es fea; es ______________________________

8. Yo ____________________ un resfriado.

9. La plaza mayor de la ciudad de México se llama el ____________________

10. ________________ veinte y cinco estudiantes en la clase.

11. El Palacio ____________________ está en el Zócalo.

12. Lupe ____________________ a casa a las cinco.

13. La clase empieza a las diez y ____________________ a las once.

14. Mi madre es simpática. Mis hermanos son ________________ también.

La columna personal de Anita Gómez (16)

Vocabulario

ganar, to earn
bastante, enough
para vivir, to live on
todo, everything
pagar, to pay
el **alquiler,** rent
el **sueldo,** salary, wage
tendrán, will have

el 1º de marzo

Querida Anita Gómez:

Estoy enamorada de Diego y él está enamorado de mí. Queremos casarnos, pero mis padres dicen que Diego no gana bastante para vivir.

¿Qué debo hacer?

Luisa La Novia

el 18 de marzo

Querida Luisa La Novia:

Sus padres tienen razón. El dinero no es todo, pero el amor no paga el alquiler. ¿Por qué no busca Ud. empleo? Con dos sueldos Ud. y Diego tendrán bastante para vivir.

Anita Gómez

G. Complete the sentences:

1. Luisa y Diego están ____________________ y quieren ________________________
2. Según los padres de Luisa, ella no debe casarse con Diego porque ______________ ____
3. Anita Gómez dice que los padres de Luisa tienen razón porque ________________ ____
4. Según Anita Gómez, los dos novios tendrán bastante para vivir si Luisa ______ ______________ también.

Lesson 53

tener que + INFINITIVE, *to have to, must*

TOPIC QUESTION 33

¿Tiene Ud. que trabajar? Do you have to work?

A. *Preguntas y respuestas*

1. ¿Tiene Ud. que trabajar?
No tengo que trabajar. Voy a la escuela.

2. ¿Tienen Uds. que trabajar?
Sí, tenemos que trabajar.

3. ¿Tiene que trabajar su padre?
Sí, mi padre tiene que trabajar.

4. ¿Tiene que trabajar su madre?
Sí, ella tiene que trabajar también. Trabaja en casa.

5. ¿Tienen que trabajar sus hermanos?
No, ellos no tienen que trabajar. Van a la escuela.

6. ¿Tiene que trabajar su amigo favorito?
No, ____

7. En su familia, ¿quiénes tienen que trabajar?
En mi familia, ______________________________________

8. ¿Tienes que hacer tus tareas?
Sí, yo ____

Vocabulario
las **tareas,** homework*
después de las clases, after school

B. *Lectura*

Ramón tiene que trabajar. Tiene que ir a la escuela también. El padre de Ramón tiene que trabajar. Los hermanos de Ramón se llaman Guillermo y Enrique. Tienen que ir a la escuela. Enrique tiene que trabajar en una tienda después de las clases. Guillermo no tiene que trabajar.

---

*One homework assignment is a **tarea,** singular. When "homework" refers to the sum of assignments received in different classes, use **tareas,** plural.

Preguntas

1. ¿Tiene que trabajar Ramón? ____________________
2. ¿Qué tiene que hacer Ramón? ____________________
3. ¿Qué tiene que hacer el padre de Ramón? ____________________
4. ¿Quién tiene que trabajar después de las clases? ____________________
____
5. ¿Tiene que trabajar Guillermo? ____________________

C. *Traduzca Ud. al español:*

1. I must go to school today. ____________________
2. Do your brothers have to go to school? ____________________
____
3. He has to work after school. ____________________
4. Do you *(tú)* have to work? ____________________
5. You *(Uds.)* have to do your homework. ____________________

Review Exercise

D. *Verdad o Mentira.* In the blank on the left, write *V* (for *Verdad*) if the statement is true, *M* (for *Mentira*) if the statement is false.

____ **1.** Los Estados Unidos consisten en cincuenta estados.
____ **2.** El primer presidente de los Estados Unidos fue Abrahán Lincoln.
____ **3.** En el Zócalo de México, D. F., hay una catedral muy vieja.
____ **4.** No bebemos cerveza en la clase.
____ **5.** Dormimos en casa.
____ **6.** Leemos español.
____ **7.** Nos gusta comer cuando tenemos hambre.
____ **8.** Queremos sacar buenas notas.
____ **9.** El Pedregal está cerca de la Ciudad Universitaria.
____ **10.** Satélite es un barrio de México, D. F.
____ **11.** Muchos pobres viven en el Pedregal.
____ **12.** Roberto tiene veinte años y su hermana tiene diez y siete años. Roberto es más joven que su hermana.
____ **13.** Los españoles tienen dos apellidos.

Vocabulario

consistir en, to consist of
sacar buenas notas, to get good marks (grades)
más joven que, younger than
los perezosos, the lazy, lazy people
se casa con, marries, gets married to

____ **14.** Una señorita se llama Margarita Sánchez y Gutiérrez. El apellido *Sánchez* es del padre y el apellido *Gutiérrez* es de la madre.

____ **15.** Margarita se casa con Rodolfo Martínez y Cárdenas. Ahora Margarita se llama Margarita Gutiérrez de Cárdenas.

____ **16.** Los perezosos trabajan mucho.

____ **17.** Estamos en la Argentina.

____ **18.** Diego Rivera fue un artista mexicano.

____ **19.** No vamos a la escuela a la una de la mañana.

____ **20.** La clase de español empieza a las once de la noche.

Lesson 54

ir a + INFINITIVE, *to be going to*

TOPIC QUESTION 34	**¿Qué va Ud. a hacer esta noche?** What are you going to do tonight?

A. *Preguntas y respuestas*

1. ¿Qué va Ud. a hacer esta noche?
Voy a estudiar.

2. ¿Qué van Uds. a hacer esta noche?
Vamos a hacer nuestras tareas.

Vocabulario
el **periódico,** newspaper
la **comedia,** comedy, play
la **película,** film, movie

3. ¿Qué va a hacer su padre esta noche?
Mi padre va a leer el periódico.

4. ¿Qué va a hacer su madre esta noche?
Ella va a ver una comedia en la televisión.

5. ¿Qué van a hacer sus hermanos esta noche?
Ellos van a mirar la televisión.

6. ¿Qué va a hacer su amiga favorita esta noche?
Ella ______________________________

7. ¿Qué van Uds. a hacer mañana?
Nosotros ______________________________

8. ¿Qué vas a hacer después de las clases?
Yo ______________________________

B. *Lectura*

Ramona va a mirar la televisión a las nueve. No tiene que estudiar. Sus hermanos van a mirar la televisión también. Van a ver una película. Los padres de Ramona no van a mirar la televisión. Van a jugar al boliche.

Preguntas

1. ¿Qué va a hacer Ramona? ______________________________

2. ¿Quién no tiene que estudiar? ______________________________

3. ¿Qué van a ver Ramona y sus hermanos?

4. ¿Quiénes no van a mirar la televisión?

5. ¿Qué van a hacer los padres de Ramona?

C. *Preguntas personales*

1. ¿Qué va Ud. a hacer esta noche?
2. ¿Va Ud. a mirar la televisión después del almuerzo?

3. ¿Cómo se dice *tonight* en español?
4. ¿Qué va a hacer su madre esta noche?

D. *Traduzca Ud. al español:*

1. I'm going to watch television tonight.

2. We're going to watch a movie. (Use *ver*.)

3. What are your friends going to do?

4. They are going to do their homework.

5. What are you *(Uds.)* going to do?

6. We're going to play soccer.

7. Is your father going to work tomorrow?

E. *Conversación*. You and your classmates take turns asking one another *¿Qué va Ud. a hacer esta noche*?

La columna personal de Anita Gómez (17)

Vocabulario

los **hijos,** children (= sons *or* sons and daughters)
irse, to leave, go away
si no, if not
no es justo, it's not fair
permitir, to permit
el **derecho,** right
invitar, to invite

el 11 de abril

Querida Anita Gómez:

Mis padres, mi hermana, su esposo y sus ocho hijos viven en nuestra casa. Mi esposo dice que ellos tienen que irse. Si no, él quiere un divorcio.

¿Qué debo hacer?

Gloria

el 22 de abril

Querida Gloria:

Su esposo tiene razón. No es justo. Si Ud. permite a su familia vivir en la casa, la familia de él debe tener el mismo derecho. ¿Por qué no invita Ud. también a la familia de su esposo a vivir con Uds.?

Anita Gómez

Ocho hijos y seis grandes en una casa.

F. Complete the sentences:

1. La familia de la hermana de Gloria consiste en ______________ personas, y viven en la casa de ____
2. El esposo de Gloria dice que la familia de ella debe ___________________________
3. Según Anita Gómez, Gloria debe ____________________ a la familia de su esposo a ____________________ con ellos.

Crucigrama (6)

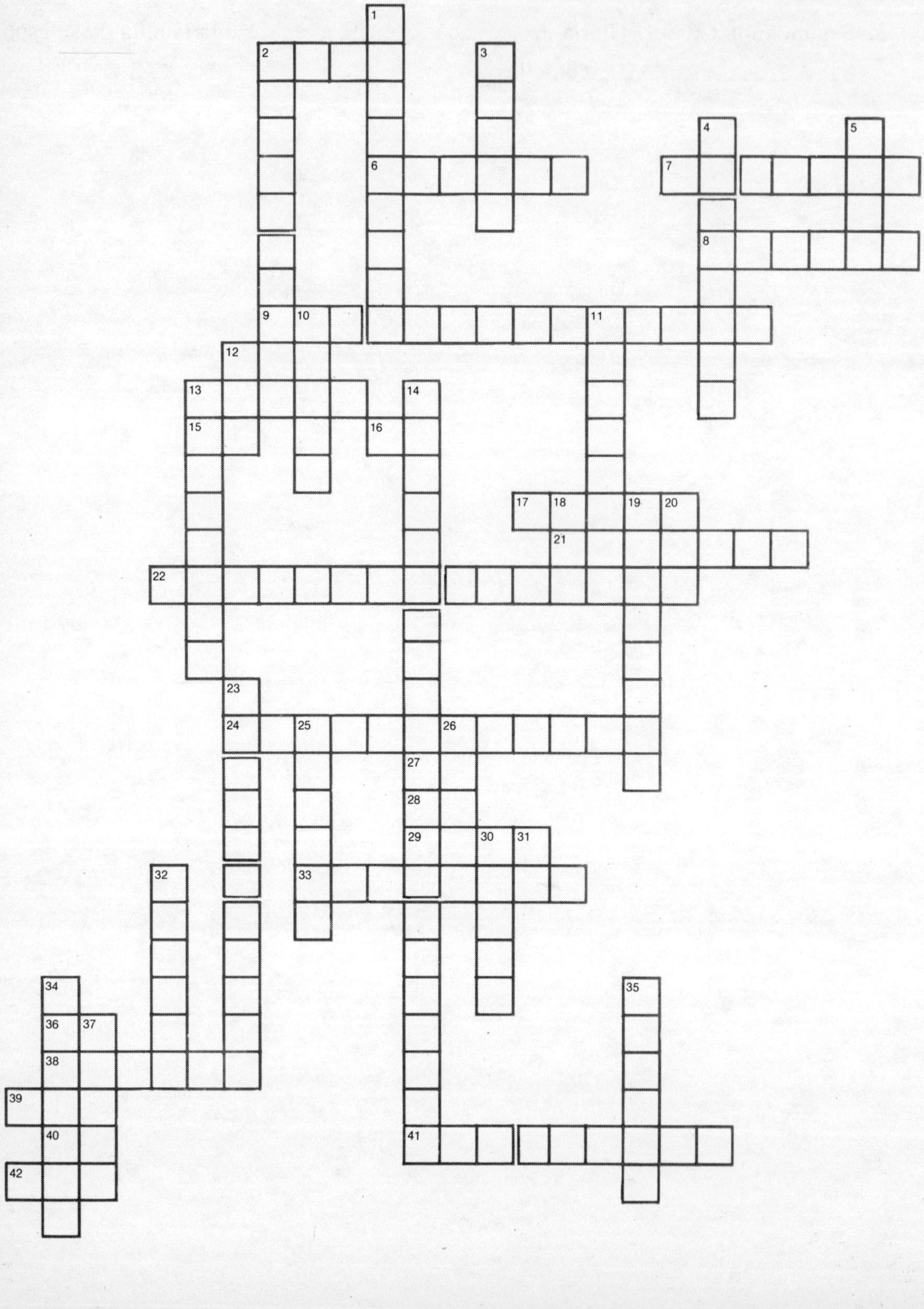

(Each blank represents one word.)

Across

2. ¿Cómo se dice *muchos* en inglés?
6. El dormitorio no está abajo; está _____.
7. la primavera, el verano, _____ _____, el invierno
8. *wife*
9. *He likes mathematics* = Le gusta _____ _____.
12. el apodo inglés de Roberto
13. *donkey*
15. Para nosotros = *for* _____.
16. ¿Qué bebida toma Ud. con el almuerzo: café, _____ o leche?
17. ¿Qué quiere decir *mes*?
21. *orange*
22. En "México, D. F.," las letras D. F. representan las palabras _____ _____.
24. *architecture*
27. iniciales de Raúl Sánchez
28. Hace frío = _____ *is cold*.
29. a kind of Mexican sandwich
33. un estado de los Estados Unidos que tiene un nombre español
36. iniciales de Ernesto Pérez
38. primero, segundo, tercero, cuarto, _____
39. Si hoy es miércoles, ayer _____ martes.
40. Para sus amigos y parientes, Edward se llama _____.
41. *four o'clock*
42. *year*

Down

1. ¿Qué quiere decir *gimnasio*?
2. *It's hot today* = Hace _____ _____ hoy.
3. enero, febrero, marzo, _____
4. *the summertime*
5. Lupita no va a la escuela porque tiene sólo cuatro _____.
10. el cuarto mes del año
11. *to end*
12. Tomar el autobús = *to take the* _____.
13. ¿Qué quiere decir *edificio*?
14. En México, ¿cómo se llama la capital del país?
18. ¿Qué quiere decir *uno*?
19. A los perezosos no les gusta _____.
20. Harold se llama _____ cuando está en casa o con sus amigos.
23. *five minutes after one o'clock*
25. Diez y cinco son _____.
26. *To be sick* = _____ enfermo(-a).
30. No me gusta vivir en la ciudad; prefiero vivir en el _____.
31. iniciales de Otelo Dante
32. ¿Qué quiere decir *estación*?
34. La cocina no es grande; es _____.
35. Hace buen tiempo en los meses de mayo, junio, julio y _____.
37. Yo no _____ ir a la escuela hoy porque estoy enfermo.

Lesson 55

poder, *to be able, can*

TOPIC QUESTION 35

¿Puede Ud. ir al cine está noche? Can you go to the movies tonight?

present tense of ***poder (ue)***	
yo **puedo**	nosotros **podemos**
tú **puedes**	vosotros **podéis**
Ud. / él / ella } **puede**	Uds. / ellos / ellas } **pueden**

A. *Preguntas y respuestas*

1. ¿Puede Ud. ir al cine esta noche?
Sí, yo puedo ir al cine esta noche.

2. ¿Pueden Uds. ir al cine esta noche?
No, no podemos ir esta noche.

3. ¿Puede su padre ir al cine esta noche?
No, mi padre no puede ir esta noche.

4. ¿Puede su madre ir al cine esta noche?
Sí, mi madre puede ir esta noche.

5. ¿Pueden sus hermanos ir al cine esta noche?
No, ellos ______________________________

6. ¿Puedes ir a la escuela mañana?
Sí, yo ______________________________

7. ¿Pueden Uds. ir a la corrida de toros el domingo?
Sí, nosotros ______________________________

8. ¿Puede su hermana ir al Parque Chapultepec mañana?
No, ella ______________________________

Vocabulario

no . . . tampoco, not . . . either, neither
celebrar, to celebrate
el **cumpleaños,** birthday

9. ¿Pueden ellos ir al cine esta noche?

Sí, ellos ____

10. ¿Puedes tú trabajar hoy?

Sí, ____

B. *Lectura*

Joaquín Sánchez quiere ir a la corrida de toros, pero no puede ir. Tiene que ir con su familia al Parque Chapultepec. El Parque Chapultepec está en la ciudad de México.

Ramón y Paco, los amigos de Joaquín, son hermanos. Ellos quieren ir a la corrida de toros también. No pueden ir tampoco porque su familia va a celebrar el cumpleaños de su hermana Dorotea.

Dorotea celebra su cumpleaños.

Preguntas

1. ¿Adónde quiere ir Joaquín? ______________________
2. ¿Por qué no puede ir Joaquín a la corrida de toros? ______________________
3. ¿Cuál es el apellido de Joaquín? ______________________
4. ¿Por qué no pueden ir Ramón y Paco? ______________________

   ____

C. *Preguntas personales*

1. ¿Puede Ud. leer un libro en una noche?

   ____

2. ¿Pueden Uds. ir al cine hoy?

   ____

3. ¿Pueden jugar al fútbol sus amigos?

   ____

4. ¿Puede trabajar mañana su padre?

   ____

5. ¿Podéis tomar el almuerzo en la cafetería de la escuela?

   ____

D. *Traduzca Ud. al español:*

1. They can't work. ______________________
2. We can go. ______________________

3. Can your friends go to the bullfight? ______________________________

____

4. Can you *(tú)* go to Chapultepec Park tomorrow? ______________________

____

5. I can't work after school. ______________________________________

E. *Conversación*. You and your classmates take turns asking one another *¿Puede Ud. ir al cine esta noche* (or *mañana*)?

Review Exercises

(Lessons 40–54)

F. Here are some answers. What are the questions?

1. Yo soy alta. ______________________________
2. Mi amigo favorito va a la escuela. ______________________________
3. Llueve mucho en el mes de abril. ______________________________
4. Sí, tengo que trabajar. ______________________________
5. Nosotros tenemos quince años. ______________________________
6. Mis hermanos vuelven a casa a las seis. ______________________________
7. Nieva mucho en el invierno. ______________________________
8. Margarita va a mirar la televisión esta noche. ______________________________

G. Write the form of the verb that goes with the indicated subject.

1. *aprender*

ella ______________________

Uds. ______________________

tú ______________________

nosotros ______________________

2. *escribir*

tú ______________________

vosotros ______________________

nosotros ______________________

él ______________________

3. *comer*

nosotros ______________________

ellos ______________________

yo ______________________

tú ______________________

4. *dormir*

nosotros ______________________

tú ______________________

Ud. ______________________

vosotros ______________________

5. *leer*
   yo ______________________________
   nosotros ______________________
   tú ______________________________
   ellas ___________________________

6. *querer*
   yo ______________________________
   tú ______________________________
   vosotros ______________________
   Uds. ___________________________

7. *fumar*
   vosotros ______________________
   ellos ___________________________
   yo ______________________________
   nosotros ______________________

8. *vivir*
   nosotros ______________________
   ella ____________________________
   vosotros ______________________
   tú ______________________________

Lesson 56

levantarse, *to get up, rise;* **acostarse,** *to go to bed*

TOPIC QUESTION 36A

¿A qué hora se levanta Ud.? At what time do you get up?

present tense of ***levantarse***			
yo	**me levanto**	nosotros	**nos levantamos**
tú	**te levantas**	vosotros	**os levantáis**
Ud. él ella	**se levanta**	Uds. ellos ellas	**se levantan**

A. *Preguntas y respuestas*

Vocabulario
temprano, early
tarde, late

1. ¿A qué hora se levanta Ud.?
Yo me levanto a las siete.

2. ¿A qué hora se levantan Uds.?
Nosotros nos levantamos a las ocho.

3. ¿A qué hora se levanta su padre?
Mi padre se levanta a las seis y media.

4. ¿A qué hora se levanta su madre?
Ella se levanta a las siete.

5. ¿A qué hora se levantan sus hermanos?
Mis hermanos se levantan a las siete.

6. ¿Se levanta temprano su amigo favorito?
No, él no se levanta temprano; se levanta tarde.

7. ¿A qué hora te levantas tú?
Yo ____ de la mañana.

8. ¿A qué hora se levantan tus padres?
Mis padres ____

9. ¿Se levantan temprano tus hermanos?
No, ellos ______________________________

10. ¿A qué hora os levantáis?
______________________________ de la mañana.

B. *Traduzca Ud. al español:*

1. At what time do you *(Uds.)* get up? ______________________________

2. We get up at seven o'clock in the morning (at 7 A.M.). ______________________________
____

3. At what time do your brothers and sisters get up? (brothers and sisters = *hermanos*)
____

4. Do you get up early? *a.* you = *Ud.* ______________________________
b. you = *tú* ______________________________
c. you = *vosotros* ______________________________

5. No, I get up late. ______________________________

TOPIC QUESTION 36B

¿A qué hora se acuesta Ud.?
At what time do you go to bed?

present tense of ***acostarse (ue)***	
yo **me acuesto**	nosotros **nos acostamos**
tú **te acuestas**	vosotros **os acostáis**
Ud. / él / ella } **se acuesta**	Uds. / ellos / ellas } **se acuestan**

C. *Preguntas y respuestas*

1. ¿A qué hora se acuesta Ud.?
Yo me acuesto a las once.

2. ¿A qué hora se acuestan Uds.?
Nosotros nos acostamos a las diez y media.

3. ¿A qué hora se acuestan sus padres?
Mis padres se acuestan a las once.

4. ¿Se acuesta su hermano a las once?
No, mi hermano no se acuesta a las once; se acuesta a las diez.

5. ¿Se acuesta tarde o temprano?
   Él se acuesta temprano.

6. ¿A qué hora te acuestas?
   Yo ____________________

7. ¿Te acuestas tarde o temprano?
   Yo ____________________

8. ¿Se acuestan Uds. tarde?
   No, nosotros ____________________ tarde; ____________________ temprano.

D. *Lectura*

Juan se acuesta a las diez y media de la noche, y se levanta a las seis y media de la mañana. Duerme ocho horas.

El padre de Juan se acuesta a las once y media. A él le gusta ver las noticias en la televisión. Se levanta a las cinco y media. Duerme seis horas.

La madre se acuesta a la una después del programa ''Esta Noche.'' Se levanta a las seis y media. Duerme cinco horas y media.

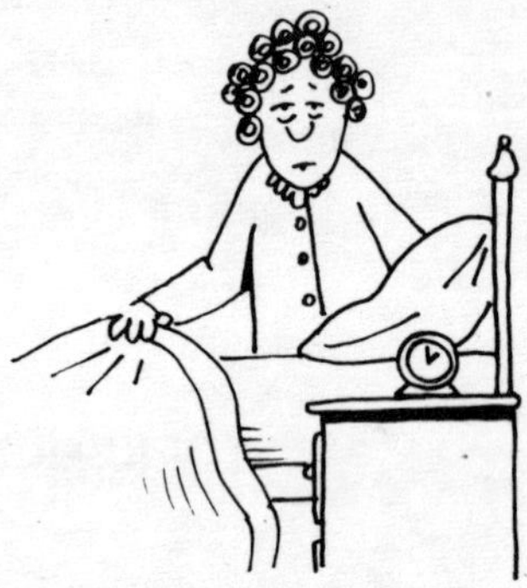

La madre de Juan se acuesta a la una.

Preguntas

1. ¿A qué hora se acuesta Juan? ____________________
2. ¿A qué hora se levanta Juan? ____________________
3. ¿Cuántas horas duerme? ____________________
4. ¿A qué hora se acuesta su padre? ____________________
5. ¿A qué hora se levanta? ____________________
6. ¿Qué le gusta ver en la televisión? ____________________
7. ¿A qué hora se acuesta la madre de Juan? ____________________

E. *Preguntas personales*

1. ¿A qué hora se acuesta Ud.? ____________________
2. ¿A qué hora se levanta su padre? ____________________
3. ¿Cuántas horas duermen sus hermanos? ____________________
4. ¿Cuántas horas duerme Ud.? ____________________
5. ¿A qué hora se acuesta su madre? ____________________

F. *Tema*. Write a composition entitled *¿Cuántas horas duerme Ud.?* Begin your *tema* as shown in the following example:

EXAMPLE:

¿Cuántas horas duerme Ud.?

Yo me llamo Pepe Gómez. Me acuesto a las once y me levanto a las siete. Duermo ocho horas.

Continue with similar paragraphs about the following subjects: *mi padre, mis hermanos,* and *mi amigo favorito* (or *amiga favorita*).

G. *Traduzca Ud. al español:*

1. I go to bed at eleven o'clock.

----

2. At what time do you *(Ud.)* go to bed?

----

3. They get up at eight.

----

4. At what time do your brothers get up?

----

5. I sleep eight hours.

----

6. How many hours does Robert sleep?

----

7. At what time do you *(Uds.)* go to bed?

----

8. We go to bed late.

----

9. We sleep late on Saturdays.

----

10. They don't sleep well.

H. Reflexive Verbs (1)

In **levantarse** and **acostarse,** the **-se** ending is a reflexive pronoun. The reflexive pronouns in English end in *-self.* Here are the Spanish reflexive pronouns and their English meanings:

me	myself
te	yourself
se	yourself, himself, herself, itself, oneself, yourselves, themselves
nos	ourselves
os	yourselves

Thus, *I get up* is expressed in Spanish as "I raise myself": **yo me levanto.**

A verb is called "reflexive" if it is used mostly with reflexive pronouns. Such verbs can be identified in vocabulary lists by the **-se** ending attached to the infinitive. *Note:* When the infinitive is used in a sentence, other endings may be attached, depending on the subject:

¿Quiere Ud. acostar**se**?	Debes levantar**te**.
Sí, quiero acostar**me**.	Vamos a casar**nos**.

Here are some other reflexive verbs. Complete the sentences with the correct reflexive pronoun. (In part *c,* write the entire infinitive.)

1. *llamarse,* to be named ("to call oneself")

a. What are your names?
("How do you call yourselves?") ¿Cómo ________ llaman Uds.?

b. Our names are John and Michael.
("We call ourselves . . .") ________ llamamos Juan y Miguel.

c. Guadalupe is going to call herself Lupe because it's shorter. Guadalupe va a ____________________ Lupe porque es más corto.

2. *lavarse,* to wash oneself, to wash up

a. I wash myself. Yo ________ lavo.

b. We are washing ourselves. Nosotros ________ lavamos.

c. Do you want to wash up? ¿Quieres ____________________?

3. *sentarse (ie),* to sit down ("to seat oneself")

a. you sit down vosotros ________ sentáis

b. they sit down ellos ________ sientan

c. We are going to sit down. Vamos a ________________________.

4. *irse,* to leave, go away*

a. I leave at one o'clock. — Yo ________ voy a la una.

b. Are you going away? — ¿________ van Uds.?

c. You can leave now. — Tú puedes ____________________ ahora.

I. *¿Cómo se sientan tres gorilas a una mesa para dos personas?* To find out how, print the Spanish words suggested by these pictures, subtracting the letters following the minus signs. Then print the remaining letters in the boxes.

 +  + 

____

−  −  + 

____

− E − IO + UL +  − A

____

+ 2 − 

____

ANSWER: ☐☐☐ ☐☐☐☐☐☐☐☐☐☐

*For some verbs, the reflexive pronoun has no separate meaning in English and cannot be translated. Other examples: **acostarse,** to go to bed; **dormirse,** to fall asleep; **quedarse,** to stay, remain.

Lesson 57
don Juan

A. *Lectura*

Vicente Torres asiste a la Universidad de Buenos Aires. Estudia para ingeniero. Es popular con las muchachas porque es guapo y muy simpático. Es moreno y no es muy alto. Tiene una personalidad agradable.

Vicente tiene muchas novias. Sus amigos dicen que él es el don Juan de la universidad.

Vocabulario

estudia para, he is studying to be
el **ingeniero,** engineer
simpático, -a, likeable, nice
moreno, -a, dark (in complexion)
agradable, pleasant, agreeable
don Juan, a legendary Spanish lover whose charm and good looks made him irresistible to women

Preguntas

1. ¿Dónde está Buenos Aires?

____

2. ¿Cuál es el apellido de Vicente?

____

3. ¿Asiste a la escuela superior?

____

4. ¿Para qué estudia?

____

5. ¿Con quiénes es popular Vicente?

____

Vicente Torres es el don Juan de la universidad.

6. ¿Por qué es popular Vicente?

____

7. ¿Es alto Vicente?

____

8. ¿Tiene Vicente muchas novias?

____

9. ¿Qué dicen los amigos de Vicente?

____

10. ¿Quién es el don Juan de la escuela de Ud.?

____

Review Exercises

(Lessons 38–57)

Traduzca Ud. al español:

B. Topic Questions

1. In what city do you live? ________________

2. Do you work? ________________

3. How old are you? ________________

4. At what time do you return home? ________________

5. In what month is it hot? ________________

6. In what season does it snow? ________________

7. What do you do? ________________

8. Do you have to work? ________________

9. What are you going to do tonight? ________________

10. Can you go to the movies tonight? ________________

11. At what time do you get up? ________________

12. At what time do you go to bed? ________________

C. Vocabulary

1. The house has two stories. ________________

2. an example of Spanish architecture ________________

3. I am very cold. ________________

4. It is warm. *(weather)* ________________

5. We are very hungry. ________________

6. How many rooms do you have? ________________

7. We have five rooms and two bathrooms. ________________

8. the kitchen ________________

9. downstairs ________________

10. the dining room ________________

11. upstairs ________________

12. the bedroom ________________

13. the fountain ________________

14. the flowers ________________

15. trees ________________

16. large ________________

17. small ________________

18. cool ________________

19. the weather ________________

20. the season ________________

21. it is raining ________________

22. it's snowing ________________

23. to be able ________________

24. the bullfight ________________

25. to celebrate ________________

26. the birthday ____________________
27. to get up ____________________
28. to go to bed ____________________
29. the news ____________________
30. early ____________________
31. late ____________________
32. the engineer ____________________
33. nice, likeable ____________________
34. dark (complexion) ____________________

D. Write the Spanish names of the months of the year:

____

____

____

E. Write the Spanish names of the four seasons. (Include the definite article.)

1. ____________________ **3.** ____________________
2. ____________________ **4.** ____________________

F. Write the opposite of each word.

1. bajo ____________________
2. feo ____________________
3. delgado ____________________
4. empezar ____________________
5. abajo ____________________
6. pequeño ____________________
7. frío ____________________
8. invierno ____________________
9. primavera ____________________
10. llueve ____________________
11. levantarse ____________________
12. temprano ____________________

G. *Preguntas personales.* Answer in Spanish:

1. ¿Qué hace Ud.? ____________________
2. ¿Qué hace su padre? ____________________
3. ¿Tiene Ud. que trabajar? ____________________
4. ¿Tiene su padre que trabajar? ____________________
5. ¿Va Ud. a mirar la televisión esta noche? ____________________

____

6. ¿Puede Ud. leer una novela en una noche? ____________________

____

7. ¿A qué hora se acuesta Ud.? ____________________
8. ¿A qué hora se levanta Ud.? ____________________
9. ¿Cuántas horas duerme Ud.? ____________________
10. ¿Estudia Ud. para ingeniero? ____________________

H. Reflexive Verbs (2)

Lectura

Son las siete de la mañana. Conchita está en la cama. No quiere levantarse. No quiere ir a la escuela hoy. Por fin se levanta y se viste. Después de lavarse, entra en la cocina y se sienta a la mesa para tomar el desayuno.

Su padre dice: —Buenos días, Conchita. ¿Cómo estás esta mañana?

—No muy bien, papá. Creo que tengo un resfriado. ¿Debo quedarme en casa?

—Sí, claro —contesta su padre—. Puedes quedarte en casa hoy si quieres.

Conchita está muy contenta. ¡Ella no tiene que ir a la escuela! Pero ¿por qué sonríe su papá?

En ese momento, su madre entra en la cocina. Ella dice:

—Buenos días, todos. Conchita, ¿por qué te levantas temprano? ¿Adónde vas?

—Debo ir a la escuela, pero . . .

—Pero hoy es sábado, hija. No hay clases hoy.

—¡Ay, me olvidé! —dice Conchita. —¡Qué bueno! Puedo ir a la playa con mis amigas esta mañana.

Su padre se ríe. —Pero no puedes irte, Conchita. No estás bien. Debes acostarte, ¿no?

—Pero, papá, el sol es bueno para los resfriados, ¿verdad?

—Sí, tienes razón, hija. ¡Especialmente los sábados y domingos!

Y todos se ríen.

Vocabulario

la **cama,** bed
por fin, finally
se viste, gets dressed
entrar en, to enter, come (go) into
la **mesa,** table
creer, to believe, think
claro, of course
contento, -a, glad, happy
sonríe, is smiling
en ese momento, at that moment
no hay clases hoy, there's no school today
me olvidé, I forgot
¡Qué bueno! How nice!
se ríe, laughs
el **sol,** sun(shine)

Preguntas

1. ¿Dónde está Conchita a las siete de la mañana? ______________________________
2. ¿Por qué no quiere levantarse? ______________________________
3. ¿Dónde toma el desayuno? ______________________________
4. ¿Dónde se sienta? ______________________________
5. ¿Por qué está contenta? ______________________________
6. ¿Por qué no tiene Conchita que levantarse temprano hoy? ______________________________
____
7. ¿Adónde quiere ir Conchita por la mañana? ______________________________

Crucigrama (7)

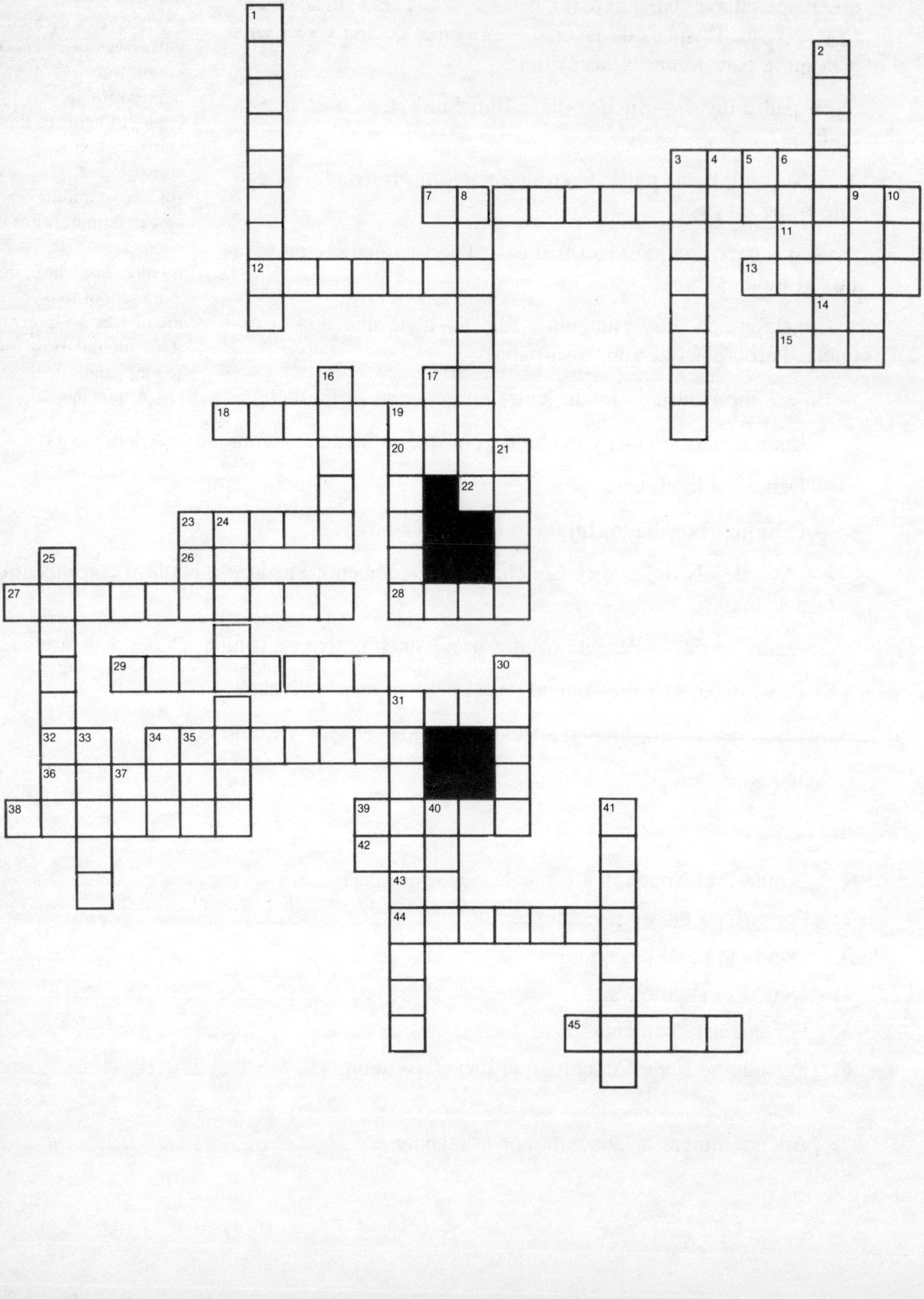

Across

3. *Helen*
7. *the personality*
11. *each*
12. "¿A qué hora se acuesta Ud.?" "Yo me _____ a las once."
13. Si tú quieres sacar buenas notas, _____ estudiar más.
14. the letter that comes after *L* in the Spanish alphabet
15. palabra inglesa que quiere decir *mar* u *océano*
17. *He's at school* = Está en _____ escuela.
18. *to celebrate*
20. "¿Cómo _____ Ud.?" "Muy bien, gracias."
22. infinitive ending
23. *to do, to make*
26. soy / estoy } = *I* _____
27. *He doesn't want to get up* = No quiere _____.
28. El profesor dice: "No escriban Uds. nada; esto es un examen _____."
29. *To have to* = _____ _____.
31. *to go away*
32. iniciales de Anita Jiménez
34. Ramón asiste a la escuela y sus padres _____ en una fábrica.
36. Los coches no son usados; son coches _____.
38. *column*
39. *to live*
42. *Anne*
43. Es alta = *She* _____ *tall.*
44. ¿Cómo se dice *esta noche* en inglés?
45. *late*

Down

1. Roberto es guapo y simpático; por eso, es muy popular con las _____.
2. *A pleasant day* = un día _____.
3. ¿Qué quiere decir *ingeniero*?
4. artículo definido femenino
5. artículo definido masculino
6. Es muy simpática = *She's very* _____.
8. "No puedo leer más; tengo mucho sueño." "¿Quieres _____?"
9. nombre de muchacha
10. ¿Cómo se dice *that* en alemán?
16. *to drink*
17. forma plural del artículo definido
19. *review*
21. *tree*
23. ¿Cómo se dice *sombrero* en inglés?
24. Él es médico y su esposa es _____ _____ _____.
25. No es tarde; es _____.
30. *to ask for*
31. In English, the _____ form of the verb usually begins with *to*.
33. el séptimo mes del año
34. iniciales de Tomasina Váldez Mendoza
35. *rum*
37. El nombre de un continente empieza con estas dos letras.
39. "¿Adónde _____ Ud. ahora?" "Yo voy a casa."
40. *A glass of milk* = un _____ de leche.
41. ¿Qué quiere decir *cumpleaños*?

Lesson 58

dar, *to give;* INDIRECT OBJECT PRONOUNS; CLARIFYING PHRASES

TOPIC QUESTION 37 | **¿Quién le da dinero a Ud.?** Who gives you money?

present tense of ***dar***	
yo **doy**	nosotros **damos**
tú **das**	vosotros **dais**
Ud. / él / ella } **da**	Uds. / ellos / ellas } **dan**

A. *Preguntas y respuestas*

Vocabulario
el **patrón,** employer, boss
mostrar (ue), to show
la **foto,** photo, snapshot
cada, each, every

1. ¿Quién le da dinero?
   Mi padre me da dinero.
2. Y María, ¿quién le da dinero *a Ud.*?
   Mi madre me da dinero a mí.
3. ¿Quién les da dinero?
   Nuestra madre nos da dinero.
4. Y muchachos, ¿quién les da dinero *a Uds.*?
   Nuestro padre nos da dinero a nosotros.
5. ¿Quién les da dinero a sus hermanos?
   Mi padre les da dinero a mis hermanos.
6. Y ¿quién les da dinero a sus amigos?
   Sus padres ______ dan dinero a mis amigos.
7. ¿Quién le da dinero a su padre?
   Su patrón le da dinero.
8. ¿Quién le da dinero a su hermano?
   Mi hermana mayor ______________________________ a él.
9. Juan, ¿quién te da dinero?
   Mi padre ______________________________.

Su madre le da dinero.

10. Y María, ¿quién te da dinero a ti?
Mi madre me da dinero.

11. ¿Le da su padre dinero a Ud.?
No, él no me da dinero a mí; le da dinero a él.

12. ¿Les da dinero a Uds.?
No, él no ________ da dinero a nosotros;
él ________ da dinero a ellas.

B. Indirect Object Pronouns

me	(to) me	**nos**	(to) us
te	(to) you	**os**	(to) you, *pl.*
le	(to) you	**les**	(to) you, *pl.*
	(to) him		(to) them
	(to) her		
	(to) it		

You have already learned how to use these pronouns with the verb **gustar** (Lessons 34 and 35).

An indirect object answers the question *to whom*? For example:

I give John the books.
I give the books *to whom*?
Answer: John.

Therefore, *John* is the indirect object of the verb *give*.

Let us replace *John* with a pronoun: "I give *him* the books." In Spanish, this sentence becomes

Yo le doy los libros.

Notice that, unlike English, the object pronoun comes *before* the verb.

Complete the Spanish sentences with the correct pronoun:

1. She gives me the book.	Ella ________ da el libro.
2. I give her the book.	Yo ________ doy el libro.
3. You give him the book.	Ud. ________ da el libro.
4. They give us the book.	Ellos ________ dan el libro.
5. We give them the book.	Nosotras ________ damos el libro.

Choose the correct way to translate *you* into Spanish:

6. Si queréis leer, ________ doy las revistas.

7. Si Ud. quiere leer, ________ doy el periódico.

8. Si tú quieres leer, ________ doy un libro interesante.
9. Si Uds. quieren leer, ________ doy los periódicos.
10. Si ella quiere leer, ____________ puede darle una revista.

C. Clarifying Phrases

As we saw, the pronouns **le** and **les** have several possible meanings. Thus, for the sake of emphasis or greater clarity, the following phrases may be added to the sentence when **le** or **les** is used:

le doy los libros	**a Ud.**	(to) you
	a él	(to) him
	a ella	(to) her
les doy el dinero	**a Uds.**	(to) you, *pl.*
	a ellos	(to) them, *m.*
	a ellas	(to) them, *f.*

Add a clarifying phrase in each sentence. The meaning of *le* or *les* is shown in parentheses:

1. (to her) ¿Le da Ud. dinero ____________________?
2. (to them, *f.*) ¿Les muestra Ud. las fotos ____________________?
3. (to him) Su madre no le da dinero ____________________.
4. (to you) ¿No le dan las revistas ____________________?
5. (to you) Yo les doy dinero ____________________.

The object pronouns **me, te, nos,** and **os** never need clarification because each of them has only one meaning, but the following phrases may be added for emphasis:

a mí **a ti** **a nosotros(-as)** **a vosotros(-as)**

Complete the Spanish sentences with phrases that add emphasis to the object pronouns:

6. You give *him* money but you never give *me* any money.
   Usted le da dinero ________________ pero nunca me da dinero ________________.
7. She shows the photos to you but not to us.
   Ella te muestra las fotos ________________ pero no nos muestra las fotos ____________________.
8. Why doesn't she show *you* the photos?
   ¿Por qué no os muestra las fotos ____________________?

D. The Redundant Object Pronoun

On page 231, we used the sentence *I give John the books* to show an example of an indirect object in English. Since we were discussing object *pronouns,* we changed the sentence to *I give him the books,* which becomes in Spanish:

Yo **le** doy los libros.

To translate the original sentence, simply add **a Juan**:

Yo **le** doy los libros **a Juan.**

Here are other examples:

She gives her daughter the money = She gives the money to her daughter.
Ella **le** da el dinero **a su hija.**

Mary shows her friends the photos = Mary shows the photos to her friends.
María **les** muestra las fotos **a sus amigas.**

In Spanish sentences like these, the pronouns **le** and **les** are still used but cannot be translated into English. They are called "redundant" because they add nothing to the meaning of the sentence.

Complete the Spanish sentences with a redundant pronoun:

1. We give the boys magazines. — Nosotros ________ damos revistas a los muchachos.
2. Do you give the teacher your compositions? — ¿________ dan Uds. sus temas a la profesora?
3. The parents give their children money. — Los padres ________ dan dinero a sus hijos.
4. They show Charlie the new car. — Ellos ________ muestran el nuevo coche a Carlitos.

E. *Lectura*

Me llamo Enrique. Yo no trabajo. Yo voy a la escuela. Mi madre me da dinero. Ella me da veinte y cinco pesos cada semana.

Mi hermano José trabaja. Mi madre no le da dinero a él.

Mi hermana Rosita trabaja también. Mi madre no le da dinero a ella.

Mis hermanos Pablo y Margarita no trabajan. Mis padres les dan dinero a ellos. Ellos les dan quince pesos cada semana.

Mi padre trabaja. Su patrón le da dinero a mi padre.

Preguntas

1. ¿Trabaja Enrique? ________________________________
2. ¿Qué hace Enrique? ________________________________
3. ¿Quién le da dinero a él? ________________________________
4. ¿Cuánto dinero le da su madre? ________________________________
5. ¿Trabaja José? ________________________________
6. ¿Le da dinero su madre? ________________________________
7. ¿Trabajan Pablo y Margarita? ________________________________

8. ¿Quiénes les dan dinero? ______________________________

9. ¿Quién le da dinero al padre? ______________________________

F. *Preguntas personales*

1. ¿Le dan sus padres dinero? ______________________________

2. ¿Les da su profesor(-ra) muchas tareas a Uds.? ______________________________

____

3. ¿Quién les da dinero a sus hermanos? ______________________________

4. ¿Les das dinero a tus amigos? ______________________________

G. *Traduzca Ud. al español:*

1. My parents give me money every week. ______________________________

____

2. Do you *(tú)* give your sister money? Does she give *you* money? ______________

____

3. I give you money. (you, *formal pl.*) ______________________________

4. My parents give them money. ______________________________

5. My parents give my brothers money. ______________________________

6. He gives us the books. ______________________________

7. How much money do they give *you* (*formal sing.*)? ______________________________

____

8. Henry shows his teachers the book. ______________________________

9. Do you *(Ud.)* show your friends the new car? ______________________________

10. She doesn't give her mother money. ______________________________

H. *Conversación.* You and your classmates take turns asking one another these questions:

¿Quién le da dinero a Ud.?
¿Quién les da dinero a Uds.?
¿Quién le da dinero a su hermano (or *hermana*)?

If you are not sure about how to form your replies, refer to pages 230–231.

Review Exercise

(Lessons 43–58)

I. *Frases revueltas*. Unscramble the sentences:

1. notas saco siempre buenas yo .

---

2. ¿ vuelve hora ? qué a Ud. casa a

---

3. televisión nosotros noche a vamos esta mirar la .

---

4. sus ¿ qué hermanos hacen ?

---

5. quince tiene mi años hermano .

---

6. mes hace ? en calor qué ¿

---

7. al yo noche cine puedo no ir esta .

---

8. en mi fábrica trabaja padre una .

---

9. tiene ? cuántos madre su años ¿

---

10. en mucho invierno nieva el .

---

11. que ? su tiene padre trabajar ¿

---

12. tres vuelven hermanos casa a las a y mis media .

---

13. llueve ? en estación ¿ qué mucho

---

14. a ? su hacer qué ¿ esta va amigo noche favorito

---

15. que yo trabajar tengo no .

---

16. acuesta las se menos mi cuarto padre a once .

---

17. nos los no nosotros levantamos sábados temprano .

----

18. al ¿ puede Ud. cine ? noche esta ir

----

19. su bajo ¿ padre alto ? es o

----

20. frío mes hace en enero de el .

Lesson 59
el peso mexicano

A. *Lectura*

El "dólar" mexicano se llama el *peso*. Si Ud. cambia un dólar norteamericano por pesos, Ud. recibe veinte pesos mexicanos.

El tipo de cambio hoy es veinte pesos en el banco y un poco menos en los hoteles.

Vocabulario

el **dólar,** dollar
cambiar, to change, exchange
por, for (= in exchange for)
recibir, to receive
el **tipo de cambio,** rate of exchange (how much you get for a dollar)
poco, little
menos, less
costar (ue), to cost
valer, to be worth; **¿cuánto vale?** how much is it worth (does it cost)?

Preguntas

1. ¿Cómo se llama el "dólar" mexicano?

____

2. ¿Cuál es el tipo de cambio?

____

3. ¿Cuántos pesos recibe Ud. por diez dólares norteamericanos?

____

4. ¿Dónde es menos el tipo de cambio?

____

5. ¿Qué quiere decir *tipo de cambio*?

____

6. Una camisa cuesta 100 pesos. ¿Cuánto vale la camisa en dólares?

____

B. *Diálogo*. In the following dialogue, play the role of Carlos. Write his responses in the blanks.

Esteban y Carlos asisten a una escuela superior en Nueva York. Esteban invita a Carlos a jugar al béisbol con sus amigos.

ESTEBAN: Mis amigos y yo vamos a jugar al béisbol el domingo. ¿Quieres jugar con nosotros?

CARLOS: ____

ESTEBAN: Jugamos en Central Park. Empezamos a jugar a las nueve de la mañana.

CARLOS: ____

ESTEBAN: Si no te gusta levantarte temprano, puedes venir más tarde. Tenemos que estar en el parque temprano si queremos hallar una cancha desocupada. ¿A qué hora vienes?

CARLOS: ____

ESTEBAN: Vamos a jugar hasta la una, y luego tomamos el almuerzo.

CARLOS: ____

ESTEBAN: Podemos comer en un restaurante cerca del parque.

CARLOS: ____

ESTEBAN: Si llueve, claro, no podemos jugar. Si hace mal tiempo, ¿quieres ir al cine con nosotros?

CARLOS: ____

Vocabulario

invitar, to invite
hallar, to find
la **cancha,** (tennis) court, (baseball) field, etc.
desocupado, -a, unoccupied, free, available
está bien, all right, O.K.

present tense of ***venir,*** *to come*	
vengo	**venimos**
vienes	**venís**
viene	**vienen**

Lesson 60

ver, *to see;* Direct Object Pronouns; the "Personal **a**"

TOPIC QUESTION 38

¿A quién ve Ud. todos los días? Whom do you see every day?

present tense of ***ver***	
yo **veo**	nosotros **vemos**
tú **ves**	vosotros **veis**
Ud. / él / ella } **ve**	Uds. / ellos / ellas } **ven**

A. *Preguntas y respuestas*

1. ¿A quién ve Ud. todos los días?
Yo veo a mi amigo favorito.
¿Dónde lo ve Ud.?
Yo lo veo en la escuela.

2. ¿A quién ven Uds. todos los días?
Vemos a la señora Martínez.
¿Dónde la ven Uds.?
La vemos en la clase de español.

3. ¿A quiénes ven Uds. todos los días?
Vemos a nuestros profesores.
¿Dónde los ven Uds.?
Los vemos en la escuela.

4. ¿A quiénes ven sus padres todos los días?
Ellos nos ven a nosotros.
¿Cuándo los ven a Uds.?
Ellos nos ven cuando estamos en casa.

5. ¿A quién ves tú todos los días?
Yo ____

¿Dónde lo/la ves? (Cross out the inappropriate pronoun.)
Yo ___________________ en la escuela.

Vocabulario

todos los días, every day
la **clase de español,** Spanish class
juntos, -as, together
después de, after
la **cena,** supper
las **noticias,** news
el **partido,** game (= match)
luego, then
escuchar, to listen (to)
saludar, to greet

6. ¿A quiénes ven tus hermanos todos los días?

   Mis hermanos ____

   ¿Dónde los/las ven ellos?

   ______________________________ en casa.

B. *Lectura*

Andrés está en la escuela. Es mediodía, la hora del almuerzo. Andrés ve a su amigo Alberto. Lo saluda y lo invita a comer con él en la cafetería. Luego Andrés ve a su amiga Susana y la invita a ella también. Los tres amigos toman el almuerzo juntos. Siempre lo toman a mediodía.

Alberto y Susana son los amigos favoritos de Andrés. Él los ve en la escuela todos los días.

A Susana le gusta mirar la televisión. Ella y su hermano Pablo la miran después de la cena. A ella le gusta ver las noticias. Las ve todas las noches. Pablo prefiere los partidos de fútbol. Los ve los sábados o los domingos.

Preguntas

1. ¿A quiénes invita Andrés a comer con él? ______________________________
2. ¿A qué hora toman el almuerzo? ______________________________
3. ¿Dónde lo toman? ______________________________
4. ¿Qué le gusta a Susana hacer? ______________________________
5. ¿Cuándo la mira ella? ______________________________
6. ¿Qué prefiere ver Pablo? ______________________________
7. ¿Cuándo los ve? ______________________________

C. Direct Object Pronouns

me	me	**nos**	us
te	you	**os**	you, *pl.*
***lo**	you, *m.* him it, *m.*	**los**	you, *m. pl.* them
la	you, *f.* her it, *f.*	**las**	you, *f. pl.* them, *f.*

You as direct object is **lo** or **la** when speaking to a person addressed as **Ud.**

*In Spain, **le** is used instead of **lo,** except when **lo** = *it*.

Note the difference between direct and indirect objects:

I see *you*.	I give *you* the books.
Yo **lo** veo *or* **la** veo.	Yo **le** doy los libros.
I see *her*.	I give *her* the books.
Yo **la** veo.	Yo **le** doy los libros.

Complete the Spanish sentences with the correct object pronouns:

1. I see him and I give him the books.	Yo ________ veo y ________ doy los libros.
2. She sees them *(m.)* and gives them the books.	Ella ________ ve y ________ da los libros.
3. You see them *(f.)* and give them the books.	Uds. ________ ven y ________ dan los libros.
4. They see me and give me the books.	Ellos ________ ven y ________ dan los libros.
5. "Do you see the books?"	—¿Ve Ud. los libros?
"No, I don't see them."	—No, yo no ________ veo.
6. "Do you see the magazine?"	—¿Ves la revista?
"No, I don't see it."	—No, yo no ________ veo.
7. "Do you see Mary?"	—¿Ven Uds. a María?
"Yes, we see her."	—Sí, ________ vemos.
8. We show her the photos.	________ mostramos las fotos.
9. They see us and show us the photos.	Ellos ________ ven y ________ muestran las fotos.

Choose the object pronouns that correspond to the subject pronoun in parentheses:

10. (Uds., *f.*) We see you and give you the books.	________ vemos y ________ damos los libros.
11. (Ud., *m.*) He sees you and gives you the books.	Él ________ ve y ________ da los libros.
12. (tú) He sees you and gives you the books.	Él ________ ve y ________ da los libros.
13. (vosotras) They see you and give you the books.	Ellos ________ ven y ________ dan los libros.
14. (Ud., *f.*) She sees you and shows you the photos.	Ella ________ ve y ________ muestra las fotos.

D. Clarifying Phrases

When one of the object pronouns **lo, la, los,** and **las** is used in a sentence, its meaning may not be clear. For example, since **la** can mean either *you (f.)* or *her,* how would you translate into Spanish "We are inviting *you* but we are not inviting *her*"? In such cases, the clarifying phrases displayed on page 232 may also be used with the direct object pronouns for emphasis or greater clarity.

La invitamos **a Ud.** pero no **la** invitamos **a ella.**

Practice reading aloud the following *preguntas y respuestas*. Supply the missing direct object pronouns or clarifying phrases:

1. ¿Me ve Ud. los lunes?
   Sí, señor, lo veo a Ud. los lunes.
2. ¿Nos ve Ud. los martes?
   Sí, señores, los veo a Uds. los martes.
3. ¿Me ve Ud. los jueves?
   Sí, señora, la veo ______________ los jueves.
4. ¿Nos ve Ud. los miércoles?
   Sí, señoritas, ________ veo a Uds. los miércoles.
5. ¿Tiene Ud. el libro?
   Sí, yo lo tengo.
6. ¿Tiene Ud. los libros?
   Sí, yo ________ tengo.
7. ¿Escribe Ud. la lección?
   Sí, yo ________ escribo.
8. ¿Escribe Ud. las lecciones?
   Sí, yo las escribo.
9. ¿________ ve Ud. a él?
   Sí, yo lo veo ______________.
10. ¿La ve Ud. a ella?
    Sí, yo la veo ______________.
11. ¿________ ve Ud. a ellos?
    No, yo no los veo ________________.
12. ¿Las ven Uds. a ellas?
    No, no ________ vemos ______________.

E. The "Personal **a**"

The direct object of a verb may be a thing or a person: "I see *the house*"; "I see *John*." If the direct object is a noun that refers to *persons,* the preposition **a** must precede it in Spanish:

—¿**A** quién ve Ud.?	—¿**A** quiénes ve Ud.?
—Yo veo **a** Juan.	—Yo veo **a** mis amigos.

This preposition is called the "personal **a**." It has no meaning in English and cannot be translated.

In the following sentences, add a personal **a** wherever necessary. If the sentence is complete without it, leave the line blank:

1. Miramos ________ las fotos.
2. Miramos ________ la profesora.
3. Escucho ________ la radio.
4. Escucho ________ mi madre.
5. Vemos ________ las noticias en la televisión.
6. Vemos ________ nuestros actores favoritos en la televisión.
7. Yo amo ________ la música.
8. Yo amo ________ Gilberto.

F. *Traduzca Ud. al español:*

1. (them = *las lecciones*) I write them. ________________
2. (it = *el libro*) I read it. ________________
3. (it = *la lección*) He studies it. ________________
4. (them = *los libros*) They read them. ________________
5. They see you on Tuesdays, Mr. Rodríguez. ________________
____
6. He sees me tomorrow. ________________
7. I see you on Saturdays, *señores*. ________________
8. He sees you on Sundays, *señora*. ________________
9. They see you on Mondays, *señoras*. ________________

Translate #10 and #11 into Spanish sentences that are not exactly the same. (You = *Ud.* in both sentences.)

10. Do you see him on Tuesdays? ________________
11. Do you see *him* on Tuesdays? ________________
12. What do they see? ________________
13. They see the cars. ________________
14. Whom do they see? ________________
15. They see the teachers. ________________
16. He greets Mary. ________________
17. He greets her and shows her the book. ________________
18. You see *them,* gentlemen, but *they* don't see *you*. ________________
____

19. "When do you have supper?" "I have it at seven o'clock." ________________

____

20. *a.* They don't see us tomorrow. ______________________________________

b. They don't see *us* tomorrow. ______________________________________

G. *Conversación.* You and your classmates take turns asking one another the following questions. In your answers, replace a part of the question with a direct object pronoun.

EXAMPLE: —¿Ve Ud. *la mesa del profesor*?
—Sí, yo *la* veo.

1. ¿Ve Ud. a sus padres todos los días?
2. ¿Ve Ud. a sus amigos todos los días?
3. ¿Estudia Ud. sus lecciones todas las noches?
4. ¿Toma Ud. el desayuno a las seis?
5. ¿Mira Ud. la televisión todas las noches?
6. ¿Tiene Ud. mi lápiz?
7. ¿Tiene Ud. mi pluma?
8. ¿Tiene Ud. mis libros?
9. ¿Tiene Ud. mis plumas?
10. *Pregunta libre.* Make up a question of your own.

Review Exercise

(Commands)

H. Here are Professor Caramba's horoscopes for next Wednesday. On the line below the last horoscope, write the infinitive forms of the eight verbs that the Professor used.

ACUARIO ....No fumen Uds. hoy.
PISCIS ....Trabajen Uds. mucho.
ARIES ....Vayan Uds. al cine hoy.
TAURO ....Hagan Uds. sus lecciones.
GÉMINIS ....No lleguen Uds. tarde a casa esta noche.
CÁNCER ....Vivan Uds. bien hoy.
LEO ....Vean Uds. los animales en el parque zoológico.
VIRGO ....No fumen Uds. un cigarro hoy.
LIBRA ....No vean Uds. a sus profesores hoy.
ESCORPIO ......No trabajen Uds. hoy.
SAGITARIO .....No beban Uds. nada hoy.
CAPRICORNIO ...No hagan sus lecciones hoy.

____

Lesson 61

necesitar, *to need;* **poner,** *to put, to put on*

TOPIC QUESTION 39

¿Necesita Ud. dinero? Do you need money?

present tense of ***necesitar***	
yo **necesito**	nosotros **necesitamos**
tú **necesitas**	vosotros **necesitáis**
Ud. / él / ella } **necesita**	Uds. / ellos / ellas } **necesitan**

A. *Preguntas y respuestas*

1. ¿Necesita Ud. dinero?
   Sí, yo necesito dinero.
   ¿Para qué lo necesita?
   Lo necesito para comprar un cuaderno.

2. ¿Necesitan Uds. dinero?
   Sí, nosotros necesitamos dinero.
   ¿Para qué lo necesitan?
   Lo necesitamos para comprar discos.

3. ¿Necesitan sus padres dinero?
   Sí, mis padres necesitan dinero.
   ¿Para qué lo necesitan?
   Lo necesitan para pagar el alquiler.

4. ¿Necesita dinero su amiga favorita?
   No, ella no necesita dinero.

5. ¿Necesitas tú dinero?
   Sí, yo ______________________________
   ¿Para qué lo necesitas?
   Yo ______________________________

6. ¿Necesita Ud. estudiar?
   Sí, yo necesito estudiar.

7. ¿Necesitan Uds. estudiar?
   Sí, ______________________________

Vocabulario

¿para qué? why? (= what for? for what purpose?)
comprar, to buy
el **cuaderno,** notebook
el **disco,** (phonograph) record

8. ¿Necesitan trabajar sus hermanos?
No, mis hermanos no necesitan trabajar.

9. ¿Quién necesita trabajar?
____

10. ¿Por qué necesita trabajar su padre?
Mi padre ____

B. *Traduzca Ud. al español:*

1. Do they need money? ________________________
2. Yes, they need it. ________________________
3. What do they need it for? ________________________
4. They need it to pay the rent. ________________________
5. Do you *(tú)* need the books? ________________________
6. No, I don't need them. ________________________
7. Do you *(Uds.)* need to study? ________________________
8. No, we don't need to study. ________________________
9. She needs to work. ________________________

TOPIC QUESTION 40

¿Pone Ud. discos mientras lee?
Do you put on (play) records while you read?

present tense of ***poner***	
yo **pongo**	nosotros **ponemos**
tú **pones**	vosotros **ponéis**
Ud. / él / ella **pone**	Uds. / ellos / ellas **ponen**

C. *Preguntas y respuestas*

1. ¿Pone Ud. discos mientras lee?
Sí, yo pongo discos mientras leo.

2. ¿Ponen Uds. discos mientras leen?
No, nosotros no ponemos discos mientras
__________________.

3. ¿Pone su padre discos mientras lee?
No, mi padre no pone discos mientras __________________.

Vocabulario

poner un disco, to put on (play) a record
poner la radio, to turn on the radio
poner la televisión, to turn on the TV set
mientras, while
algunas veces, sometimes
se lo dan (a ella), give it to her

4. ¿Pone su hermana discos mientras lee?
   No, ella pone la radio.

5. ¿Ponen sus amigos discos mientras leen?
   No, ellos ponen la televisión.

6. ¿Pones tú discos mientras lees?
   No, yo ________________________________
   mientras leo.

7. ¿Qué ponen tus amigos?
   Mis amigos ______________________________.

Mi padre pone discos mientras lee.

D. *Lectura*

Linda va a la escuela a las siete y media de la mañana y vuelve a casa a las tres de la tarde. Después de la cena, estudia sus lecciones y las escribe. Mientras estudia, pone unos discos.

Algunas veces Linda va al cine con su amiga Elena. Si necesita dinero, sus padres se* lo dan a ella.

Los hermanos de Linda vuelven a casa a las seis y su padre vuelve a las siete. A las ocho su padre pone la televisión para ver las noticias.

Preguntas

1. ¿A qué hora va Linda a la escuela? ______________________________________
2. ¿A qué hora vuelve a casa? ____
3. ¿Cómo se dice *supper* en español? _______________________________________
4. ¿Qué hace Linda mientras estudia? _______________________________________
5. ¿Con quién va Linda al cine? ____
6. Si Linda necesita dinero, ¿quiénes se lo dan? ___________________________
7. ¿A qué hora vuelven sus hermanos a casa? ___________________________
8. ¿A qué hora vuelve su padre? ____
9. ¿A qué hora pone su padre la televisión? ___________________________
10. ¿Para qué la pone? ____

E. *Preguntas personales*

1. ¿A qué hora vuelve Ud. a casa? ____
2. ¿Prefiere su padre poner discos o la televisión? ______________________
   ____
3. ¿Pone Ud. discos mientras estudia? _____________________________________

---

*See Lesson 62.

4. ¿Ponen Uds. la radio algunas veces? ________________________________
5. ¿Necesitan sus padres dinero? ________________________________
6. ¿A qué hora pone Ud. la televisión? ________________________________
7. ¿La pone Ud. todas las noches? ________________________________
8. ¿Qué necesita Ud.? ________________________________
9. ¿Qué necesita Ud. hacer? ________________________________

F. *Traduzca Ud. al español:*

1. I return home at four o'clock. ________________________________
2. Do you *(Uds.)* need the magazines? ________________________________
   No, we don't need them. ________________________________
3. Do you *(tú)* need to do your homework? ________________________________
4. They play records while they study. ________________________________
5. Do her parents give her money? ________________________________
6. I don't put on records. ________________________________
7. We turn on the TV set. ________________________________
8. If we need money, our parents give it to us *(nos lo dan)*. ________________________________
   ____
9. (them = *las lecciones*) Do you *(tú)* write them? ________________________________

G. *Conversación.* You and your classmates take turns asking one another the following questions:

1. ¿Necesita Ud. dinero? ¿Para qué lo necesita?
2. ¿Pone Ud. discos mientras lee?
3. ¿Cuándo pone Ud. la televisión?
4. ¿Necesita Ud. estudiar todas las noches?

In your replies, use an object pronoun whenever you can.

EXAMPLE: —¿Pone Ud. discos mientras lee?
—No, yo *los* pongo mientras escribo mis lecciones.

Review Exercise

(Lessons 49–56)

H. *Vocabulario.* Complete the sentences:

1. La casa de la señora Ibáñez es un ejemplo de la ___________________ española.
2. En el centro de la casa española hay un ___________________.
3. Nosotros comemos en el comedor y en la ___________________.
4. Nosotros nos lavamos en el _______________ de _______________.
5. Los dormitorios no están abajo. Están ___________________.
6. Hace frío en el ___________________.
7. Hace ___________________ en el verano.
8. Llueve mucho en la _______________________.
9. Nieva mucho en el _____________________.
10. Yo voy a estudiar _________________ noche.
11. Nosotros vamos a la ___________________ de toros los domingos.
12. Vamos a ___________________ el cumpleaños de mi hermano.
13. Yo me levanto a las siete y me ___________________ a las once.
14. Me levanto temprano los lunes. Me levanto _______________ los domingos.

COGNATES (8)

I. Read these words aloud and write an English cognate for each of them:

1. alfabeto _______________________
2. astronauta _____________________
3. anestésico _____________________
4. aviación _______________________
5. bomba atómica _________________
6. cafeína _______________________
7. caloría _______________________
8. cristiano _____________________
9. delicado _______________________
10. desastre _______________________
11. diálogo _______________________
12. dieta _________________________
13. disciplina _____________________
14. electricista ____________________
15. eléctrico _______________________
16. electrónico _____________________
17. epidemia _______________________
18. esquiar _________________________
19. eternidad _______________________
20. etiqueta ________________________
21. filósofo ________________________
22. fisiología ______________________
23. garantizar ______________________
24. helicóptero ____________________
25. homicidio ______________________
26. internacional __________________
27. japonés ________________________
28. justicia ________________________

29. justo ____________________
30. kilómetro ____________________
31. líquido ____________________
32. luna ____________________
33. lunático ____________________
34. mayonesa ____________________
35. mercurio ____________________
36. microscopio ____________________
37. molécula ____________________
38. monólogo ____________________
39. monótono ____________________
40. músculo ____________________
41. nervioso ____________________
42. optimismo ____________________
43. paréntesis ____________________
44. plataforma ____________________
45. selección ____________________
46. sermón ____________________
47. sílaba ____________________
48. teoría ____________________
49. último ____________________
50. vitamina ____________________

Lesson 62

devolver, *to return, give back;* Direct and Indirect Object Pronouns Used Together

A. **Devolver (ue)** is conjugated in the same way as **volver:**

devuelvo	**devolvemos**
devuelves	**devolvéis**
devuelve	**devuelven**

B. *Lectura*

El señor Mendoza es nuestro profesor de español. En la clase, nos explica la nueva lección. Mientras nos la explica, la escribimos en nuestros cuadernos.

El profesor ve que Felipe no escribe nada.

—¿Por qué no escribe Ud. la lección? —le pregunta.

—No tengo lápiz —contesta Felipe.

El Sr. Mendoza saca un lápiz del bolsillo y se lo da.

—Es mi lápiz favorito —le dice a Felipe—. ¿Cuándo me lo devuelve Ud.?

—Se lo devuelvo mañana —contesta Felipe.

—Bueno —dice el profesor. Explica la lección otra vez.

Pero Felipe todavía no escribe nada.

—Ya tiene Ud. lápiz. ¿Por qué no escribe Ud.?

—No tengo cuaderno —contesta Felipe.

Vocabulario

explicar, to explain
no . . . nada, nothing, not . . . anything
preguntar, to ask
contestar, to answer
sacar, to take out
del bolsillo, from his pocket
otra vez, again
ya, already
el **alumno**, la **alumna** } pupil, student
el **cuaderno,** notebook

Preguntas

1. ¿Qué les explica el Sr. Mendoza a los alumnos? ______________________________
2. Mientras se la explica, ¿qué hacen los alumnos? ______________________________
3. ¿Qué le da el profesor a Felipe? ______________________________
4. ¿Por qué se lo da? ______________________________
5. ¿Por qué no usa Felipe el lápiz? ______________________________

C. Direct and Indirect Object Pronouns Used Together

A verb may have both a direct and an indirect object, as in the sentence "He gives me the books." In this sentence, the direct object is *the books,* the indirect object is *me*. (Test this by saying: He gives *what?* The books. *To whom?* me.) If we substitute a pronoun for *the books,* the sentence becomes "He gives them to me":

he gives them	**los** da
to me	**me**

In Spanish, the indirect object comes first:

He gives them to me.	**Me los** da.

Here are other examples. Write the missing parts of the incomplete sentences:

1. I show you the photo.	Te muestro la foto.
I show *it to you*.	*Te la* muestro.
2. They give us the money.	Nos dan el dinero.
They give it to us.	________________ dan.
3. We give you the flowers.	Os damos las flores.
We give them to you.	________________ damos.
4. She returns the magazine to me.	Me devuelve la revista.
She returns it to me.	________________ devuelve.
5. Does he show you his room?	¿Te muestra su cuarto?
Does he show it to you?	¿________________ muestra?

D. Combining **le** or **les** with a Direct Object Pronoun

In "I give her the book," if we replace *the book* with a pronoun, the sentence becomes "I give it to her":

I give it	**lo** doy
to her	**le**

Spanish does not permit combinations like "le lo." If both object pronouns begin with the letter *l,* the indirect object pronoun changes from **le** or **les** to **se**:

I give it to her.	**Se lo** doy.

Here are other examples. Write the missing parts of the incomplete sentences:

1. We give her the flowers.	Le damos las flores.
We give *them to her*.	*Se las* damos.
2. You give him the notebook.	Ud. le da el cuaderno.
You give *it to him*.	Ud. *se lo* da.
3. She gives them the pencils.	Ella les da los lápices.
She gives them to them.	Ella ____________ da.

4. I give him back the photos. — Le devuelvo las fotos.
   I give them back to him. — ____________ devuelvo.
5. Don't you show her your work? — ¿No le muestra Ud. su trabajo?
   Don't you show it to her? — ¿No ____________ muestra Ud.?

E. Clarifying Phrases

Since **se** in expressions like **se lo doy** has several possible meanings, one of the clarifying phrases shown on page 232 may be added for emphasis or greater clarity:

No **se** lo doy **a Ud.**; **se** lo doy **a ella**. — I'm not giving it to *you*; I'm giving it to *her*.

Similar phrases may be added when using **me, te, nos,** or **os,** if emphasis is desired:

No **me** la muestra **a mí**; **te** la muestra **a ti**. — She isn't showing it to *me*; she is showing it to *you*.

Complete each sentence with the appropriate clarifying phrases:

1. (it = *el libro*)
   I'm showing it to you *(pl.)*; I'm not showing it to them.
   Se lo muestro ________________; no se lo muestro ____________________.
2. (them = *las fotos*)
   We show them to him, but sometimes we show them to her.
   Se las mostramos ____________, pero algunas veces se las mostramos ____________.
3. (it = *el coche*)
   They show it to you but they don't show it to us.
   Te lo muestran ________________ pero no nos lo muestran ________________.

F. For further practice, study the following dialogue and read it aloud several times:

ERNESTO: ¿Tiene Ud. mi lápiz?
ANDRÉS: Sí, yo lo tengo.
ERNESTO: ¿Me lo devuelve hoy?
ANDRÉS: Sí, yo se lo devuelvo hoy.

ERNESTO: ¿Tiene Ud. mi pluma?
ANDRÉS: Sí, yo la tengo.
ERNESTO: ¿Me la devuelve Ud. hoy?
ANDRÉS: Sí, yo se la devuelvo a Ud. hoy.

ERNESTO: ¿Tiene Ud. mis libros?
ANDRÉS: Sí, yo los tengo.
ERNESTO: ¿Me los devuelve Ud. hoy?
ANDRÉS: Sí, yo se los devuelvo hoy.

ERNESTO: ¿Tiene Ud. mis plumas?
ANDRÉS: Sí, yo las tengo.
ERNESTO: ¿Me las devuelve Ud. hoy?
ANDRÉS: Sí, yo se las devuelvo a Ud. hoy.

G. Practice reading aloud the following sentences so that you can say them fluently:

(1) Mi amigo me da un libro.
Mi amigo me lo da.

Mi amigo me da dos libros.
Mi amigo me los da.

Mi amigo me da una pluma.
Mi amigo me la da.

Mi amigo me da dos plumas.
Mi amigo me las da.

(2) Nuestro amigo nos da un libro.
Nuestro amigo nos lo da.

Nuestro amigo nos da dos libros.
Nuestro amigo nos los da.

Nuestro amigo nos da una botella de vino.
Nuestro amigo nos la da.

Nuestro amigo nos da dos botellas de vino.
Nuestro amigo nos las da.

H. *Traduzca Ud. al español:*

(*you* = formal singular; *you (pl.)* = formal plural)

EXAMPLE: (it = *el lápiz*)
I give it to you. *Yo se lo doy.*

1. (it = *el libro*)
I return it to her. ________________________

2. (them = *los lápices*)
I return them to you *(pl.)*. ________________________

3. (them = *las flores*)
I give them to her. ________________________

4. (it = *el coche*)
We show it to him. ________________________

5. (it = *la licencia*)
I show it to them. ____

6. (them = *las fotos*)
She returns them to you. ____

7. (them = *los cuadernos*)
You *(tú)* return them to them. ____

8. (it = *la casa*)
I show it to you *(pl.)*. ____

9. (them = *los libros*)
We return them to him. ____

10. (it = *la carta*)
She reads it to you. ____

Lesson 63

los apodos, *nicknames*

Vocabulario
se usan apodos, nicknames are used
se usa, is used
el **sufijo,** suffix
-ito, -ita, the Spanish equivalent of *-y* or *-ie,* as in *Johnny* or *Charlie*
Juan, John
Juana, Joan, Jane, Jean
Juanito, Johnny
Juanita, Jeannie, Jennie, Jeannette
Miguel, Michael
Miguelito, Mickey
Andrés, Andrew
Andresito, Andy

En inglés, el apodo de Robert es *Bob* y el apodo de Charles es *Chuck. Ted* es el apodo de Theodore, y *Hank* es el apodo de Henry.

También se usan apodos en los países de habla española. El apodo de José es *Pepe,* y el apodo de Francisco es *Paco* o *Pancho*.

Lupe es el apodo de Guadalupe, y *Panchita* es el apodo de Francisca. El apodo de Dolores es *Lola* o *Lolita*.

Se usa mucho el sufijo *-ito* o *-ita* con muchos nombres:

Juanito, Miguelito, Juanita, Andresito

Preguntas

1. ¿Cuál es el apodo de José? ______________________________
2. ¿Cuál es el apodo de Francisco? ______________________________
3. ¿Cuál es el apodo de Henry en inglés? ______________________________
4. ¿Cuál es el apodo de Charles en inglés? ______________________________
5. ¿Tiene Ud. un apodo? ¿Cuál es? ______________________________
6. ¿Tiene un apodo su amigo favorito? ______________________________

Review Exercises

(Lessons 55–61)

A. *Preguntas y respuestas.* Here are some answers. What are the questions?

EXAMPLE: Mi madre me da dinero. *¿Quién le da dinero a Ud.?*

1. No podemos ir al cine esta noche. ______________________________
2. Nuestros padres nos dan dinero. ______________________________
3. Necesito dinero para comprar una revista. ______________________________
4. Yo me levanto a las seis. ______________________________

5. Yo veo a mi amigo favorito todos los días. ________________

6. No, María no quiere ir al cine esta noche. ________________

7. Nosotros nos acostamos a las once. ________________

8. Margarita pone discos mientras lee. ________________

B. *Verbs* (Lessons 39–61). Write the verb form that goes with the indicated pronoun:

1. *trabajar*
   tú ________________
   vosotras ________________
2. *ser*
   ellos ________________
   Uds. ________________
   tú ________________
   yo ________________
   ella ________________
3. *hacer*
   vosotros ________________
   yo ________________
   tú ________________
4. *poder*
   tú ________________
   vosotros ________________
   yo ________________
   ellos ________________
5. *levantarse*
   vosotros ________________
   tú ________________
   yo ________________
   nosotras ________________
6. *acostarse (ue)*
   yo ________________
   nosotros ________________
   ella ________________
   tú ________________
7. *necesitar*
   nosotros ________________
   ellos ________________
8. *poner*
   vosotros ________________
   yo ________________
   ella ________________
   ellas ________________

C. *Object Pronouns* (Lesson 62). Complete the sentences:

1. Yo le digo a Ud. un chiste.
   Yo ________ ________ digo a Ud. (*it to you*)
2. Yo le digo a Ud. muchos chistes.
   Yo ________ ________ digo a Ud. (*them to you*) (el **chiste,** joke)
3. Yo les digo a Uds. una mentira.
   Yo ________ ________ digo a Uds. (*it to you*)
4. Yo le digo a Ud. muchas mentiras.
   Yo ________ ________ digo a Ud. (*them to you*)

Rimas Locas

1

En el pueblo de Aguascalientes
Los toros son muy valientes,
Pero pierden su valor
Cuando hace calor
Y tienen dolor de dientes.

2

En Tampico, Puerto Rico y Chicago
Los toreros no reciben mucho pago,
Viven vidas aburridas
Porque nunca hay corridas
en Tampico, Puerto Rico y Chicago.

3

En la plaza de toros de Piesta
Los toros duermen la siesta,
Si ustedes protestan,
Ellos contestan:
—Pero, hombre, ¡es día de fiesta!

Vocabulario

la **rima,** rhyme
loco, -a, crazy
el **pueblo,** town
valiente, brave
perder (ie), to lose
el **valor,** bravery
dolor de dientes, toothache
el **torero,** bullfighter
el **pago,** pay
aburrido, -a, bored, boring
la **plaza de toros,** bullring
dormir la siesta, to take an afternoon nap
el **día de fiesta,** holiday

Lesson 64

escuchar, *to listen (to);* **relajar,** *to relax*

TOPIC QUESTION 41

> **¿Escucha Ud. la radio?**
> Do you listen to the radio?

present tense of	
escuchar	***relajar***
escucho	**relajo**
escuchas	**relajas**
escucha	**relaja**
escuchamos	**relajamos**
escucháis	**relajáis**
escuchan	**relajan**

A. *Preguntas y respuestas*

1. ¿Escucha Ud. la radio?
Sí, yo escucho la radio.

2. ¿Escuchan Uds. la radio?
No, nosotros escuchamos discos.

3. ¿Escucha su padre la radio?
Sí, mi padre escucha la radio.

4. ¿Escucha su madre la radio?
Sí, ella la escucha también.

5. ¿Escucha su hermana la música clásica?
No, ella escucha la música popular.

6. ¿Escucha su hermano la música de rock?
No, él escucha la música de jazz.

7. ¿Escuchas tú la música de jazz?
No, yo ____

8. ¿Escuchan Uds. las noticias en la radio?
Sí, nosotros las escuchamos en la radio.

9. En tu familia, ¿quiénes escuchan la radio?
En mi familia, ____

10. ¿Escuchas mucho los discos?
No, yo ____

Vocabulario

por la tarde, in the afternoon
por la noche, in the evening, at night
el **tocadiscos,** phonograph, record player

B. *Lectura*

Cuando Inés vuelve a casa, le gusta relajar. Por la tarde le gusta poner la radio. Escucha la música en la radio. Algunas veces pone unos discos en el tocadiscos. Por la noche prefiere mirar la televisión. A ella le gustan muchos programas en la televisión.

Preguntas

1. ¿Cuándo le gusta a Inés relajar? ______________________________
2. ¿Qué escucha en la radio? ______________________________
3. ¿Qué pone en el tocadiscos? ______________________________
4. ¿Qué quiere decir *tocadiscos*? ______________________________
5. ¿Qué prefiere hacer Inés por la noche? ______________________________

C. *Traduzca Ud. al español:*

1. I like to relax at home. ______________________________
2. In the afternoon they like to turn on the radio. ______________________________

   ____
3. We listen to music on the radio. ______________________________

   ____
4. Do you like to listen to records? (you = *familiar sing.*) ______________________________

   ____
5. He prefers to watch television. ______________________________
6. We like many programs on television. ______________________________
7. I can't relax in school. ______________________________
8. They don't have a record player. ______________________________
9. Are you *(Uds.)* going to listen to the radio? ______________________________

   ____
10. I listen to the radio in the evening; my sister listens to it also. ______________________________

    ____

D. *Conversación.* You and your classmates take turns asking one another the questions of the *Preguntas y respuestas* on page 259. Try to give your answers without looking at the page.

E. *Preguntas para un examen oral.* Write an answer in Spanish for each question, and prepare to answer these questions orally without looking at your paper.

1. ¿Quién le da dinero a Ud.?

   ____
2. ¿Quién le da dinero a ella?

   ____

3. ¿Cómo se llama el ''dólar'' mexicano?

----

4. ¿Cuántos pesos recibe Ud. por dos dólares norteamericanos?

----

5. ¿Cómo se dice *rate of exchange* en español?

----

6. ¿Me ve Ud. los lunes?

----

7. ¿Cómo se llama su amiga favorita?

----

8. ¿La ve Ud. en la escuela?

----

9. ¿Necesita Ud. dinero?

----

10. ¿Pone Ud. la radio muchas veces?

----

11. ¿Tiene Ud. dinero? (Answer affirmatively.)

----

12. ¿Quién se lo da a Ud.?

----

13. ¿Tiene Ud. un apodo? ¿Cuál es?

----

14. ¿Cuál es el apodo de José?

----

15. ¿Escuchan Uds. mucho la radio?

Crucigrama (8)

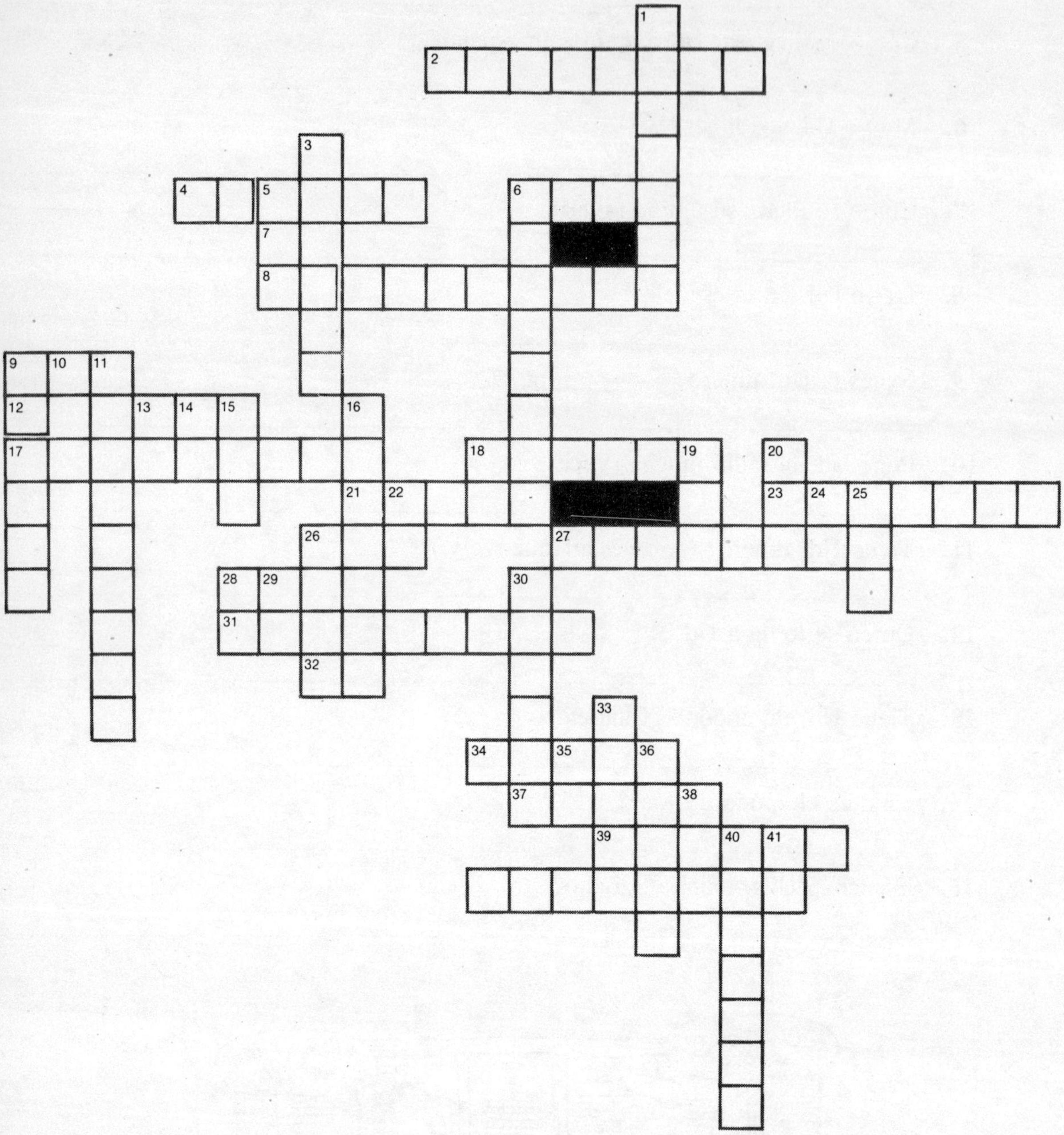

(Each blank represents one word.)

Across

2. *while*
4. Quieren dar dinero = *They want* _____ _____ *money.*
6. Yo entro en el restaurante, me siento a una mesa y _____ el menú.
7. *in, on*
8. _____ _____ el libro = *They show you the book.*
9. ¿Qué quiere decir *pierna*?
12. *pupil*
17. *Pancho* es el apodo de _____.
18. ¿Qué quiere decir *disco*?
21. No debes lavarte en la cocina; ¿por qué no te _____ en el cuarto de baño?
23. "¿Escucha Ud. la radio?" "Sí, yo la _____."
26. Si Ud. va a México, debe cambiar sus dólares _____ pesos mexicanos.
27. *notebook*
28. *to use*
31. *to need*
32. Siempre _____ levantáis tarde.
34. *A 3-story house* = una casa de tres _____.
37. *Anita* en inglés
39. nombre de pila de Gloria Vanderbilt
42. *to give back, return*

Down

1. *Se* is used instead of *le* when the next word is a 3rd-person direct object _____.
3. No puedo pagar el alquiler porque no tengo _____.
5. casarse = *to* _____ *married.*
6. papas / patatas } = _____ en inglés.
9. *the snapshot*
10. iniciales de Enrique López Ramírez
11. *Lupe* es el apodo de _____.
13. iniciales del autor de este libro
14. iniciales de Natalia Cohen
15. Lo ponemos en las ensaladas y en el motor del coche; ¿cómo se llama en inglés?
16. *Lola* o *Lolita* es el apodo de _____.
18. iniciales de Raquel Álvarez
19. *papá* en inglés
20. *to see*
22. infinitive ending
24. iniciales de Sammy Navarro
25. *with*
26. El apodo de Francisco es Pancho o _____.
28. artículo indefinido
29. Whenever the indirect object pronoun *le* or *les* is used with a 3rd-person object pronoun, *le* or *les* changes to _____.
30. Cuando está en México, el Sr. Smith va a un banco y _____ sus dólares por dinero mexicano.
33. "¿Qué discos pones?" "Yo _____ mis discos favoritos."
35. same as 24 Down
36. ¿Qué quiere decir *tonto*?
38. iniciales de Ernesto Oliverio Vargas
40. *to relax*
41. *to go*

Lesson 65

salir (de),* *to leave, go out;* el almuerzo, *lunch*

TOPIC QUESTION 42

¿A qué hora sale Ud. de casa? At what time do you leave home?

present tense of ***salir***	
salgo	**salimos**
sales	**salís**
sale	**salen**

A. *Preguntas y respuestas*

1. ¿A qué hora sale Ud. de casa?
Yo salgo de casa a las ocho.

2. ¿A qué hora salen Uds.?
Nosotros salimos a las nueve.

3. ¿A qué hora sale su padre?
Mi padre sale a las siete y media.

4. ¿A qué hora salen sus hermanos de la escuela?
Ellos salen de la escuela a las tres.

5. ¿A qué hora sale su madre de la oficina?
Ella sale de la oficina a las cinco.

6. ¿Sales tú de casa esta noche?
No, yo ________________________________.

7. ¿Salís de la escuela a las dos?
No, nosotros ____________________________.

Vocabulario

la **oficina,** office
el **banco,** bank
llegar a casa, to arrive (get) home

Mi padre sale de casa a las ocho menos cuarto.

---

*__Salir__ is folowed by **de** if you mention the place you are leaving:

Yo **salgo** a las tres.	I leave at 3 o'clock.
But:	
Yo **salgo de** la escuela a las tres.	I leave school at 3 o'clock.

B. *Lectura*

Luisa no sale mucho de casa por la noche porque tiene que estudiar. Algunas veces sus padres salen de casa después de la cena. Visitan a sus amigos o van al cine.

La madre de Luisa trabaja en una oficina. Sale de la oficina a las cinco y llega a casa a las cinco y media.

El padre de Luisa trabaja en un banco. Sale del banco a las cinco y media y llega a casa a las seis.

Clara, la hermana mayor de Luisa, sale con su novio los sábados por la noche. Algunas veces no salen. Se quedan en casa para mirar la televisión.

Preguntas

1. ¿Por qué no sale Luisa mucho de casa? ______________________________

2. ¿Quiénes salen de casa algunas veces? ______________________________

3. ¿A qué hora sale su padre del banco? ______________________________

4. ¿A qué hora llega su madre a casa? ______________________________

5. ¿Qué hacen Clara y su novio cuando no salen? ______________________________

____

TOPIC QUESTION 43

¿Qué quiere Ud. para el almuerzo?
What do you want for lunch?

C. *Preguntas y respuestas*

1. ¿Qué quiere Ud. para el almuerzo?
Yo quiero una hamburguesa, un vaso de leche y un helado.

2. ¿Qué quieren Uds. para el almuerzo?
Queremos sopa de legumbres, un emparedado de pollo y café. De postre queremos un pastel.

3. ¿Qué quiere su padre para el almuerzo?
Él quiere sopa, una ensalada de lechuga y queso, y pescado con papas. De postre quiere un helado.

4. ¿Qué quieren sus amigos para el almuerzo?
Mis amigos quieren una hamburguesa con queso, una gaseosa y papas fritas.

5. ¿Qué quieres tú para el almuerzo?
Yo ____

6. ¿A qué hora toman tus padres el almuerzo?
Mis padres ____

7. ¿Qué toman tus padres para beber?
Mi padre toma cerveza; mi madre toma vino.

8. ¿Qué tomas tú para beber?
Yo ____

D. *Vocabulario.* Learn these words and expressions:

el **pan,** bread
pan con mantequilla, bread and butter
la **sopa,** soup
sopa de legumbres, vegetable soup
la **ensalada,** salad
ensalada de lechuga y queso, lettuce and cheese salad
el **queso,** cheese
la **carne,** meat
la **hamburguesa,** hamburger
el **pollo,** chicken
el **pescado,** fish
el **emparedado,** sandwich
emparedado de pollo, chicken sandwich
la **legumbre,** vegetable
la **lechuga,** lettuce
el **tomate,** tomato
el **arroz,** rice
la **papa,** potato (**patata** in Spain)
papas fritas, French fried potatoes
la **leche,** milk
la **taza de café,** cup of coffee
el **postre,** dessert
de postre, for dessert
las **frutas,** fruit
el **helado,** ice cream
el **pastel,** pastry, pie
el **plato mixto,** combination plate
incluye, includes
la **comida típica,** typical food
la **clase,** *(2nd meaning)* kind, sort, type

E. *Lectura*

Luisa asiste a la Universidad Nacional en México, D.F. Ella toma el almuerzo en la cafetería de la Universidad. Siempre toma sopa, carne, legumbres, arroz o papas, ensalada y un vaso de leche. A Luisa le gustan los postres. Toma un helado o un pastel.

Algunas veces Luisa toma el plato mixto. El plato mixto incluye la comida típica de México: tamales, enchiladas, tacos, frijoles, arroz y tortillas.

Algunas veces Luisa toma un emparedado de queso o de pollo. También le gustan las hamburguesas.

Preguntas

1. ¿Dónde toma Luisa el almuerzo? ________________________________
2. ¿Qué toma ella para beber? ________________________________
3. ¿Qué toma de postre? ________________________________
4. ¿Qué incluye el plato mixto? ________________________________
____
5. ¿Qué clase de emparedado toma ella algunas veces? ____________________
____
6. ¿Le gustan a ella las hamburguesas? ____________________________

La comida mexicana

Here are descriptions of the typical Mexican foods included in Luisa's *plato mixto:*

el **arroz,** rice
la **tortilla,** a cornmeal pancake
el **taco,** a folded tortilla filled with chopped meat, chicken, or cheese
la **enchilada,** a taco covered with a hot sauce and sprinkled with cheese
el **tamal,** a corn husk wrapped around cornmeal mixed with seasoned pork or chicken
los **frijoles,** boiled beans

F. *Preguntas personales*

1. ¿Dónde toma Ud. el almuerzo? ______________________________
2. ¿A qué hora sale Ud. de casa? ______________________________
3. ¿Prefiere Ud. carne o pescado? ______________________________
4. ¿Le gustan a Ud. las hamburguesas? ______________________________
5. ¿Prefiere Ud. un emparedado de pollo o de queso? ______________________________
____
6. ¿Le gusta a Ud. el helado? ______________________________
7. ¿Prefiere Ud. sopa de tomate o sopa de legumbres? ______________________________
____

G. *Traduzca Ud. al español:*

1. She has* soup, meat, a salad and a glass of milk for lunch. ______________________________
____
2. He doesn't like desserts. ______________________________
3. They prefer hamburgers. ______________________________
4. Do you *(Ud.)* want a cheese sandwich? ______________________________
5. We prefer ice cream. ______________________________
6. I like salads. ______________________________
7. Do they want a chicken sandwich? ______________________________
8. We don't leave the house at night. ______________________________
9. I leave school at three o'clock and get home at four. ______________________________
____
10. I have* a hamburger and a soda for lunch. ______________________________
____

Reminder:* To have something to eat or drink is expressed in Spanish with the verb **tomar, not **tener.** In Spanish, one *takes* lunch, soup, etc. (See Lesson 26.)

H. *Conversación.* You and your classmates take turns asking one another these two sets of questions:

(1) **1.** ¿A qué hora sale Ud. de la escuela?
2. ¿A qué hora llega Ud. a casa?
3. ¿Sale Ud. de casa por la noche?

(2) **1.** ¿Qué quiere Ud. para el almuerzo?
2. ¿Prefiere Ud. sopa de tomate o sopa de legumbres?
3. ¿Prefiere Ud. un emparedado de pollo, de queso, o una hamburguesa?
4. ¿Prefiere Ud. ensalada de lechuga o de frutas?
5. ¿Prefiere Ud. pastel o helado?
6. ¿Prefiere Ud. café, té o leche?

Lesson 66

decir, *to say, to tell*

TOPIC QUESTION 44 — **¿Siempre dice Ud. la verdad?**
Do you always tell the truth?

present tense of ***decir***	
digo	**decimos**
dices	**decís**
dice	**dicen**

A. *Preguntas y respuestas*

Vocabulario
la **verdad,** truth
la **mentira,** lie
al encontrar, on meeting, when I (you, etc.) meet
al encontrarlo, on meeting him (you, *m.*)

1. ¿Siempre dice Ud. la verdad?
   Sí, yo siempre digo la verdad.
2. ¿Siempre dicen Uds. la verdad?
   No, nosotros no decimos siempre la verdad.
3. ¿Siempre dice su padre la verdad?
   Sí, mi padre siempre dice la verdad.
4. ¿Siempre dice su madre la verdad?
   Sí, ella también dice la verdad.
5. ¿Siempre dicen sus hermanos la verdad?
   No, ellos ______________________________
6. ¿Siempre dice la verdad su amigo favorito?
   Mi amigo favorito ______________________________
7. ¿Me dices tú la verdad?
   Sí, te digo la verdad.
8. ¿Dicen mentiras sus amigas?
   No, ellas ______________________________
9. ¿Nos dices mentiras?
   No, no os digo mentiras.
10. ¿Qué le dices a tu padre al encontrarlo?
    Yo le digo ''Buenos días, papá.''
11. ¿Qué le dices a tu madre al encontrarla?
    Le digo que no tengo dinero.

12. ¿Qué les dices a tus amigos al encontrarlos?
    Yo les digo "Hola, ¿qué tal?"

13. ¿Qué les dicen Uds. a sus hermanas al encontrarlas?
    Nosotros ______________________________

14. ¿Qué le decís a vuestro profesor al encontrarlo por la mañana?
    Al encontrar a nuestro profesor, ______________________________

B. *Lectura*

Tomás va a la escuela el lunes. Al encontrar a sus amigos, Tomás les dice "Hola." Ellos le dicen "¿Qué tal?" o "¿Cómo estás?" Al encontrar a su profesora de español, Tomás le dice "Buenos días, señorita Torres. ¿Cómo está Ud.?"

Preguntas

1. ¿Adónde va Tomás el lunes? ______________________________
2. ¿Qué les dice Tomás al encontrar a sus amigos? ______________________________
3. ¿Qué le dicen sus amigos? ______________________________
4. ¿Qué le dice Tomás a su profesora al encontrarla? ______________________________
   ____

C. *Preguntas personales*

1. ¿Qué les dice Ud. a sus amigos al encontrarlos? ______________________________
   ____
2. ¿Dice Ud. mentiras algunas veces? ______________________________
3. ¿Siempre dice Ud. la verdad? ______________________________

4. ¿Qué les dice Ud. a sus padres al salir de casa por la mañana? ________________

____

D. *Traduzca Ud. al español:*

1. They always tell the truth. ________________________
2. He always tells lies. ________________________
3. Do you *(tú)* always tell the truth? ________________________
4. They say "Hello." ________________________
5. We tell them the truth. ________________________
6. I say "Good morning" to my friends when I meet them. ________________

____

Review Exercises

(Commands)

In Lesson 33, we learned that commands are formed by changing the **-o** ending of the first person singular to **-e** (for *ar* verbs) or **-a** (for *er* and *ir* verbs). The three examples on page 120 show how this is done. Here are three more examples:

mostr**ar**, to show	yo muestr**o**
	¡muestr**e** Ud.! ¡muestr**en** Uds.!
hac**er**, to do, make	yo hag**o**
	¡hag**a** Ud.! ¡hag**an** Uds.!
dec**ir**, to say, tell	yo dig**o**
	¡dig**a** Ud.! ¡dig**an** Uds.!

E. Make sentences of the following phrases by using the singular and plural command forms of the verb.

EXAMPLE: hablar con Pedro — *Hable Ud. con Pedro.* *Hablen Uds. con Pedro.*

1. vivir en México ________________________
____
2. trabajar mucho ________________________
____
3. tener cuidado (to be careful) ________________________
____
4. hacer la lección ________________________
____

5. ver a sus amigos mañana ____
____

6. poner la televisión ____
____

7. devolver el libro ____
____

8. escuchar la radio ____
____

9. salir temprano ____
____

10. no decir nada (not to say anything) ____
____

F. Here are Professor Caramba's horoscopes for next Thursday. On the line below the last horoscope, write the infinitive forms of the six verbs that the Professor used.

ACUARIO ....Pongan Uds. discos esta noche.
PISCIS ....No relajen Uds. hoy.
ARIES ....No digan Uds. muchas mentiras hoy.
TAURO ....Escuchen Uds. a sus profesores hoy.
GÉMINIS ....Haga Ud. muchas preguntas a sus profesores hoy.
CÁNCER ....No digan Uds. la verdad hoy.
LEO ....Escuchen Uds. la radio esta noche.
VIRGO ....No pongan Uds. la televisión esta noche.
LIBRA ....No hagan Uds. preguntas hoy.
ESCORPIO ....Relajen Uds. desde las ocho de la mañana hasta las doce de la noche.
SAGITARIO ......Devuelvan Uds. el dinero de sus amigos.
CAPRICORNIO ....No devuelvan Uds. el dinero de sus amigos.

____

La columna personal de Anita Gómez (18)

Vocabulario
el **viudo,** widower
la **viuda,** widow
tanto, -a, so much
correr, to run

el 10 de diciembre

Querida Anita:

Yo soy viudo. Estoy enamorado de una viuda. Ella tiene diez hijos, y yo tengo nueve hijos. Quiero casarme con la señora pero tengo miedo de tanta responsabilidad.

¿Qué debo yo hacer?

Alberto Muchoshijos

Alberto Muchoshijos tiene miedo de tanta responsabilidad.

el 20 de diciembre

Querido Sr. Muchoshijos:

¡¡Corra Ud., hombre!!

Anita Gómez

G. Complete the sentences:

1. Alberto ama a una ______________ que tiene ______________________________
2. Alberto quiere ____________ con ella pero tiene miedo de __________________
3. Anita Gómez le dice a Alberto que él debe ______________________________

Lesson 67

saber, *to know;* **saber** + INFINITIVE, *to know how (to do something)*

TOPIC QUESTION 45A

¿Sabe Ud. la lección? Do you know the lesson?

TOPIC QUESTION 45B

¿Sabe Ud. nadar? Do you know how to swim?

present tense of ***saber***	
sé	**sabemos**
sabes	**sabéis**
sabe	**saben**

Vocabulario

el **número de teléfono,** phone number
la **hora,** hour, time
la **dirección,** address

A. *Preguntas y respuestas*

1. ¿Sabe Ud. la lección?
Sí, yo la sé.

2. ¿Saben Uds. la lección?
Sí, nosotros la sabemos.

3. ¿Sabe él las lecciones?
No, él no las sabe.

4. ¿Sabes mi número de teléfono?
Sí, lo sé.

5. ¿Sabes la hora?
No, no la sé.

6. ¿Sabes qué hora es?
No, no lo* sé.

Ernesto sabe la lección.

---

*In the answer to #5, the pronoun **la** stands for **la hora.** In the answer to #6, **lo** stands for **qué hora es.** (No **lo** sé = No sé **qué hora es.**) The pronoun **lo,** when used as the object of **saber,** represents either a masculine noun or a group of words that form a question.

7. ¿Saben ellos tu dirección?

   No, ellos no ________ saben.

8. ¿Saben ellos dónde vives?

   Sí, ellos ________ saben.

9. ¿Sabe Ud. nadar?
   Sí, yo sé nadar.

10. ¿Saben Uds. nadar?

    Sí, nosotros ____

11. ¿Saben manejar sus padres?
    Sí, mis padres saben manejar.

12. ¿Sabe manejar su amiga favorita?

    No, ella ____

13. ¿Sabéis manejar?

    No, ____

14. ¿Sabes jugar al boliche?

    Sí, ____

B. *Lectura*

Ernesto asiste a la escuela superior. Su primera clase es inglés. La clase empieza a las ocho. Si Ernesto estudia, sabe bien la lección. Si no estudia, no la sabe bien.

A Ernesto le gusta nadar. Sabe nadar bien.

Ernesto sabe manejar pero no tiene coche. Maneja el coche de su padre.

Preguntas

1. ¿Cuál es la primera clase de Ernesto? ________________________________
2. ¿A qué hora empieza la clase de inglés? ________________________________
3. ¿Sabe bien la lección si no estudia? ________________________________
4. ¿Qué le gusta hacer? ________________________________
5. ¿Tiene Ernesto un coche? ________________________________
6. ¿Sabe manejar? ________________________________

C. *Preguntas personales*

1. ¿Sabe Ud. la lección para hoy? ________________________________
2. ¿Saben Uds. qué día es hoy? ________________________________
3. ¿Sabe Ud. manejar? ________________________________
4. ¿Sabe manejar su madre? ________________________________
5. ¿Sabe nadar su padre? ________________________________

D. *Traduzca Ud. al español:*

1. I know how to swim. ________________________
2. Does your brother know how to drive? ________________________
3. (them = *las lecciones*) Do you *(Ud.)* know them? ________________________
4. (it = *la lección*) I know it. ________________________
5. We know how to write. ________________________
6. "Do you *(Uds.)* know the address?" "Yes, we know it." ________________________

   ____
7. "Do you *(tú)* know at what time the class begins?" "No, I don't know." ________

   ____

E. *Conversación.* You and your classmates take turns asking one another the two topic questions on page 274, and the question "¿Sabe Ud. manejar?"

F. What's the punch line? To find out, solve the puzzle below, then write the rest of Miguelito's reply.

Vocabulario

el **escritorio,** desk
el **papel,** paper
no importa, it doesn't matter

Miguelito tiene cinco años y vive en Madrid, la capital de España. Su prima Lupita tiene cuatro años y vive en Barcelona. Un día, el muchacho se sienta al escritorio de su padre, toma papel y lápiz, y empieza a escribir.

Su madre pregunta: —Miguelito, ¿qué haces?

—Escribo una carta a Lupita.

—Pero, niño, tú no sabes escribir.

—No importa; ________________________.

1. la tercera persona femenina
2. palabra negativa
3. SARA + BENITO − RANITO = ?
4. ¿Quiere Ud. ________ la revista?

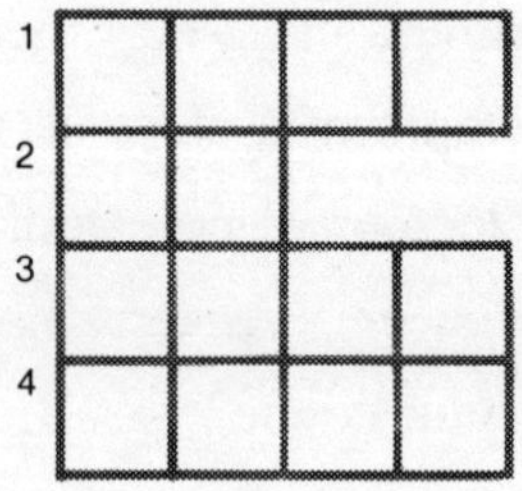

Lesson 68

Irregular Commands; Forming Commands With Reflexive Verbs

A. Irregular Commands

The following commands are irregular because they cannot be formed from the first person singular:

dar: **dé** Ud.	estar: **esté** Ud.	ir: **vaya** Ud.
den Uds.	**estén** Uds.	**vayan** Uds.

ser: **sea** Ud.	saber: **sepa** Ud.
sean Uds.	**sepan** Uds.

Complete the Spanish sentences. Make the command singular or plural as shown in parentheses.

1. (Ud.) Give Mary the books. ________________ los libros a María.
2. (Ud.) Be here at one o'clock. ________________ aquí a la una.
3. (Uds.) Don't go with them. No ________________ con ellos.
4. (Uds.) Don't be silly! ¡________________ tontos!
5. (Ud.) Know the names of your classmates. ________________ los nombres de sus compañeros de clase.

B. Forming Commands With **-gar** Verbs

Verbs whose infinitives end in **-gar** form commands in the regular way, but the letter **u** is inserted between **g** and **e** to keep the hard sound of **g**:

ju**gar**: yo juego	lle**gar**: yo llego	pa**gar**: yo pago
jueg**u**e Ud.	lleg**u**e Ud.	pag**u**e Ud.
jueg**u**en Uds.	lleg**u**en Uds.	pag**u**en Uds.

Complete the Spanish sentences:

1. (Ud.) Don't play soccer today. ________________________ al fútbol hoy.
2. (Uds.) Arrive on time. ________________________ a tiempo.
3. (Ud.) Pay the bill. ________________________ la cuenta.

C. Forming Commands With Reflexive Verbs

Reflexive verbs form commands in the same way as other verbs but are used with **se.** The reflexive pronoun **se** is attached to the verb in an affirmative command but precedes the verb in a negative command:

		Affirmative	*Negative*
levantarse to rise, get up, stand up	yo me levanto ↓ levante	levánt**ese** Ud. levánt**ense** Uds.	no **se** levante Ud. no **se** levanten Uds.
acostarse (ue) to go to bed; to lie down	yo me acuesto ↓ acueste	acuést**ese** Ud. acuést**ense** Uds.	no **se** acueste Ud. no **se** acuesten Uds.
irse to leave, go away	yo me voy ↓ **vaya**	váya**se** Ud. váyan**se** Uds.	no **se** vaya Ud. no **se** vayan Uds.

Note: When **se** is attached to the command, an accent mark must be written over the stressed vowel.

Here are other reflexive verbs that you have learned. Supply the affirmative and negative commands:

	Affirmative	*Negative*
1. lavarse to wash oneself, wash up	____________________ Ud. ____________________ Uds.	____________________ Ud. ____________________ Uds.
2. sentarse (ie) to sit down	____________________ Ud. ____________________ Uds.	____________________ Ud. ____________________ Uds.
3. dormirse (ue) to fall asleep	____________________ Ud. ____________________ Uds.	____________________ Ud. ____________________ Uds.
4. quedarse to stay, remain	____________________ Ud. ____________________ Uds.	____________________ Ud. ____________________ Uds.

Traduzca Ud. al español:

5. (Ud.) Don't get up. ____

6. (Uds.) Go away! ____

7. (Ud.) Go to bed. ____

8. Wash yourselves. ____

9. (Ud.) Sit down. ____

10. (Uds.) Don't sit down there. ____________________________________ allí.

11. (Ud.) Don't fall asleep in class. ______________________________ en la clase.

12. (Uds.) Stay home tomorrow. __________________________ en casa mañana.

D. Make sentences of the following phrases by using the singular and plural command forms of the verb.

EXAMPLE: hablar con Pedro — *Hable Ud. con Pedro.* *Hablen Uds. con Pedro.*

1. estar en casa esta noche ______________________________ ______________________________

2. ir al cine hoy ______________________________ ______________________________

3. ser bueno(s) ______________________________ ______________________________

4. saber la lección ______________________________ ______________________________

5. dar dinero a los pobres ______________________________ ______________________________

6. levantarse a las siete ______________________________ ______________________________

7. acostarse temprano ______________________________ ______________________________

8. jugar al tenis ______________________________ ______________________________

9. pagar la cuenta ______________________________ ______________________________

10. llegar a tiempo ______________________________ ______________________________

11. irse a mediodía ______________________________ ______________________________

12. no dormirse en el cine ______________________________ ______________________________

13. no lavarse en la fuente ______________________________ ______________________________

14. quedarse aquí ______________________________ ______________________________

Wherever you attached the pronoun **se** to the verb, *make sure you have written an accent mark over the stressed vowel!*

E. Here are Professor Caramba's horoscopes for next Friday. On the line below the last horoscope, write the infinitive forms of the nine verbs that the Professor used.

ACUARIO ....No se queden Uds. en casa hoy.
PISCIS ....Estén Uds. en la escuela hoy a las seis y media de la mañana.
ARIES ....Jueguen Uds. al boliche hoy.
TAURO ....Siempre sean Uds. amables *(kind)*.
GÉMINIS ....Sepan Uds. bien sus lecciones.
CÁNCER ....Si Uds. no quieren quedarse en la escuela, váyanse.
LEO ....No jueguen Uds. al boliche hoy.
VIRGO ....No se levanten Uds. esta mañana.
LIBRA ....No den Uds. dinero a su profesora de español.
ESCORPIO ....No se acuesten Uds. esta noche.
SAGITARIO ......No estén Uds. en casa a la una de la mañana.
CAPRICORNIO ....No den Uds. dinero a los ricos.

La columna personal de Anita Gómez (19)

Vocabulario
todavía, still
usar, to use
ya, already, now

el 6 de julio

Querida Anita Gómez:

Yo vivo en la casa de mis padres. Tengo cuarenta años pero mi padre todavía no me permite usar su coche. Yo necesito un coche para ir al cine y a los restaurantes con mis novias.

¿Qué debo hacer?

Diego Sin Coche

el 12 de julio

Querido Diego Sin Coche:

Ya es Ud. un muchacho grande. No debe vivir con sus padres. ¿Por qué no compra Ud. un coche? Si Ud. no trabaja, ¿por qué no?

Anita Gómez

P.D. Mis novios siempre toman un taxi cuando yo salgo con ellos.

F. Complete the sentences:

1. Diego tiene ________________ años pero su padre no le permite ____________
2. Diego necesita un coche para ______________________________________
3. Anita Gómez le dice a Diego que él no debe ____________________________
4. Según Anita Gómez, Diego debe ____________________________________
5. Los novios de Anita Gómez no necesitan coche porque toman ________________

Lesson 69

conocer, *to know, be acquainted with;* **saber** AND **conocer**

TOPIC QUESTION 46	**¿Conoce Ud. al señor . . .?** Do you know Mr. . . .?

present tense of ***conocer***	
conozco	**conocemos**
conoces	**conocéis**
conoce	**conocen**

A. *Preguntas y respuestas*

Vocabulario

el (la) **estudiante,** student
el **nombre,** name
el **compañero** / la **compañera** } **de clase,** classmate
la **fecha,** date

1. ¿Conoce Ud. al señor Prado?
   Sí, yo lo conozco.
2. ¿Conocen Uds. a la señora Pérez?
   No, no la conocemos.
3. ¿Conoce su padre a los señores Mendoza?
   Sí, mi padre los conoce.
4. ¿Conoce su madre a mis hermanas?
   Sí, mi madre las conoce.
5. ¿Conocen sus padres a María y Carlos?
   No, mis padres no los conocen.
6. ¿Conoce Ud. a Miguel?
   No, yo ______________________________
7. ¿Conocen Uds. a mi amiga Felisa?
   Sí, ______________________________
8. ¿Conoces a las muchachas de tu clase?
   No, no las conozco.
9. ¿Conocéis a vuestros compañeros de clase?
   Sí, ______________________________
10. ¿Conocen ellos al señor Gómez?
    No, ellos ______________________________

B. *Lectura*

Miguel conoce a muchos estudiantes. Él sabe los nombres de todos sus compañeros en la clase de español. Sus amigos favoritos son Luis y Dorotea. Miguel los conoce bien. Los tres amigos saben hablar inglés y español.

Preguntas

1. ¿Qué sabe Miguel? ____________________
2. ¿Cómo se llama su amigo favorito? ____________________
3. ¿Lo conoce bien? ____________________
4. ¿Quién es Dorotea? ____________________
5. ¿La conoce bien Miguel? ____________________
6. ¿Qué saben hacer los tres amigos? ____________________

C. Saber and **conocer**

Saber means to know facts, information, or how to do something. **Conocer** means to know persons or places.

Complete the sentences. In each case, decide whether *saber* or *conocer* is the right verb to use, then write it in the correct form:

1. —¿____________________ Ud. la fecha?
   —Sí, yo la ____________________; es el 9 de febrero.
2. —¿____________________ Ud. al nuevo profesor?
   —No, yo no lo ____________________.
3. —¿____________________ Ud. el nombre del nuevo profesor?
   —No, yo no lo ____________________.
4. —¿____________________ tú qué hora es?
   —Sí, lo ____________________; son las dos y cuarto.
5. —¿____________________ Uds. la lección para hoy?
   —No, no la ____________________.
6. —¿____________________ vosotras a mis hermanos?
   —Sí, los ____________________.
7. María no ____________________ bien la ciudad. Por eso, necesita un plano *(street map)*.
8. —¿____________________ Ud. a Nueva York?
   —No, no la ____________________, pero ____________________ que es una ciudad muy grande.

D. Like all verbs, **conocer** is followed by the personal **a** when the direct object is a noun that refers to persons. (See Lesson 60.) The personal **a** is also used before the *names of places*:

Ella conoce **a** Madrid.	She knows (is familiar with) Madrid.
But:	
Ella conoce la ciudad.	She knows the city.

E. The article **el** or **la** is used before titles when mentioning a person by name. The article is omitted when speaking directly to the person:

El señor Rivas es alto.	**La** señorita Gómez es baja.
But:	*But:*
—Buenos días, señor Rivas.	—Buenas tardes, señorita Gómez.

F. *Preguntas personales*

1. ¿A quién conoce Ud. bien? ______________________
2. ¿Conocen Uds. al presidente de los Estados Unidos? ______________________
____
3. ¿Saben Uds. quién es el presidente de los Estados Unidos? ______________________
____
4. ¿Conoce su padre a sus profesores? ______________________
5. ¿Saben Uds. hablar inglés? ______________________
6. ¿Sabe Ud. la lección para hoy? ______________________

G. *Traduzca Ud. al español:*

1. I know the lesson. ______________________
2. I know John. ______________________
3. Do you *(Uds.)* know Mr. and Mrs. Rivera? ______________________
4. Do you *(Uds.)* know Mr. González? ______________________
5. Do you *(tú)* know him? ______________________
6. Do you *(Ud.)* know her? ______________________
7. Do you *(Uds.)* know how to swim? ______________________
8. (them = *las muchachas*) We know them. ______________________
9. (it = *la lección*) I know it. ______________________
10. He knows the lesson. ______________________
11. They know the city well. ______________________
12. We know how to drive. ______________________
13. Do you *(Ud.)* know Mexico City? ______________________
14. Do you *(Uds.)* know what time it is? ______________________
15. I know that he needs money. ______________________

H. *Conversación.* You and your classmates take turns asking one another the following questions:

1. *¿A quién conoce Ud. bien?*
Reply in the form *Yo conozco bien a . . .* (name of friend, relative, etc.).

2. *¿Qué sabe Ud. hacer?*
Reply in the form *Yo sé . . .* (*nadar, hablar inglés,* etc.)

Vary the questions by using the plural subject *Uds*. The replies should then, of course, start with *Nosotros*.

3. *¿Conoce Ud. al señor (a la señora, a mi amiga . . .)?*
Use direct object pronouns in your replies: *Sí, yo lo (la,* etc.) *conozco*.

Review Exercises

Object and Prepositional Pronouns*

I. Supply the missing pronouns. In 9 and 10, use the familiar singular. Otherwise, use the formal singular to translate the pronoun *you*.

1. El señor Marín es mi abogado. Yo ____________ (him) veo los jueves. Yo trabajo con ____________ (him) por la mañana.

2. Señor Álvarez, yo ____________ (you) veo mañana. Voy a hablar con ____________ (you) en mi oficina.

3. Ella ____________ (us) visita los domingos.

4. Ellos van a escuchar la música con ________________ (us).

5. María vive en Costa Rica. Yo no ____________ (her) veo mucho.

6. Yo voy a trabajar con ____________ (her) el año que viene *(next year)*.

7. Señora, yo ____________ (you) veo mañana.

*A prepositional pronoun is a pronoun that follows a preposition. You have already learned to use such pronouns in several types of phrases: "a **Ud.**," "de **ella**," "con **nosotros**," etc. The prepositional pronouns are the same as the subject pronouns with two exceptions: (1) **yo** becomes **mí** ("me hablan a **mí**"), (2) **tú** becomes **ti** ("ellos van sin **ti**").

Also note these two special forms, which are not used in this book:

with me = **conmigo** with you, *familiar sing.* = **contigo**

8. Señora, voy a trabajar con ____________ mañana.
(you)

9. Juan, yo ____________ veo los lunes.
(you)

10. María, el libro es para ____________.
(you)

11. El libro es para ____________.
(her)

12. (them = *los muchachos*) Yo voy con ____________.
(them)

Direct and Indirect Object Pronouns Used Together

J. Complete the sentences:

1. Ellos me dan el libro.	Ellos me __________ dan.
2. Roberto nos da la pluma.	Roberto nos __________ da.
3. Yo doy el libro a María.	Yo __________ __________ doy a ella.
4. Yo doy los libros a Juan.	Yo __________ __________ doy a él.
5. Juan les da cinco pesos.	Juan __________ __________ da.
6. Juan les da una carta.	Juan __________ __________ da.

Rimas Locas

1

La vampiresa Elena
Come de manera ajena,
A la luz de la luna
Se desayuna
Y al alba toma la cena.

Vocabulario

la **vampiresa,** female vampire
la **manera,** manner, fashion
ajeno, -a, different, alien
la **luz,** light
la **luna,** moon
desayunarse, to have breakfast
al alba, at dawn

2

La lista Conchita Rebaños
Relata cuentos extraños,
Si Ud. la frecuenta
Tenga en cuenta
Que tiene solamente seis años.

listo, -a, clever
relatar, to report, tell
el **cuento,** story
extraño, -a, strange
frecuentar, to visit frequently
tener en cuenta, to take into account

3

Reginaldo, rey de los charros,
Tiene dos hijos chaparros
Que se quejan de sus callos
Cuando montan sus caballos
Y prefieren caminar en sus carros.

el **rey,** king
el **charro,** Mexican cowboy
chaparro, -a, short and chubby
quejarse, to complain
el **callo,** callus
montar, to mount
el **caballo,** horse
el **carro** = el **coche**

Lesson 70

entender, *to understand*

TOPIC QUESTION 47

¿Entiende Ud. la lección?
Do you understand the lesson?

present tense of ***entender (ie)***	
entiendo	**entendemos**
entiendes	**entendéis**
entiende	**entienden**

A. *Preguntas y respuestas*

Vocabulario
hacer preguntas, to ask questions
al día siguiente, the next day
la clase más difícil, the most difficult class
este, -a, this

1. ¿Entiende Ud. la lección?
Sí, yo la entiendo.

2. ¿Entienden Uds. la lección?
No, nosotros no la entendemos.

3. ¿Entiende ella la lección?
Sí, ______________________________________.

4. ¿Qué hace Ud. si no entiende la lección?
Si no entiendo la lección, le hago preguntas al profesor.

5. ¿Qué hacen Uds. si no entienden la lección?
Si no la entendemos, le hacemos preguntas a nuestra profesora.

6. ¿Entienden los estudiantes la lección?
Sí, ellos la entienden.

7. ¿Entiendes tú la lección?
No, no la entiendo.

8. ¿Qué haces si no entiendes la lección?
Si no ______________________, le ______________________________________.

9. ¿Qué hacen tus compañeros de clase si no entienden la lección?
Ellos ____.

B. *Lectura*

Roberto Vargas estudia sus lecciones por la noche. Algunas veces las escribe. Si no entiende la lección, le hace preguntas al profesor al día siguiente. Su clase más difícil es la clase de física. Hace muchas preguntas en esta clase. Otros estudiantes hacen preguntas también.

Preguntas

1. ¿Cuándo estudia Roberto sus lecciones?

   ____

2. Mientras las estudia, ¿qué hace Roberto algunas veces?

   ____

3. ¿Qué hace Roberto si no entiende la lección?

   ____

4. ¿Cuál es su clase más difícil?

   ____

5. ¿Por qué hace Roberto muchas preguntas?

   ____

C. *Preguntas personales*

1. ¿Entiende Ud. la lección para hoy? ______________________________
2. ¿Qué hace Ud. si no entiende la lección? ______________________________

   ____

3. ¿En qué clase hace Ud. muchas preguntas? ______________________________

   ____

4. ¿Quién hace muchas preguntas en esta clase? ______________________________

   ____

5. Cuando Ud. hace una pregunta, ¿quién le contesta a Ud.? ______________________________

   ____

D. *Traduzca Ud. al español:*

1. They ask a lot of questions. ______________________________
2. I don't understand the lesson. ______________________________
3. (it = *la lección*) Do you *(Ud.)* understand it? ______________________________
4. I don't like to ask questions. ______________________________
5. (them = *las lecciones*) We understand them. ______________________________
6. Are you *(tú)* going to ask a question? ______________________________

   ____

7. If I don't understand the lesson, I ask questions. ______________________________

   ____

E. *Conversación*. You and your classmates take turns asking one another the following questions:

1. ¿Entiende Ud. la lección para hoy?
2. ¿Qué hace Ud. si no entiende la lección?

Lesson 71

la tarjeta de turismo, *tourist card*

A. *Lectura*

México tiene un embajador en Wáshington, D. C. En las ciudades más importantes de los Estados Unidos, México tiene consulados.

Para ir a México, no se necesita pasaporte. Se necesita una tarjeta de turismo. Para ir a México, no se necesitan inyecciones.

Para obtener una tarjeta de turismo, se necesita el certificado de nacimiento. Es posible obtener la tarjeta de turismo en el consulado mexicano o en una agencia de turismo.

Vocabulario

el **embajador,** ambassador
el **consulado,** consulate
se necesita(n), one needs
el **pasaporte,** passport
la **inyección,** injection, shot
obtener, to obtain, get
el **certificado de nacimiento,** birth certificate
es posible, it is possible

Preguntas

1. ¿Dónde está el embajador mexicano?

----

2. ¿Dónde tiene México consulados?

----

3. ¿Se necesita un pasaporte para ir a México?

----

4. ¿Cómo se dice *tourist card* en español?

----

5. ¿Se necesitan inyecciones para ir a México?

----

6. ¿Qué se necesita para obtener una tarjeta de turismo?

----

7. ¿Dónde es posible obtener una tarjeta de turismo?

No se necesitan inyecciones para ir a México.

Review Exercises

(Lessons 58–70)

Topic Questions

B. *Traduzca las frases al español.* "You" is formal singular in each case.

1. Who gives you money? ______________________________

2. Whom do you see every day? ______________________________

3. Do you need money? ______________________________

4. Do you play records while you read? ______________________________

5. Do you listen much to the radio? ______________________________

6. At what time do you leave the house? ______________________________

____

7. What do you want for lunch? ______________________________

8. Do you always tell the truth? ______________________________

9. Do you know how to swim? ______________________________

10. Do you know Miss Sánchez? ______________________________

11. What do you do if you don't know the lesson? ______________________________

____

12. Whom do you know well? ______________________________

Preguntas y respuestas

C. Here are some answers. What are the questions?

1. Yo salgo de casa a las siete menos cuarto.

____

2. Sí, mis amigos siempre dicen la verdad.

____

3. Sí, nosotros sabemos nadar.

____

4. Mi hermano quiere sopa, un emparedado, café y helado para el almuerzo.

____

5. No, no conozco bien a mis profesores.

____

6. No, mi amigo no escucha mucho la radio.

____

7. Si Ramiro no entiende la lección, hace muchas preguntas.

---

8. Mi madre no sabe nadar.

Frases revueltas

D. Unscramble the sentences:

1. ve ¿ a todos quién días los Ud. ?

---

2. siempre mi verdad dice madre la .

---

3. de y nosotros media salimos casa las a nueve .

---

4. mientras mis ponen leen hermanos discos .

---

5. ¿ conoce a bien quién Ud. ?

---

6. Ud. ? almuerzo qué para quiere el ¿

---

7. si siempre preguntas yo entiendo hago no lección la .

---

8. dan mis dinero me padres .

---

9. a no mis bien conocen padres profesores mis .

---

10. sus mi días a todos amigas los ve madre .

---

11. mentiras Ud. diga no .

---

12. mucho yo radio la escucho no .

---

13. un mi para quiere amigo almuerzo el emparedado .

---

14. saben mis nadar hermanos .

---

15. ¿ les sus quién a hermanos dinero da ?

____

16. salen ? a casa de qué Uds. hora ¿

____

Vocabulario

E. *Traduzca Ud. al español:*

1. to give ______________________
2. to change ______________________
3. to be worth ______________________
4. rate of exchange ______________________
5. the shirt ______________________
6. to need ______________________
7. to put (on) ______________________
8. the supper ______________________
9. the records ______________________
10. while ______________________
11. if ______________________
12. to return, give back ______________________
13. the nickname ______________________
14. to leave, go away ______________________
15. to listen (to) ______________________
16. to relax ______________________
17. the classical music ______________________
18. the record player ______________________
19. to leave, go out ______________________
20. the soup ______________________
21. the meat ______________________
22. the vegetables ______________________
23. the rice ______________________
24. the potatoes ______________________
25. the salad ______________________
26. the dessert ______________________
27. the ice cream ______________________
28. the pastry ______________________
29. the combination plate ______________________

30. the sandwich ______________________________________
31. the cheese ______________________________________
32. the chicken______________________________________
33. the hamburger ______________________________________
34. the fish ______________________________________
35. the lettuce ______________________________________
36. to say, tell ______________________________________
37. to meet ______________________________________
38. on meeting______________________________________
39. the lies ______________________________________
40. the truth ______________________________________
41. to know (information) ______________________________
42. to know (people, places) ___________________________
43. to understand ______________________________________
44. to ask a question __________________________________
45. difficult ______________________________________
46. the tourist card __________________________________
47. the consulate ______________________________________
48. the passport ______________________________________
49. the injection ______________________________________
50. to get, obtain ______________________________________
51. the birth certificate _______________________________
52. the tourist agency _________________________________

F. Complete the sentences:

1. Mis padres me _______________ dinero.
2. El tipo de _______________ es veinte pesos por un dólar.
3. Mi padre necesita _______________ porque quiere comprar un coche.
4. No pongo la ___________________ mientras estudio.
5. El ___________________ de José es Pepe.
6. Mi hermano pone discos y yo ___________________ la música.
7. Me ___________________ relajar.
8. Ellos escuchan la ___________________ clásica.
9. Nosotras ___________________ de casa a las ocho.
10. A Juan le gusta el plato ___________________.
11. Les gusta el ___________________ de queso.
12. Nosotros siempre ___________________ la verdad.

13. Al ____________________ a un amigo, yo digo "hola".
14. Yo no sé la ____________________ porque yo no estudio.
15. ¿____________________ Ud. al señor Jiménez?
16. Yo hago preguntas si no ____________________ la lección.
17. No se necesita pasaporte para ir a México; se necesita una ____________________ de turismo.
18. No se ____________________ inyecciones para ir a México.
19. Se necesita un certificado de ____________________.
20. Es posible obtener una tarjeta de turismo en el consulado mexicano o en una ________________ de turismo.

Verbs

G. Write the form of the verb that goes with the indicated subject:

1. *escuchar*
   vosotros ________________________
   yo ____________________________
2. *relajar*
   tú ____________________________
   ella ____________________________
3. *salir*
   tú ____________________________
   vosotros ________________________
   nosotros ________________________
   yo ____________________________
4. *saber*
   nosotros ________________________
   vosotros ________________________
   yo ____________________________
5. *decir*
   nosotros ________________________
   ellos ____________________________
   tú ____________________________
   vosotros ________________________
   yo ____________________________
6. *conocer*
   tú ____________________________
   vosotros ________________________
   yo ____________________________
7. *entender*
   ellos ____________________________
   tú ____________________________
   vosotros ________________________
   nosotros ________________________

H. *Preguntas para un examen oral.* Write an answer in Spanish for each question, and prepare to answer these questions orally without looking at your paper.

1. ¿A qué hora sale Ud. de casa?

   ____

2. ¿A qué hora sale su hermano(-a) de casa?

   ____

3. ¿Le gustan los postres?

   ____

4. En un restaurante mexicano, ¿qué comidas incluye el plato mixto?

----

5. ¿Siempre dice Ud. la verdad?

----

6. ¿Sabe Ud. nadar?

----

7. ¿Conocen Uds. a todos los estudiantes de su escuela?

----

8. ¿Me conoce Ud. bien?

----

9. ¿Qué hace Ud. si no entiende la lección?

----

10. ¿Qué se necesita para ir a México?

----

11. ¿Tiene Ud. un certificado de nacimiento?

----

12. ¿Cuál es el apodo de su amigo favorito?

La columna personal de Anita Gómez (20)

el 7 de agosto

Querida Anita Gómez:

Yo paso muchas horas en un café al aire libre porque me gusta mucho mirar a las muchachas bonitas que pasan en la calle. Mientras las miro, tomo mucho café . . . ¡veinte tazas al día! Fumo mucho también. Mi problema es que no puedo dormir nada.

¿Qué debo hacer?

Juan Fumacafé

el 30 de agosto

Querido Juan Fumacafé:

La solución de su problema es muy fácil. Ud. no debe mirar a las muchachas bonitas. Mire Ud. a las muchachas feas. De este modo no va Ud. a quedarse mucho tiempo en el café.

Anita Gómez

Vocabulario

pasar, to pass; to spend (time)
al aire libre, in the open air, outdoors
café al aire libre, sidewalk cafe
no puedo dormir nada, I can't sleep at all
fácil, easy
feo, -a, ugly
de este modo, in this way

Juan Fumacafé mira a las muchachas.

I. Complete the sentences:

1. Juan Fumacafé pasa mucho tiempo en un café al aire libre porque ______________ ____

2. Juan no puede dormir porque ______________________________________

3. Anita Gómez le dice a Juan que él debe ______________________________ ____

J. What's the punch line? To find out, solve the puzzle below, then write the rest of the waiter's reply.

Vocabulario

de repente, suddenly
gritar, to shout
el **camarero,** waiter
la **mosca,** fly
la **sopa,** soup
¿y qué? what of it?
la **cantidad,** quantity
el **tazón,** bowl
caliente, warm, hot

Un hombre toma la cena en un restaurante elegante. De repente grita: "Camarero, ¡hay una mosca en mi sopa!"

El camarero mira la sopa y dice:

"¿Y qué? ¿____?"

1. ¿Qué cantidad?
2. La cena empieza con un tazón de ________ caliente.
3. Ella no ________ comprar la revista porque no tiene dinero.
4. "¿Qué toma Ud. para ________?" "Tomo una gaseosa."
5. La Sra. Méndez es ________ profesora muy buena.
6. insecto

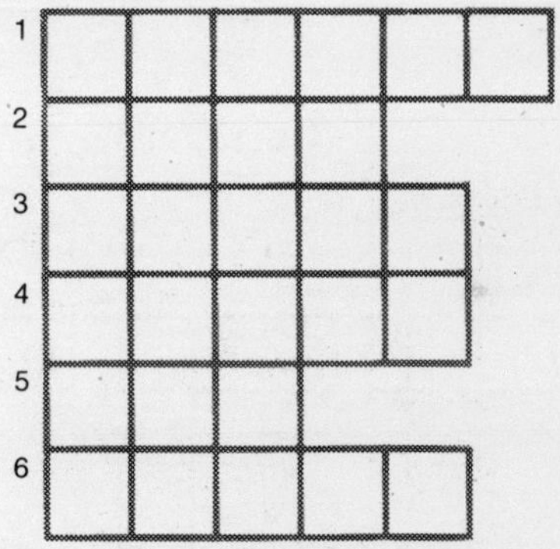

Crucigrama (9)

(Each blank represents one word.)

Across

1. el cuarto mes del año
5. *She is alone* = Ella está _____.
8. *house*
11. *The Pacific Coast* = la costa _____ _____.
13. *pupil*
16. iniciales de Elena López Espinosa
17. ¡No puedo estudiar cuando tú _____ discos!
18. "¿Dónde encuentras a tus amigas?" "_____ encuentro en la escuela."
19. la capital de los Estados Unidos
21. reflexive pronoun
23. ¿Quién _____ tú?
25. *She sits down* = Ella se _____.
28. abreviatura de *posdata*
29. ¡_____ Uds.! = *Read!*
30. ¿Cómo se dice *hijo* en inglés?
32. ¡_____ Ud.! = *Run!*
33. primera persona singular
35. iniciales de Olga Jiménez
36. *the record player*
37. *the vegetable*
38. *each, every*
39. *the hamburger*
43. "buen amigo" en inglés
46. Yo _____ muestro mi trabajo a la profesora.
47. *the sandwich*
49. iniciales de "National Gallery" en español
50. El plato mixto incluye tamales, frijoles, tortillas y _____.
52. iniciales de un estado al norte de South Carolina
54. iniciales de Olivia Calderón McGillicuddy
55. Yo _____ de casa a las ocho.
56. Él entra en el cuarto = *He comes* _____ *the room.*
57. Seis y cinco son _____.
58. Las clases _____ a las tres, y vuelvo a casa.
60. _____ levanto a las seis.
61. *Claro* and the English word _____ are cognates.
62. *to sing*
63. ¿Qué quiere decir *hacer preguntas*?

Down

1. *the next day*
2. ellas es / ella está } = *she* _____.
3. *crazy*
4. Para ir a México, no se necesita _____.
6. No _____ conozco a Ud., señorita; ¿quién es Ud.?
7. Si quieres mis revistas, _____ _____ _____ mañana.
9. Juan está solo = *John is* _____.
10. ¿Qué quiere decir *respuesta*?
11. El coche _____ señor López es muy grande.
12. A ellos no _____ gusta nadar.
14. artículo indefinido
15. ¿Por qué no _____ muestra la foto a mí?
20. ¿A qué hora _____ levantas?
21. "¿Cuándo me devuelve Ud. mi libro?" "Yo _____ _____ devuelvo a Ud. hoy."
22. el primer mes del año
24. Nieva mucho = *It* _____ *a lot.*
26. Para ir a México, se necesita una _____ _____ _____.
27. *Anne*
28. abreviatura de *postscript* (en inglés)
31. palabra negativa
34. *in the afternoon*
40. iniciales de Enrique Pérez
41. Si Ud. quiere irse, ¡_____ Ud.!
42. *On meeting John* = _____ _____ a Juan.
44. *the dessert*
45. La verdad es lo contrario *(the opposite)* de _____ _____.
48. Yo _____ la radio para escuchar las noticias.
51. abreviatura del décimo mes del año
53. "¿Conocen Uds. a la señora González?" "Sí, nosotros la _____."
59. *we need*

Lesson 72

REPASO GENERAL

A. *Verdad o Mentira.* In the blank on the left, write *V* (for *Verdad*) if the statement is true, *M* (for *Mentira*) if the statement is false.

____ **1.** Nosotros dormimos en la cocina.
____ **2.** Nos lavamos en el cuarto de baño.
____ **3.** Los dormitorios generalmente están arriba—si no están abajo.
____ **4.** Jugamos al béisbol en el comedor.
____ **5.** Hace frío en enero.
____ **6.** Nieva en julio en la Florida.
____ **7.** Llueve en la primavera.
____ **8.** No tenemos que estudiar.
____ **9.** La corrida de toros es popular sólo en España.
____ **10.** El parque de Chapultepec está en Filadelfia.
____ **11.** Nos acostamos por la noche.
____ **12.** Don Juan no tiene novias.
____ **13.** Un dólar norteamericano vale más que un peso mexicano.
____ **14.** Nunca necesitamos dinero.
____ **15.** Lupe es el apodo de Guadalupe.
____ **16.** Pepe es el apodo de José.
____ **17.** No salimos de la escuela por la tarde.
____ **18.** Siempre decimos mentiras.
____ **19.** Sabemos decir mentiras.
____ **20.** Para ir a México es necesario obtener un pasaporte.

B. *Preguntas temáticas.* Here are English translations of the Topic Questions that you have learned in *Para Servirle.* How many of them can you recall? Write the Topic Question in blank *a,* and answer it in blank *b.* Be prepared to answer the questions orally, without looking at your paper.

1 What is your name? *a.* ____________________
b. ____________________

2A How are you? *a.* ____________________
b. ____________________

2B	Are you in good health?	*a.* ______________________
		b. ______________________
3	Do you have a car?	*a.* ______________________
		b. ______________________
4	Do you drive?	*a.* ______________________
		b. ______________________
5	What does . . . mean? (Choose a word.)	*a.* ______________________
		b. ______________________
6	How does one say . . . in Spanish? (Supply an English word.)	*a.* ______________________
		b. ______________________
7A	How much is five and three?	*a.* ______________________
		b. ______________________
7B	How much is six minus two?	*a.* ______________________
		b. ______________________
8	Do you go to the movies a lot?	*a.* ______________________
		b. ______________________
9A	What day is today?	*a.* ______________________
		b. ______________________
9B	What day is tomorrow?	*a.* ______________________
		b. ______________________
9C	What day was yesterday?	*a.* ______________________
		b. ______________________
10	Do you swim?	*a.* ______________________
		b. ______________________
11	What sports do you play?	*a.* ______________________
		b. ______________________
12A	Do you speak Spanish?	*a.* ______________________
		b. ______________________
12B	Do you talk a lot on the telephone?	*a.* ______________________
		b. ______________________
13	Do you prefer coffee, tea or milk?	*a.* ______________________
		b. ______________________
14A	What language are you studying?	*a.* ______________________
		b. ______________________
14B	What subjects are you studying?	*a.* ______________________
		b. ______________________

14C	What courses are you taking?	*a.*	______________________________
		b.	______________________________
15	What are you learning?	*a.*	______________________________
		b.	______________________________
16	What are you writing?	*a.*	______________________________
		b.	______________________________
17A	Do you eat a lot?	*a.*	______________________________
		b.	______________________________
17B	Where do you have breakfast?	*a.*	______________________________
		b.	______________________________
18	How many hours do you sleep?	*a.*	______________________________
		b.	______________________________
19	What do you drink?	*a.*	______________________________
		b.	______________________________
20	What do you read?	*a.*	______________________________
		b.	______________________________
21	Do you like coffee?	*a.*	______________________________
		b.	______________________________
22	What sports do you like?	*a.*	______________________________
		b.	______________________________
23	Do you want a new car?	*a.*	______________________________
		b.	______________________________
24	Do you smoke?	*a.*	______________________________
		b.	______________________________
25A	Where do you live?	*a.*	______________________________
		b.	______________________________
25B	Do you live to eat or do you eat to live?	*a.*	______________________________
		b.	______________________________
26	Do you work?	*a.*	______________________________
		b.	______________________________
27	How old are you?	*a.*	______________________________
		b.	______________________________
28A	Are you tall or short?	*a.*	______________________________
		b.	______________________________
28B	Do you prefer to be rich or intelligent?	*a.*	______________________________
		b.	______________________________

29A	At what time do you return home?	*a.* ________________ *b.* ________________
29B	At what time does the class begin?	*a.* ________________ *b.* ________________
29C	At what time does it end?	*a.* ________________ *b.* ________________
30	In what months is it warm (cold)?	*a.* ________________ *b.* ________________
31	How is the weather?	*a.* ________________ *b.* ________________
32	What do you do?	*a.* ________________ *b.* ________________
33	Do you have to work?	*a.* ________________ *b.* ________________
34	What are you going to do tonight?	*a.* ________________ *b.* ________________
35	Can you go to the movies tonight?	*a.* ________________ *b.* ________________
36A	At what time do you get up?	*a.* ________________ *b.* ________________
36B	At what time do you go to bed?	*a.* ________________ *b.* ________________
37	Who gives you money?	*a.* ________________ *b.* ________________
38	Whom do you see every day?	*a.* ________________ *b.* ________________
39	Do you need money?	*a.* ________________ *b.* ________________
40	Do you put on (play) records while you read?	*a.* ________________ *b.* ________________
41	Do you listen to the radio?	*a.* ________________ *b.* ________________
42	At what time do you leave home?	*a.* ________________ *b.* ________________
43	What do you want for lunch?	*a.* ________________ *b.* ________________

44	Do you always tell the truth?	*a.*	--
		b.	--
45A	Do you know the lesson?	*a.*	--
		b.	--
45B	Do you know how to swim?	*a.*	--
		b.	--
46	Do you know Mr. . . .? (Supply a surname.)	*a.*	--
		b.	--
47	Do you understand the lesson?	*a.*	--
		b.	--

Spanish-English Vocabulary

Note. Nouns that have a masculine and a feminine form are displayed in the same style as adjectives. For example, **autor, -ra** represents the forms **el autor** and **la autora.**

abajo, downstairs
abandonar, to abandon
abogado, -a, lawyer
la **abreviatura,** abbreviation
abril, April
absurdo, -a, absurd
la **abuela,** grandmother
el **abuelo,** grandfather; **los abuelos,** grandparents
la **abundancia,** abundance
aburrido, -a, bored, boring
el **acento,** accent
acompañar, to accompany
acostarse (ue), to go to bed; to lie down
la **actriz,** actress
Acuario, Aquarius
adiós, good-bye
el **adjetivo,** adjective
admirar, to admire
¿adónde? (to) where?; **¿adónde va Ud.?** where are you going?
el **aeroplano,** airplane
el **aeropuerto,** airport
aficionado, -a, fan; **aficionado(-a) de béisbol,** baseball fan
afuera, outside; **las afueras,** suburbs, outskirts
la **agencia,** agency
agosto, August
agradable, pleasant, agreeable, nice
el **agua** *(f),* water
ahora, now
el **aire,** air; **al aire libre,** in the open air, outdoors
ajeno, -a, different, alien
al, to the; (+ *inf.*) on, upon: **al entrar,** on (upon) entering
Alberto, Albert
alemán, alemana, German
el **alfabeto,** alphabet
el **álgebra** *(f),* algebra
algunos, -as, some, a few; **algunas veces,** sometimes
el **almuerzo,** lunch; **la hora del almuerzo,** lunchtime
alto, -a, tall
¡Alto! Halt! Stop!
alumno, -a, pupil, student
el **ama** *(f)* **de casa,** housewife
el (la) **amante,** lover
amar, to love
amigo, -a, friend
el **amor,** love
andar, to walk, ride, travel
Andrés, Andrew; **Andresito,** Andy
el **anestésico,** anesthetic
Anita, Annie
ansioso, -a, anxious
anticipar, to anticipate
Antonio, Anthony, Tony
el **año,** year; **tengo 15 años,** I am 15 years old
el **apartamento,** apartment
el **apellido,** surname, family name
el **apodo,** nickname
aprender, to learn
el **árbol,** tree
Aries, Aries
aristocrático, -a, aristocratic
la **aritmética,** arithmetic
la **arqueología,** archeology
la **arquitectura,** architecture
arriba, upstairs
arrogante, arrogant
el **arroz,** rice
el **arte** *(m* and *f),* art; **artes industriales,** industrial arts, "shop"
el **artículo,** article; **artículo definido,** definite article (= *the* in English); **artículo indefinido,** indefinite article (= *a* or *an* in English)
el (la) **artista,** artist
así, thus, in that way; **así así,** so-so

la **asignatura,** (school) subject
asistir a, to attend
el **atleta,** athlete
atómico, -a, atomic
autor, -ra, author
atribuir, to attribute
ayer, yesterday
ayudar, to help

el **baile,** dance
bajo, -a, short
el **banco,** bank
la **banda,** band
bañarse, to take a bath
el **baño,** bath; **el cuarto de baño,** bathroom
el **barrio,** neighborhood
bastante, enough; quite; **bastante bien,** quite well
Beatriz, Beatrice
beber, to drink
la **bebida,** beverage, drink
el **béisbol,** baseball
el **beisbolero,** baseball player
la **bicicleta,** bicycle
bien, well
la **biología,** biology
la **blusa,** blouse
la **boca,** mouth
el **boliche,** bowling, bowling ball; **jugar al boliche,** to bowl
el **bolsillo,** pocket
la **bomba,** bomb
bonito, -a, pretty
borracho, -a, drunk, drunkard
la **botella,** bottle
el **botones,** bellhop
el **boxeador,** boxer
boxear, to box
brillar, to shine
bueno, -a, good
el **burro,** donkey
buscar, to look for; **buscar empleo,** to look for a job

el **caballo,** horse
cada, each, every
el **cadáver,** corpse, cadaver
el **café,** coffee; cafe; **café al aire libre,** sidewalk cafe
la **cafeína,** caffein
la **cafetería,** cafeteria
la **cajetilla,** (cigarette) pack
el **calendario,** calendar
el **calor,** heat; **hace calor,** it's warm (weather); **hace mucho calor,** it's hot; **tengo calor,** I'm warm
la **caloría,** calorie
la **calle,** street
el **callo,** callus
la **cama,** bed
cambiar, to change, exchange
el **camello,** camel
caminar, to walk, ride, travel
el **campo,** country (opposite of ''city'')
la **canción,** song; **canción de cuna,** lullaby, cradle song
la **cancha,** (tennis) court, (baseball) field
cantar, to sing
la **capacidad,** capacity
el **carácter,** character
la **cárcel,** jail
Carlos, Charles, Karl; **Carlitos,** Charlie
la **carne,** meat
el **carro,** car
la **carta,** letter
la **casa,** house; **en casa,** at home; **en la casa,** in the house; **ir a casa,** to go home
casarse (con), to get married (to)
casi, almost
la **catedral,** cathedral
católico, -a, Catholic
catorce, fourteen
la **cavidad,** cavity
celebrar, to celebrate
el **cementerio,** cemetery
la **cena,** supper; **tomar la cena,** to have supper
centígrado, centigrade, Celsius
cerca de, near
cero, zero
la **cerveza,** beer
la **ciencia,** science

científico, -a, scientific
ciento (cien), one hundred
el **cigarrillo,** cigarette
cinco, five
cincuenta, fifty
el **cine** (= **cinema**), movies, movie theater; **ir al cine,** to go to the movies
la **ciudad,** city
¡claro! of course!
la **clase,** class; sort, kind: **¿qué clase de emparedado?** what kind of sandwich?; **la clase de español,** Spanish class
el **clima,** climate
la **cocina,** kitchen
cocinero, -a, cook
el **coche,** car
el **comedor,** dining room
comer, to eat
la **comida,** food; meal; dinner or main meal of the day
compañero, -a, companion; **compañero(-a) de clase,** classmate
comprar, to buy
la **comunidad,** community
con, with
Concha, Conchita, nicknames for *María de la Concepción*
conocer (conozco), to know, be acquainted with; to meet (for the first time), make the acquaintance of
consistir en, to consist of
construido, -a, constructed, built
el **consulado,** consulate
contar (ue), to count
contento, -a, glad, happy
contestar, to answer
contribuir, to contribute
el **corazón,** heart
el **coro,** choir, chorus
correo aéreo, airmail
correr, to run
la **corrida de toros,** bullfight
la **cortesía,** courtesy
costar (ue), to cost
creer, to believe, think
el **crimen,** crime
el **cristianismo,** Christianity
cristiano, -a, Christian
Cristóbal, Christopher
el **cuaderno,** notebook
¿cuál? ¿cuáles? what? which?
cuando, when, whenever; **¿cuándo?** when?
¿cuánto, -a? how much?; **¿cuántos, -as?** how many?
cuarenta, forty
cuarto, -a, quarter, fourth
el **cuarto,** room; **cuarto de baño,** bathroom
cuatro, four
la **cuenta,** check (restaurant)
el **cuento,** story
cuidado: con cuidado, carefully
la **cultura,** culture
el **cumpleaños,** birthday
la **curiosidad,** curiosity

chaparro, -a, short and chubby
el **charro,** Mexican cowboy
Chavela, a Mexican nickname for "Betty"
el **cheque,** check
la **chica,** girl
el **chicle,** gum
el **chico,** boy
el **chiste,** joke
el **chófer,** driver, chauffeur

la **dama,** lady
dar, to give; **dar a,** to face
deber, ought (to), should; **¿qué debo hacer?** what should I do?
de, of, from; **de nada,** you're welcome; **de veras,** really
décimo, -a, tenth
decir (i, digo), to say, to tell; **¿Cómo se dice . . .?** How does one (do you) say . . .?
declarar, to declare
dedicado, -a, dedicated
delgado, -a, slim, slender
delicado, -a, delicate
delicioso, -a, delicious
democrático, -a, democratic
el (la) **dependiente,** clerk

el **deporte,** sport
el **derecho,** right
el **desastre,** disaster
desayunarse, to have breakfast
el **desayuno,** breakfast; **tomar el desayuno,** to have breakfast
desde, from; **desde . . . hasta,** from . . . to
la **desgracia,** misfortune; **por desgracia,** unfortunately
el **desierto,** desert
desocupado, -a, unoccupied, free
después de, after; **después de las clases,** after school
detestar, to detest, hate
devolver (ue), to return, give back
el **día,** day; **al día,** per day; **al día siguiente,** on the following day, next day; **el día de fiesta,** holiday; **todo el día,** all day; **todos los días,** every day; **buenos días,** good morning
el **diálogo,** dialogue
diario, -a, daily
el **dibujo mecánico,** mechanical drawing
diciembre, December
el **dictador,** dictator
Diego, James
el **diente,** tooth
la **dieta,** diet
diez, ten; **por dieces,** by tens
difícil, difficult
la **dificultad,** difficulty
la **dinamita,** dynamite
el **dinero,** money
Dionisio, Dennis
la **dirección,** address
el **disco,** record
el **distrito,** district
doce, twelve
el **dólar,** dollar
el **dolor,** pain, ache
domingo, Sunday
Domingo, Dominic
donde, where; **¿dónde?** where?
dormir (ue), to sleep; **dormirse,** to fall asleep; **dormir la siesta,** to take an afternoon nap
el **dormitorio,** bedroom
Dorotea, Dorothy
dos, two
la **droga,** drug
duro, -a, hard

el **ecuador,** equator
el **edificio,** building
la **educación física,** physical education
el **ejecutivo,** executive
el **ejemplo,** example
el **ejercicio,** exercise
el **ejército,** army
el, the
él, he, him
el **electricista,** electrician
eléctrico, -a, electrical
el **elefante,** elephant
Elena, Helen
ella, she, her
ellas, they, them *(f)*
ellos, they, them
el **emparedado,** sandwich
empezar (ie), to begin
emplear, to use; to employ, hire
empleo, job
en, in, on, at; **en casa,** at home; **en la clase,** in class; **en la escuela,** in (at) school; **en la mesa,** on the table
enamorado, -a, in love
encontrar (ue), to find; to meet
enemigo, -a, enemy
enero, January
enfermo, -a, sick, ill
Enrique, Henry
Enriqueta, Henrietta
la **ensalada,** salad
entender (ie), to understand
entrar (en), to enter
la **epidemia,** epidemic
escolar, *adj.,* school; **libro escolar,** schoolbook
Escorpio, Scorpio
escribir, to write
el **escritorio,** desk
escuchar, to listen (to)
la **escuela,** school; **escuela superior,** high school; **(escuela) primaria,** elementary school

ese, -a, that
España, Spain
español, -la, Spanish; *m,* Spanish (language), male Spaniard; *f,* female Spaniard
especialmente, especially
esperar, to wait (for); to hope
la **esposa,** wife
el **esposo,** husband; los **esposos,** husband and wife
esquiar, to ski
la **estación,** season
el **estado,** state; **los Estados Unidos,** the United States
estar (estoy), to be
este, -a, this; **esta noche,** tonight
Esteban, Steven, Stephen
la **estenografía,** stenography
el **estilo,** style
el (la) **estudiante,** student
estudiar, to study; **estudiar para,** to study to be
estudioso, -a, studious
la **etiqueta,** etiquette; tag, label
el **examen** (*pl.* exámenes), examination, test
excepto, except
explicar, to explain
extraño, -a, strange

la **fábrica,** factory
fácil, easy
la **falda,** skirt
la **familia,** family
favorito, -a, favorite
febrero, February
la **fecha,** date
Felipe, Philip
femenino, -a, feminine
feo, -a, ugly
la **filosofía,** philosophy
el **filósofo,** philosopher
el **fin,** end; **por fin,** finally
la **física,** physics
físico, -a, physical
la **fisiología,** physiology
flaco, -a, thin, skinny
la **flor,** flower
el **fonógrafo,** phonograph, record player
la **formalidad,** formality
la **foto,** photo, snapshot
la **fotografía,** photograph; photography
francés, francesa, French; *m,* French (language), Frenchman; *f,* Frenchwoman
Francia, France
Francisco, Francis; **Francisca,** Frances
la **frase,** sentence, phrase
fresco, -a, cool; **hace fresco,** it is cool (weather)
frío, -a, cold
el **frío,** cold; **hace frío,** it's cold (weather); **tengo frío,** I'm cold
frito, -a, fried
frustrado, -a, frustrated
las **frutas,** fruit(s)
fue, was
la **fuente,** fountain
fumar, to smoke
el **fútbol,** soccer; (*in U.S.*) football

garantizar, to guarantee
la **gaseosa,** soda
Géminis, Gemini
generoso, -a, generous
la **geografía,** geography
el **gimnasio,** gymnasium, gym
el **gobierno,** government
gordo, -a, fat
gracias, thanks, thank you; **muchas gracias,** thank you very much
Gran Bretaña, Great Britain
grande, gran, large, big, great
gritar, to shout
Gualterio, Walter
guapo, -a, *(m)* handsome, *(f)* pretty, attractive
Guillermo, William
gustar, to please (used when translating *to like:* **me gusta,** I like it, etc. See Lessons 34 and 35.)

la **habitación,** room
hablar, to speak, talk; **de habla española,** Spanish-speaking

hacer (hago), to do, to make; **¿qué tiempo hace?** how's the weather?; **hace calor,** it's warm; **hace mucho calor,** it's hot; **hace fresco,** it's cool; **hace (mucho) frío,** it's (very) cold; **hace sol,** it's sunny; **hace viento,** it's windy; **hace buen (mal) tiempo,** the weather is nice (bad); **hacer una pregunta,** to ask a question
hallar, to find
el **hambre** *(f),* hunger; **tener (mucha) hambre,** to be (very) hungry
la **hamburguesa,** hamburger
hasta, until; **hasta luego,** see you later; **hasta la vista,** I'll be seeing you; **hasta mañana,** see you tomorrow
hay, there is, there are
el **hecho,** fact
el **helado,** ice cream
Heriberto, Herbert
la **hermana,** sister
el **hermano,** brother; **los hermanos,** brothers *or* brother(s) and sister(s)
el **héroe,** hero
el **higo,** fig
la **hija,** daughter
el **hijo,** son; **los hijos,** sons *or* children (= sons and daughters): **los hijos de la Sra. Pérez,** Mrs. Pérez's children
la **hipocresía,** hypocrisy
hispánico, -a, Spanish-speaking, Hispanic
la **historia,** history; **la historia mundial,** world history
¡hola! hello! hi!
el **hombre,** man
la **hora,** hour, time; **la hora del almuerzo,** lunchtime; **¿qué hora es?** what time is it?
el **horario,** schedule
hoy, today
el **huevo,** egg
húngaro, -a, Hungarian

la **iglesia,** church; **ir a la iglesia,** to go to church
ilustrar, to illustrate
imaginar, to imagine
la **imitación,** imitation
importa: no importa, it doesn't matter, never mind
incluye, it includes
Inés, Inez, Agnes (a girl's name)
el **ingeniero,** engineer
Inglaterra, England
inglés, inglesa, English; *m,* English (language), Englishman; *f,* Englishwoman
las **iniciales,** initials
inocente, innocent
el **instituto,** institute; **Instituto Politécnico,** Polytechnical Institute
la **instrucción cívica,** civics
inteligente, intelligent, smart
el **interés,** interest
interesante, interesting
interesar, to interest
el **invierno,** winter
invitar, to invite
la **inyección,** shot, injection
ir (voy), to go; **irse,** to leave, go away
Irlanda, Ireland
la **isla,** island
Italia, Italy

jai alai, a game similar to handball but played off four walls
Jaime, James
el **jamón,** ham
Jorge, George
José, Joseph
Josefina, Josephine
joven (*pl,* **jóvenes**), young
Juan, John; **Juanito,** Johnny
Juana, Joan, Jane, Jean; **Juanita,** Jennie, Jeanette, Joanie
el **jueves,** Thursday
jugar (ue), to play; **jugar al tenis,** to play tennis
el **jugo,** juice; **jugo de naranja,** orange juice
julio, July
junio, June
juntos, -as, together
justo, -a, just, fair

la, the; you *(f),* her, it *(f)*

ladrar, to bark
la **lámpara,** lamp
el **lápiz** (*pl,* **lápices**), pencil
las, the; you *(f pl),* them *(f)*
latinoamericano, -a, Latin American
lavar, to wash; **lavarse,** to wash oneself, get washed, wash up
le, (to) you, (to) him, (to) her; **les,** (to) you *(pl),* (to) them
la **lección,** lesson
la **leche,** milk
la **lechuga,** lettuce
leer, to read
la **legumbre,** vegetable
la **lengua,** language
la **letra,** letter (of the alphabet)
levantarse, to rise, get up, stand up
la **liberación,** liberation
la **libertad,** liberty, freedom
el **libro,** book; **libro escolar,** schoolbook
la **licencia para manejar,** driver's license
la **liga,** league
el **líquido,** liquid
listo, -a, clever
lo, you *(m),* him, it *(m)*; **los,** the; you *(pl),* them
loco, -a, crazy
Lola, Lolita, nicknames for *Dolores*
Londres, London
Lorenzo, Lawrence
Lucía, Lucy
luego, then, afterward
la **luna,** moon
lunático, -a, lunatic
el **lunes,** Monday
Lupe, short for *Guadalupe,* a girl's name
la **luz** (*pl,* **luces**), light

llamar, to call; **llamarse,** to be called, named: **me llamo Sam,** my name is Sam
llegar, to arrive; **llegar a casa,** to get home
llorar, to cry
llover (ue), to rain

la **madre,** mother
la **majestad,** majesty
malo, -a, bad
manejar, to drive
el **manejo de la casa,** home economics
la **manera,** manner, fashion
la **mano,** hand
la **mantequilla,** butter
mañana, tomorrow
la **mañana,** morning; **de la mañana,** in the morning, A.M.; **por la mañana,** in (= during) the morning
el *or* la **mar,** sea
maravilloso, -a, marvelous
la **marca,** make
Marcos, Mark
Margarita, Margaret, Margery, Daisy
María, Mary, Miriam
Marta, Martha
el **martes,** Tuesday
marzo, March
más . . . que, more . . . than
masculino, -a, masculine
masticar, to chew
las **matemáticas,** mathematics
Mateo, Matthew
mayo, May
la **mayonesa,** mayonnaise
mayor, larger, older, oldest; **la plaza mayor,** main square
me, me, to me, myself
la **mecanografía,** typewriting
la **media,** stocking
la **medianoche,** midnight
médico, -a, doctor, physician
medio, -a, half
el **mediodía,** noon
menor, younger, youngest
menos, less, minus
la **mentira,** lie
el **mercado,** market
la **mermelada,** marmalade
el **mes,** month
la **mesa,** table
mexicano, -a, Mexican
mi(s), my
mí, me
el **micrófono,** microphone
el **miedo,** fear; **tener miedo,** to be afraid
mientras, while

el **miércoles,** Wednesday
Miguel, Michael; **Miguelito,** Mickey
la **milla,** mile
mirar, to look at; to watch (TV)
mismo, -a, same
el **misterio,** mystery
misterioso, -a, mysterious
el **modo,** manner, way; **de este modo,** in this way
el **momento,** moment; **en ese momento,** at that moment
la **monarquía,** monarchy
el **monólogo,** monologue
monótono, -a, monotonous
el **monstruo,** monster
montar, to mount
morder (ue), to bite
moreno, -a, dark (complexion); brunette
la **mosca,** fly
mostrar (ue), to show
la **motocicleta,** motorcycle
la **muchacha,** girl
el **muchacho,** boy
mucho, -a, a lot, much; **muchos, -as,** many; **muchas veces,** often
el **mundo,** world; **todo el mundo,** everybody
el **mural,** wall painting
el **músculo,** muscle
la **música,** music
muy, very

el **nacimiento,** birth
la **nación,** nation; **Naciones Unidas,** United Nations
la **nacionalidad,** nationality
nada, nothing; **no . . . nada,** nothing, not . . . anything; **de nada,** you're welcome
nadar, to swim
nadie, no one
la **naranja,** orange
la **natación,** swimming
el (la) **naturalista,** naturalist
necesitar, to need; **se necesita(n),** one needs, is (are) needed
nervioso, -a, nervous
nevar (ie), to snow
la **nevera,** refrigerator
niño, -a, child
la **noche,** night; **esta noche,** tonight; **buenas noches,** good evening, good night; **toda la noche,** all night; **todas las noches,** every night; **de la noche,** in the evening, P.M.; **por la noche,** in (= during) the evening, at night
el **nombre,** name; **nombre de pila,** first name
el **norte,** north; **al norte de,** north of
norteamericano, -a, American
nos, us, to us; ourselves
nosotros, -as, we, us
la **nota,** grade, mark; **sacar buenas (malas) notas,** to get good (bad) grades
la **noticia,** news item, piece of news; **las noticias,** news
noveno, -a, ninth
noventa, ninety
la **novia,** girlfriend, sweetheart, fiancée
noviembre, November
el **novio,** boyfriend, sweetheart, fiancé
nuestro, -a, our
Nueva York, New York
nueve, nine
nuevo, -a, new
el **número,** number
nunca, never

o, or; **o . . . o,** either . . . or
obtener (ie, obtengo), to obtain, get
el **océano,** ocean
octavo, -a, eighth
octubre, October
ochenta, eighty
ocho, eight
la **oficina,** office
olímpico, -a, olympic
olvidar, to forget
once, eleven
la **oportunidad,** opportunity
el **oro,** gold
la **orquesta,** orchestra

os, you, to you, yourselves
el **otoño,** autumn
otro, -a, other, another; **otra vez,** again

Pablo, Paul
el **Pacífico,** Pacific
Paco, Frank
el **padre,** father; **los padres,** parents
pagar, to pay
la **página,** page
el **pago,** pay
el **país,** country
el **pájaro,** bird
la **palabra,** word
el **palacio,** palace
las **palomitas,** popcorn
el **pan,** bread; **pan dulce,** sweet roll; **pan tostado,** toast
el **panecillo,** roll
la **papa,** potato; **papas fritas,** fried potatoes
papá, dad, daddy
para, for, to, in order to; **¿para qué?** why? what for?
para servirle, "to serve you," at your service
el **paréntesis,** parenthesis
el **pariente,** relative
el **parque,** park
el **partido,** game (match)
el **pasaporte,** passport
pasar, to pass; to spend (time)
el **pastel,** pastry, pie
la **patata,** potato *(in Spain)*
el **patio,** inner courtyard
el **patrón** } employer, boss
la **patrona** }
pedir (i), to ask for
el **Pedregal,** a wealthy residential district in Mexico City built on lava
Pedro, Peter
la **película,** film, movie
Pepe (nickname for *José*), Joey
pequeño, -a, little, small
perder (ie), to lose; **perder peso,** to lose weight
perezoso, -a, lazy
el **periódico,** newspaper
permitir, to permit
pero, but
el **perro,** dog
la **personalidad,** personality
pesado, -a, heavy
el **pescado,** fish
la **peseta,** monetary unit of Spain
el **peso,** monetary unit of Mexico and some South American countries
el (la) **pianista,** pianist
el **pie,** foot
la **pila,** baptismal font; **el nombre de pila,** first name
la **piscina,** swimming pool
Piscis, Pisces
el **piso,** floor, story; **el piso bajo,** ground floor
la **plata,** silver
la **plataforma,** platform
el **plato,** dish, plate; **el plato mixto,** combination plate
la **playa,** beach
la **plaza,** square; **la plaza de toros,** bullring; **la plaza mayor,** main square
la **pluma,** pen
pobre, poor
poco, little (in quantity); **un poco de leche,** a little milk
poder (ue), to be able, can
la **política,** politics
el **pollo,** chicken
poner (pongo), to put, put on, turn on
por, for (= in exchange for); in (= during): **por la mañana,** in the morning; **por desgracia,** unfortunately; **por eso,** for that reason, therefore; **por favor,** please; **por fin,** finally; **¿por qué?** why?
el **porcentaje,** percentage
porque, because
posdata (P.D.), postscript (P.S.)
poseer, to possess
el **postre,** dessert; **de postre,** for dessert
el **precio,** price
precioso, -a, precious

preferir (ie), to prefer
la **pregunta,** question; **hacer una pregunta,** to ask a question; **preguntas temáticas,** topic questions
preguntar, to ask (a question)
la **primavera,** spring(time)
primero, -a, (primer), first
primo, -a, cousin
el **problema,** problem
producir, to produce
profesor, -ra, teacher
prohibir, to prohibit
protestante, Protestant
la **psicología,** psychology
el **pueblo,** town
el **pulmón,** lung

que, than, which, that; **¿qué?** what?; **¿Qué tal?** How's everything?; **¡Qué bueno!** How nice!
quedarse, to remain, stay
quejarse, to complain
querer (ie), to wish, want; **querer decir,** to mean
querido, -a, dear
el **queso,** cheese
¿quién(-es)? who?; **¿de quién(-es)?** whose?
la **química,** chemistry
quince, fifteen
quinto, -a, fifth

Ramón, Raymond
Raquel, Rachel
el **ratón,** mouse
la **razón,** reason; **tener razón,** to be right
recibir, to receive
reciente, recent
recordar (ue), to remember; to remind
el **refresco,** soft drink (with or without carbonation)
regalar, to present as a gift; **regalado,** given as a gift
Reginaldo, Reginald
reírse (í, me río), to laugh
relajar, to relax
relatar, to report, tell
religioso, -a, religious
Renaldo, Ronald
el **resfriado,** cold (illness)
la **respuesta,** reply, answer
revelar, to reveal
la **revista,** magazine
revuelto, -a, scrambled
el **rey,** king
Ricardo, Richard
rico, -a, rich
ridículo, -a, ridiculous
la **rima,** rhyme
el **ritmo,** rhythm
robar, to rob, steal
la **roca,** rock
romántico, -a, romantic
Rosita, Rosie

el **sábado,** Saturday; **el sábado por la noche,** Saturday night
saber (sé), to know, to know how
sacar: sacar buenas (malas) notas, to get good (bad) grades
el **sacrificio,** sacrifice
Sagitario, Sagittarius
sagrado, -a, sacred
la **sal,** salt
la **sala,** living room
salir (salgo), to leave, go out
la **salud,** health; **¡Salud!** Bless you! (said when someone sneezes), to your health (said in giving a toast); **bien de salud,** in good health
saludar, to greet, say hello
san, shortened form of **santo** used before the names of male saints (*exceptions:* Santo Domingo, Santo Tomás)
santo, -a, saint; **santo patrón (santa patrona),** patron saint
se, yourself, himself, herself, itself, yourselves, themselves
la **sección,** section
la **sed,** thirst; **tener sed,** to be thirsty
según, according to
segundo, -a, second

seis, six
la **semana,** week
el **semestre,** (school) term, semester
sentarse (ie), to sit down
sentir (ie), to regret, be sorry; **lo siento,** I'm sorry
el **señor,** gentleman, Mr.
la **señora,** lady, madam, Mrs.
la **señorita,** young lady, Miss
septiembre, September
séptimo, -a, seventh
sesenta, sixty
setenta, seventy
sexto, -a, sixth
si, if
sí, yes
siempre, always
siete, seven
la **sílaba,** syllable
simpático, -a, likeable, nice
sin, without
el **sinónimo,** synonym
el **sistema,** system
el **sitio,** site, place
situado, -a, situated
la **sobrina,** niece
el **sobrino,** nephew
la **sociedad,** society
¡Socorro! Help!
el **sol,** sun; **hacer sol,** to be sunny
solo, -a, alone
sólo, only
el **sombrero,** hat
sonreír (í, sonrío), to smile
la **sopa,** soup
sudamericano, -a, South American
el **sueño,** sleep; **tener sueño,** to be sleepy
la **suerte,** luck; **¡Buena suerte!** Good luck!
suficiente, sufficient
sufrir, to suffer
el **sur,** south; **al sur de,** south of

tal, such, such a; **tal vez,** perhaps; **¿qué tal?** how's everything?
el **taller,** shop
también, also, too
tampoco, either, neither
tanto, -a, so much
la **taquigrafía,** shorthand
tarde, late
la **tarde,** afternoon; **buenas tardes,** good afternoon; **de la tarde,** in the afternoon, P.M.; **por la tarde,** in (= during) the afternoon
la **tarea,** task; homework assignment; **las tareas,** homework
la **tarjeta,** card; **tarjeta de turismo,** tourist card
Tauro, Taurus
la **taza,** cup
te, you, to you, yourself
el **té,** tea
el **teatro,** theater
tecnológico, -a, technological
el **teléfono,** telephone; **el número de teléfono,** phone number
la **televisión,** television; **mirar la televisión,** to watch television
el **televisor,** television set
el **tema,** theme, composition
temático, -a: preguntas temáticas, topic questions
temprano, early
la **teneduría,** bookkeeping
tener (ie, tengo), to have; **tener . . . años,** to be . . . years old; **tener calor,** to be warm; **tener frío,** to be cold; **tener hambre,** to be hungry; **tener miedo,** to be afraid; **tener razón,** to be right; **tener sed,** to be thirsty; **tener simpatía a,** to like (a person); **tener sueño,** to be sleepy; **tener vergüenza,** to be ashamed; **tener que** + *inf.,* to have to, must
la **tentación,** temptation
la **teoría,** theory
la **tequila,** Mexican alcoholic beverage made from the maguey plant
tercero, -a (tercer), third
terminar, to end
ti, you
la **tía,** aunt
el **tiempo,** weather; time
la **tienda,** store

Timoteo, Timothy
el **tío,** uncle
típico, -a, typical
el **tipo,** type, kind; **el tipo de cambio,** rate of exchange
el **tocadiscos,** phonograph, record player
el **tocino,** bacon
todavía, still, yet
todo, -a, all, every; **todo el día,** all day; **todos los días,** every day; **todo el mundo,** everybody
tomar, to take; to have (a meal, a beverage, etc.): **tomar el almuerzo (la cena),** to have lunch (supper); **tomar (una taza de) café,** to have (a cup of) coffee
Tomás, Thomas
el **tomate,** tomato
tonto, -a, silly, foolish
el **torero,** bullfighter
el **toro,** bull; **la corrida de toros,** bullfight; **la plaza de toros,** bullring
trabajar, to work
el **trabajo,** work, job
traducir (traduzco), to translate; **traduzca Ud. al español,** translate into Spanish
el **traidor,** traitor
trece, thirteen
treinta, thirty
tres, three
el **trecho,** stretch, distance; while
la **trigonometría,** trigonometry
el **trofeo,** trophy
tu(-s), your
tú, you
el (la) **turista,** tourist

u, or (used instead of **o** before a word beginning with **o** or **ho**)
último, -a, last, ultimate
la **unidad,** unity
la **universidad,** college, university
un, uno, -a, a, an, one
usado, -a, used
usar, to use; **se usa(n),** is (are) used, one uses
usted, ustedes, you

valer, to be worth; **¿cuánto vale?** how much does it cost?
valiente, valiant, brave
el **valor,** value; bravery
el **valle,** valley
varios, -as, several
el **vaso,** glass
¡vaya(n) Ud(s)! (command form of *ir*) go!; **¡váya(n)se!** go away! leave!
veinte, twenty
venir (ie, vengo), to come
ver, to see; to watch (a film, game, program, etc.)
el **verano,** summer(time)
veras: de veras, really, truly
la **verdad,** truth; **¿verdad?** isn't that so? doesn't he? aren't you? etc.
la **vergüenza,** shame; **tener vergüenza,** to be ashamed
el **vestido,** dress
la **vez** (*pl,* **veces**), time; **algunas veces,** sometimes; **de vez en cuando,** from time to time; **en vez de,** instead of; **muchas veces,** often; **otra vez,** again, once more; **tal vez,** perhaps, maybe
la **vida,** life
viejo, -a, old
el **viento,** wind; **hacer viento,** to be windy
el **viernes,** Friday
el **vino,** wine
la **virgen,** virgin
la **viuda,** widow; **el viudo,** widower
vivir, to live
volar (ue), to fly; **volando,** flying
volver (ue), to return, go (come) back; **volver a casa,** to return home
vosotros, -as, you *(pl)*
vuestro, -a, your

y, and
ya, already, now
yo, I

el **zapato,** shoe
la **zona,** zone

English-Spanish Vocabulary

a, un, una
able: to be able, poder (ue)
address, la dirección
afraid: to be afraid, tener miedo
after, después (de); **it's ten after two,** son las dos y diez
afternoon, la tarde; **good afternoon,** buenas tardes; **in the afternoon,** por la tarde; (= *P.M.*) de la tarde
agency, la agencia; **tourist agency,** la agencia de turismo
airmail, correo aéreo
all, todo, -a; **all day,** todo el día
alone, solo, -a
also, también
always, siempre
A.M., de la mañana
American, norteamericano, -a
and, y
Anne, Ana; **Annie,** Anita
April, abril
architecture, la arquitectura
army, el ejército
arrive, llegar
art, el arte *(m* and *f)*
ashamed: to be ashamed, tener vergüenza
ask, preguntar; **to ask a question,** hacer una pregunta; **to ask for,** pedir (i)
at, a, en; **at home,** en casa; **at night,** por la noche; **at school,** en la escuela; **at the table,** a la mesa; **at what time?** ¿a qué hora?
attend, asistir (a)
August, agosto
aunt, la tía
autumn, el otoño
away: to go away, irse

bacon, el tocino
bad, malo, -a
baseball, el béisbol
baseball player, el beisbolero
bathroom, el cuarto de baño
be, ser (soy), estar (estoy); **to be able,** poder (ue); **to be afraid,** tener miedo; **to be ashamed,** tener vergüenza; **to be cold,** (= *feel cold*) tener frío, *(weather)* hacer frío; **to be warm,** (= *feel warm*) tener calor, *(weather)* hacer calor; **to be hungry,** tener hambre; **to be thirsty,** tener sed; **to be right,** tener razón; **to be sleepy,** tener sueño; **to be . . . years old,** tener . . . años; **to be worth,** valer
because, porque
bed, la cama; **to go to bed,** acostarse (ue)
bedroom, el dormitorio
beer, la cerveza
before, antes de
begin, empezar (ie)
bellboy, el botones
beverage, la bebida
big, grande
biology, la biología
birth, el nacimiento; **birth certificate,** el certificado de nacimiento
birthday, el cumpleaños
bless: Bless you! Salud!
book, el libro
bowl, jugar al boliche
bowling, el boliche
boy, el muchacho, el chico
bread, el pan
breakfast, el desayuno; **to have breakfast,** tomar el desayuno
brother, el hermano
building, el edificio
bullfight, la corrida de toros
but, pero
butter, la mantequilla
buy, comprar

call, llamar; **to be called,** llamarse
can, poder (ue)
car, el coche

card, la tarjeta
Catholic, católico, -a
celebrate, celebrar
certificate, el certificado
change, cambiar
check; el cheque
cheese, el queso
chemistry, la química
chicken, el pollo
church, la iglesia
city, la ciudad
class, la clase; **in class,** en la clase
classical, clásico, -a; **classical music,** la música clásica
clerk, el dependiente
coffee, el café
cold, frío, -a; **to be cold,** (= *feel cold*) tener frío, *(weather)* hacer frío; **to have a cold,** tener un resfriado
college, la universidad
column, la columna
combination plate, el plato mixto
consulate, el consulado
cool, fresco, -a
count, contar (ue)
country, el país; *(opposite of city)* el campo
course, la asignatura
cousin, primo, -a
crazy, loco, -a

dark (complexion), moreno, -a
daughter, la hija
day, el día; **all day,** todo el día; **every day,** todos los días; **on the following day,** al día siguiente
December, diciembre
delicious, delicioso, -a
dessert, el postre
difficult, difícil
dining room, el comedor
do, hacer (hago)
do, does, *are not translated when used as auxiliary verbs:* **do you drive?** ¿maneja Ud.?; **he does not smoke,** él no fuma, *etc.*
doctor, doctor, -ra, médico, -a
dog, el perro
donkey, el burro
downstairs, abajo
dress, el vestido; **to dress,** vestirse (i)
drink, la bebida; **to drink,** beber
drive, manejar
driver's license, la licencia para manejar

each, cada
early, temprano
eat, comer
egg, el huevo
eight, ocho
eighth, octavo, -a
eighty, ochenta
eleven, once
end, terminar
engineer, el ingeniero
English, inglés, inglesa; *(language)* el inglés
equals, son
evening, la noche; **good evening,** buenas noches; **in the evening,** por la noche; (= *P.M.*) de la noche
every, cada, todos los, todas las
everybody, todo el mundo, todos
example, el ejemplo
exchange, cambiar

factory, la fábrica
fall, el otoño
fall asleep, dormirse (ue)
famous, famoso, -a
fat, gordo, -a
father, el padre
favorite, favorito, -a
February, febrero
few: a few, unos, -as, algunos, -as
fifteen, quince
fifth, quinto, -a
fifty, cincuenta
find, encontrar (ue), hallar
fine, bien
first, primero, -a (primer)
fish, el pescado

five, cinco
flower, la flor
fly, la mosca
following, siguiente; **the following day,** al día siguiente
football, el fútbol
for, para; (= *in exchange for*) por
forty, cuarenta
fountain, la fuente
four, cuatro
fourteen, catorce
fourth, cuarto, -a
Frank, Paco, Pancho
French, francés, francesa; *(language)* el francés
Friday, el viernes
fried, frito, -a
friend, amigo, -a
from, de; **from . . . to,** desde . . . hasta
fruit, la fruta

generous, generoso, -a
German, alemán, alemana; *(language)* el alemán
get, obtener (ie, obtengo); **to get home,** llegar a casa; **to get married,** casarse; **to get up,** levantarse
girl, la muchacha, la chica
give, dar; **to give back,** devolver (ue)
glass, el vaso
go, ir (voy); **to go away,** irse; **to go to bed,** acostarse (ue)
going to (do something), ir a + *inf.*: **I'm going to study,** voy a estudiar
gold, el oro
good, bueno, -a
goodbye, adiós
grandfather, el abuelo
greet, saludar

half, medio, -a; **at half past six,** a las seis y media
ham, el jamón
hamburger, la hamburguesa
handsome, guapo, -a
have, tener; **to have to,** tener que; **to have** *(food or drink),* tomar
he, él
health, la salud; **to be in good health,** estar bien de salud
heart, el corazón
Helen, Elena
Hello! ¡Hola!
Henry, Enrique
her, la, su(-s), de ella; **to her,** le, a ella
Hi! ¡Hola!
high school, la escuela superior
him, lo; **to him,** le, a él
Hispanic, hispánico, -a
history, la historia; **world history,** la historia mundial
home: at home, en casa; **to return home,** volver a casa
homework, las tareas; **homework assignment,** la tarea
hot: to be hot, (= *feel hot*) tener mucho calor; *(weather)* hacer mucho calor
hour, la hora
house, la casa
housewife, el ama *(f)* de casa
how? ¿cómo?; **how goes it? (how's everything?)** ¿qué tal?; **how much?** ¿cuánto(-a)?; **how many?** ¿cuántos(-as)?; **how's the weather?** ¿qué tiempo hace?; **to know how,** saber
hundred, ciento, cien
hungry: to be hungry, tener hambre
husband, el esposo

I, yo
ice cream, el helado
if, si
ill, enfermo, -a
in, en; **in class,** en la clase; **in the morning,** por la mañana; (= *A.M.*) de la mañana; **in the afternoon (evening),** por la tarde (noche); (= *P.M.*) de la tarde (noche)
Inez, Inés
intelligent, inteligente

it, *(object pronoun)* lo, la; *(as subject pronoun,* él, ella, *but usually not expressed:* **it is on the table,** está en la mesa)

James, Diego
January, enero
John, Juan
Joseph, José; **Joey,** Pepe
juice, el jugo
July, julio
June, junio

kitchen, la cocina
know, *(facts or information)* saber (yo sé); (= *to be acquainted with*) conocer (conozco); **to know how,** saber

language, la lengua
large, grande
late, tarde
Latin American, latinoamericano, -a
league, la liga
learn, aprender
leave, salir (de), irse
lesson, la lección
letter, la carta; *(of the alphabet)* la letra
lettuce, la lechuga
lie, la mentira; **to lie down,** acostarse (ue)
like: I like, me gusta(n), **you like,** te gusta(n), **she likes,** le gusta(n) (a ella), etc.; **do you like coffee?** ¿le gusta (a Ud.) el café? (*See Lessons 34 and 35.*)
like, como; **what is he (she, it) like?** ¿cómo es?
listen, escuchar
little, pequeño, -a; **a little (bit of),** un poco de
live, vivir
lot: a lot (of), mucho, -a; **a lot** (= *often*), mucho
love, el amor; **to love,** amar
lunch, el almuerzo; **to have lunch,** tomar el almuerzo
lung, el pulmón (*pl.* pulmones)

magazine, la revista
make, la marca; **to make,** hacer (hago)
many, muchos, -as
March, marzo
Margaret, Margarita
marmalade, la mermelada
marry, casarse (con)
Mary, María
mathematics, las matemáticas
Matthew, Mateo
May, mayo
me, me, a mí
mean, querer decir
meat, la carne
meet, encontrar (ue); (= *to become acquainted with*) conocer (conozco)
Michael, Miguel
midnight, la medianoche; **at midnight,** a medianoche
milk, la leche
minus, menos
miss, la señorita
mister, el señor
Monday, el lunes
money, el dinero
month, el mes
morning, la mañana; **good morning,** buenos días; **in** (= *during*) **the morning,** por la mañana; **6 o'clock in the morning,** las seis de la mañana
mother, la madre
motorcycle, la motocicleta
movie, la película
movies, el cine
Mrs., la señora
much, mucho
music, la música
must, tener que + *inf.:* **I must leave,** tengo que irme
my, mi(-s)
mysterious, misterioso, -a

name, el nombre; **to be named,** llamarse; **first name,** nombre de pila
national, nacional

near, cerca de
need, necesitar
neighborhood, el barrio
neither, *(= not . . . either)* tampoco, no . . . tampoco; **neither . . . nor,** ni . . . ni: **he's neither rich nor poor,** no es ni rico ni pobre
nephew, el sobrino
new, nuevo, -a
news, las noticias
newspaper, el periódico
next: (on) the next day, al día siguiente
nice, *(person)* simpático, -a; **the weather is nice,** hace buen tiempo
nickname, el apodo
niece, la sobrina
night, la noche; **good night,** buenas noches; **at night,** por la noche
nine, nueve
ninety, noventa
ninth, noveno, -a
noon, el mediodía; **at noon,** a mediodía
nor, ni
north, el norte; **north of,** al norte de
notebook, el cuaderno
November, noviembre

ocean, el océano
o'clock: at two o'clock, a las dos; **it's one o'clock,** es la una; **it's three o'clock,** son las tres
October, octubre
of, de
office, la oficina
Oh! Ay!
old, viejo, -a
older, mayor
on, en; **on meeting (her),** al encontrar(la); **on Monday,** el lunes; **on Mondays,** los lunes
one, un, uno, una
orange, la naranja; **orange juice,** jugo de naranja
our, nuestro, -a
outside, afuera
outskirts, las afueras

the **Pacific,** el Pacífico
parents, los padres
park, el parque
passport, el pasaporte
pastry, el pastel
Paul, Pablo
pay, pagar
pencil, el lápiz (*pl.* lápices)
personality, la personalidad
Philip, Felipe
phone, el teléfono; **on the phone,** al teléfono
photo, la foto; **photograph,** la fotografía
physics, la física
play, *(sports)* jugar; *(musical instrument)* tocar
pleasant, agradable
plus, y
P.M., *(before sunset)* de la tarde; *(after sunset)* de la noche
pool, la piscina
potato, la papa, la patata
precious, precioso, -a
prefer, preferir (ie)
problem, el problema
professional, profesional
program, el programa
pupil, alumno, -a
put, poner (pongo); **to put on,** poner

quarter, cuarto; **at a quarter past two,** a las dos y cuarto
question, la pregunta; **to ask a question,** hacer una pregunta

radio, la radio
rain, llover (ue)
ranch, el rancho
rate of exchange, el tipo de cambio
read, leer
record, el disco
record player, el tocadiscos
relax, relajar
rent, el alquiler
restaurant, el restaurante

return, (= *come back*) volver (ue); (= *give back*) devolver (ue)
review, el repaso
rice, el arroz
rich, rico, -a
right: to be right, tener razón
Robert, Roberto
roll, el panecillo
room, el cuarto, la habitación
Rose, Rosa
rum, el ron
run, correr

sacred, sagrado, -a
salad, la ensalada
salt, la sal
sandwich, el emparedado
Saturday, el sábado
say, decir (i, digo); **how do you say . . .?** ¿cómo se dice . . .?
school, la escuela; **at school,** en la escuela; **to go to school,** ir a la escuela; **elementary school,** la (escuela) primaria; **high school,** la escuela superior
schoolbook, el libro escolar
science, la ciencia
scrambled, revuelto, -a
season, la estación
second, segundo, -a
secretary, secretario, -a
see, ver (veo); **see you later,** hasta luego
seeing: I'll be seeing you, Hasta la vista
September, septiembre
service: at your service, para servirle
seven, siete
seventh, séptimo, -a
seventy, setenta
she, ella
shirt, la camisa
shop, la tienda; *(school subject)* las artes industriales
short, bajo, -a
show, mostrar (ue)
sick, enfermo, -a
sing, cantar
sister, la hermana
sit down, sentarse (ie)
six, seis
sixth, sexto, -a
sixty, sesenta
sleep, el sueño; **to sleep,** dormir (ue); **to fall asleep,** dormirse
sleepy: to be sleepy, tener sueño
slim, delgado, -a
small, pequeño, -a
smart, inteligente
smoke, fumar
snapshot, la foto
snow, nevar (ie)
so-so, así así
soccer, el fútbol
soda, la gaseosa
soft drink, el refresco
some, unos, -as, algunos, -as
sometimes, algunas veces
son, el hijo
song, la canción
sorry: I'm sorry, lo siento
soup, la sopa
south, el sur; **south of,** al sur de
Spanish, español, -la; *(language)* el español
Spanish-speaking, hispánico, -a, de habla española
speak, hablar
sport, el deporte
spring(time), la primavera
state, el estado
stay, quedarse
store, la tienda
story (= *floor*), el piso
street, la calle
student, el (la) estudiante
study, estudiar
subject, la asignatura
suburbs, las afueras
summer(time), el verano
Sunday, el domingo
supper, la cena; **to have supper,** tomar la cena
surname, apellido
sweet roll, el pan dulce

sweetheart, novio, -a
swim, nadar
swimming pool, la piscina

take, tomar
talk, hablar
tall, alto, -a
tea, el té
tell, decir (i, digo)
ten, diez
tennis, el tenis
tenth, décimo, -a
term, el semestre
thank you, gracias; **thank you very much,** muchas gracias
the, el, la, los, las
their, su(-s), de ellos, de ellas
them, los, las
there is, there are, hay
they, ellos, ellas
third, tercero, -a (tercer)
thirsty: to be thirsty, tener sed
thirteen, trece
thirty, treinta
this, este, -a
Thomas, Tomás
three, tres
Thursday, el jueves
time, la hora; **at what time?** ¿a qué hora?
to, a; (= *in order to*) para
toast, el pan tostado
today, hoy
tomorrow, mañana
tonight, esta noche
too, también
tourist, el turista; **tourist agency,** la agencia de turismo
town, el pueblo
tree, el árbol (*pl.* árboles)
truth, la verdad
Tuesday, el martes
turn on, poner (pongo)
twelve, doce
twenty, veinte
two, dos

ugly, feo, -a
understand, entender (ie)
United States, los Estados Unidos
university, la universidad
upstairs, arriba
us, nos, a nosotros
use, usar
used, usado, -a

vegetable, la legumbre
very, muy

want, querer (ie)
warm: to be warm, (= *feel warm*) tener calor, *(weather)* hacer calor
was, fue
wash, lavar; to **wash oneself, get washed,** lavarse
watch, mirar, ver
water, el agua *(f)*
we, nosotros, -as
weather, el tiempo; **how's the weather?** ¿qué tiempo hace?; **the weather is nice,** hace buen tiempo
Wednesday, el miércoles
week, la semana
welcome: you're welcome, de nada
well, bien
what? ¿qué?; **what is your name?** ¿cómo se llama Ud.?; **what time is it?** ¿qué hora es?
where? ¿dónde?; *(with verb of motion)* ¿adónde?
while, mientras
who? ¿quién(-es)? **whom?** ¿a quién(-es)?
why? ¿por qué?
wife, la esposa
wind, el viento
windy: it is windy, hace viento
wine, el vino
winter, el invierno
with, con
word, la palabra
work, el trabajo; **to work,** trabajar

world, el mundo; **world history,** la historia mundial
worth: to be worth, valer
write, escribir

year, el año; **to be . . . years old,** tener . . . años
yes, sí
yesterday, ayer
you, tú, vosotros, Ud., Uds., te, os, lo, la, los, las; **to you,** le, les
younger, menor
your, su(-s), de Ud., de Uds., tu(-s), vuestro, -a

zero, cero